The Adaptive School:
A Sourcebook for Developing Collaborative Groups

The Adaptive School:
A Sourcebook for Developing Collaborative Groups

Robert Garmston
Bruce Wellman

Page Design by Michael Buckley

Christopher-Gordon Publishers, Inc.
Norwood, Massachusetts

Credits

Every effort has been made to contact copyright holders for permission to reproduce borrowed material where necessary. We apologize for any oversights and would be happy to rectify them in future printings.

Permission for adaptation of material from pages 75 and 90 of *The Skilled Facilitator: Practical Wisdom for Developing Effective Groups,* by Roger Schwarz, © 1994 By Jossey-Bass, Inc., Publishers is granted with permission of the author and publisher.

Table 2.3, The Norms of Collaboration, from Arthur L. Costa and R.M. Liebmann, Editors, *The Process-Centered School: Sustaining a Renaissance Community,* published © 1997, by Corwin Press, reproduced with permission.

Appendix F, The Facilitator's Contracting Conversation, is taken from *Flawless Consulting: A Guide to Getting Your Expertise Used,* by Peter Block © 1981 by Jossey-Bass, Inc., Publishers is used with permission of the author and publisher.

Material from Robert Garmston and Bruce Wellman, "Teacher Talk That Makes a Difference", *Educational Leadership,* April 1998, Volume 55, Number 7, pp. 30–34, used with the permission of the Association for Supervision and Curriculum Development.

Material from "Places to Intervene in a System (in increasing order of effectiveness)", *Whole Earth,* Winter, 1997, pp. 79–83 used with permission.

Material in Chapter 8, specifically Table 8-1, adapted from R. Sternberg and J. Horvath (1995, August-September), *A Prototype View of Expert Teaching, Educational Researcher, II,* 9–17. Copyright © 1995 by the American Educational Research Association and used with permission.

Christopher-Gordon Publishers, Inc.
1502 Providence Highway, Suite #12
Norwood, MA 02062
(800) 934-8322

Printed in the United States of America

10 9 8 7 6 5   04 03 02

ISBN: 0-926842-91-9
Library of Congress Catalogue Card Number: 98-74795

For Sue Garmston and Leslie Cowperthwaite

This book is dedicated to our wives. Without them we would be tufts of windborne dandelions, soaring aloft with little hope of touching ground.

Contents

Index   301

Foreword

THE QUESTION with which we are all confronted at the beginning of the new century is how to reinvent the bureaucratically controlled world of work. *The Adaptive School* both captures the essence of what the new science and systems thinking are contributing to a new world view and prepares us to move into a far more fluid world than most of us have been prepared to traverse.

As we leave the industrial age with its model of a school as a well-run factory, we enter into an era that is defined by new ways to link, organize, create, and communicate. Technology is reshaping every institution. The flow of information is overwhelming traditional boundaries (such as textbooks and classroom doors), job descriptions are changing, and stress is rampant. The need for guidance in the facilitation of learning communities is becoming critical.

Robert Garmston and Bruce Wellman have done a superb job of writing a book that directs us toward many of the necessary skills for working and living in such systems. This is an important book for the age of intelligent self-organizing systems. It informs us about the nature of self-reference and living with different learning and cultural styles. It shows us how critical it is to surface assumptions and how such assumptions can sabotage the best of projects and positive efforts. In addition, the authors help us to see that the fully participating individual leads to greater fulfillment of group and systems goals and identity.

By articulating the difference between dialogue, discussion, and conversations, as well as by identifying the responsibilities of various functions such as facilitator, consultant, presenter, and coach, they give us clear parameters for roles and functions. Yet such delineations enhance rather than restrict the possibilities for communication.

There are an unending number of gems in this book. The distinctions between role authority and knowledge authority help facilitators to establish authenticity when working with others. The reader will be challenged by the suggestions and guidance for developing sophisticated metacognitive skills. The chapter on conflict is a powerful and effective exploration of this topic and is well geared to the more interconnected and fluid world that we already entering.

Indeed, throughout the book, Garmston and Wellman are advocates for an idea that we cherish. It is simply no longer enough to focus on "knowing about." The goal for all of us is the same as the goal for all our students. Beyond preparing students for work and equipping them with knowledge and skills is the need for them to become human beings who can function together intelligently and compassionately. What we ask of them is what we need for ourselves. What readers and users will realize is that working with the skills and processes embodied in this book can help us to become better human beings.

—Renate Nummela Caine and Geoffrey Caine

Acknowledgments

To write is to learn. We are grateful for the enormous lessons encountered in writing this book. We have learned from each other, from thousands of educators in seminars over the last 8 years, from numerous facilitators, cabinets, site councils, and citizen groups we've had the pleasure of facilitating.

Challenging us in our thinking are many friends from the Institute for Intelligent Behavior: Bill Baker, from whom we first learned that we should be training group members in facilitative behaviors, not training leaders to facilitate groups; Art Costa, mentor and cofounder with Bob of cognitive coaching, the principles of which are recognizable in this work; Laura Lipton, creatively critical friend and cofounder with Bruce of Pathways to Understanding; Diane Zimmerman, who provides intellectual stimulation and pragmatic guidance; and several colleagues who have tested the adaptive schools work with us in a variety of settings: Jane Ellison, from her base in Colorado; Rachel Billmeyer and Sue Presler, from the Midwest, Bill Sommers in Minnesota, and Bill Powell, who has led the development of an adaptive school at the International School of Tanganyika in East Africa.

We are also grateful to valued colleagues who expanded our thinking in this area. We are especially appreciative to Suzanne Bailey for the vision, creativity, and gifts that she continually shares with us and the educational community. We are also indebted to Linda Lambert, Carolee Hayes, and Jim Toole for fresh perspectives and thoughtful reading of earlier versions of the manuscript.

This book would not be the book you are holding in your hands were it not for Sue Canavan and Hiram Howard at Christopher-Gordon Publishers, who believed in this project from the beginning and consistently went the extra mile in its conception and production. Nor would it be the book that it is without the copyediting skills of Judith Antonelli, formatting talents of Lynne Schueler and the design intelligence of Michael Buckley. Their craftsmanship and tenacity helped all of us think clearly about what it could look like.

Finally, with awe and gratitude, we thank Debbi Miller for her incredible gifts and dedication to keeping us on schedule, revising endless pages of manuscript, putting up with our lapses, gracefully coordinating our work with publishers, copyeditors, clients, and others and ensuring that, in the midst of everything, this project moved forward.

—Robert Garmston and Bruce Wellman

Introduction

THIS BOOK is for those who believe that schools can be better and who have a reasonable sense of optimism about what is possible. It is a sourcebook for moving beyond slogans such as "all children can learn" and actually making this happen.

Teacher or parent, principal or professor, superintendent or staff developer, if you believe that individual teacher talent and energy is essential for student learning but not sufficient, this is your book. If you sense that the cumulative effect of what teachers focus on together can improve grade level and department and schoolwide achievement, you will want this book at your fingertips as you support schools in doing a better job.

The Adaptive School is about developing strong schools in which collaborative faculties are capable of meeting the certain challenges of today and the uncertain challenges of tomorrow. Some schools are already strong. Others are making remarkable gains in improving student achievement, increasing attendance, attaining higher post-school accomplishments, and developing satisfying relationships with communities. Some schools produce only fair results; others do poorly. We believe that all can be better.

As realists, we recognize that difficult and different challenges beset schools and communities in their quest to serve students. Issues differ. Urbanism and ruralism bring their own special problems. Defeatism, extremism, apathy, or politics infect some schools. Others struggle to overcome the effects of extreme poverty, neglected children, or the burdens of ponderous bureaucracy. Money can bring its own problems. Some affluent communities lobby for traditional definitions of success at the expense of other needs. In some districts teachers and students struggle daily with inadequate and outdated materials and facilities. Regardless of the nature of the issues, our premise is that the means for improvement exist within the school community. The practical ideas and tools in this book show how to activate these resources if they are dormant and focus them if they are scattered.

We believe that leadership is important and that the most effective leadership is informed, skilled, and widely distributed. To be adaptive and meet the demands of omnipresent change requires more than linear thought, tired problem-solving formulas, and recycled strategic plans. In the work of school improvement, human energy matters as much as the elements of good management— maybe more.

How to Use This Book

This book is designed as a sourcebook to support you in developing and facilitating collaborative groups to improve student learning. You can use it as a basic text for yourself or with a study group and as a reference book for diagnosis and problem solving. We encourage you to choose approaches that best serve your interests and needs.

Options and Possibilities

Read front to back. Chapter content is designed sequentially with each chapter building on the preceding sections.

Follow any of six themes throughout the book. Each chapter is introduced by a figure showing the themes featured therein.

> Getting work done
> **Doing the right work**
> Working collaboratively
> **Adapting to change**
> Managing systems
> Developing groups

Use icons to locate principles relating to systems or strategies and moves to achieve goals within systems. Because each type of icon appears at a specific level in the margin, you can "thumb" the pages to locate specific types of information.

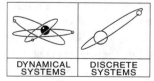

Towards top of page

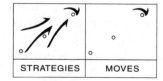

Near bottom of page

Principles explain why. A principle is the ult!imate source or cause of something. A principle is about how things work within systems. A principle informs the selection of strategies and moves.

We call attention to two levels of principles. First, *Overarching principles* govern nonlinear *dynamical* systems, like economies, weather patterns, and schools. On a smaller scale, *specific principles* govern *discrete* systems and how they work. At this level you will find principles that keep meetings on track, conflict contained, or groups cohesive.

Principles guide the development of strategies. Strategies are blueprints for action. They are preplanned, learned patterns of behavior. A strategy has structure, multiple steps and sequence. For example, brainstorming is a strategy. Its structure consists of ground rules (hot ideas only, no cold water), and its sequence is to review the topic and define the task, clarify the process, give time to think, brainstorm, and seek clarification or elaboration on brainstormed items.

Moves are different from strategies in that they are quick, discrete remarks or behaviors that take only a moment to perform. Instead of being planned, they are often spontaneous. Group leaders use them to intervene, amplify, or direct. For example, the facilitator question "Can you help the group to understand the relationship of that comment to the topic?" is a verbal move to keep a discussion on track. Taking a step away from the space in which you have delivered bad news is a move to separate the messenger from the message.

Refer to the problem-based user's guide (Table I-2) to search the text for information about specific problems.

Organization

Twelve chapters make up the body of the text, followed by several appendices and an author and subject index.

The book is organized by six themes that, taken together, focus and generate productive group results. Each chapter addresses one or more of these themes with a set of practical tools and organizing principles. Each chapter is headed with a box highlighting the themes emphasized in that chapter. Table I-1 provides a summary of which themes are covered in each chapter.

Getting Work Done

Educators are busy, time is precious, and there is often too much to do. This theme incorporates ideas and tools for getting necessary work done efficiently and effectively. Readers will find tools for developing collective understanding and making decisions, saving time, responding constructively to conflict, planning for accomplish-

Table I-1. Themes and Chapters

Themes	Chapters											
	1	2	3	4	5	6	7	8	9	10	11	12
Getting work done			•	•	•	•	•					
Doing the right work	•								•	•	•	
Working collaboratively		•	•	•	•	•			•			•
Managing systems									•	•	•	•
Developing groups			•	•	•			•	•			•
Adapting to change	•								•	•	•	•

ment, and developing high-performing groups. This theme illustrates the dynamic relationship between task accomplishment and process skills development. Groups skilled in this domain assume that their work is manageable.

Doing the Right Work

Groups often work hard but not always wisely. This theme provides guidelines for doing the work that matters most. It helps groups to reduce fragmentation and overload, distinguish between solvable and persistent problems, learn strategies appropriate for each, focus work on values and vision, and develop the capacities for adaptivity in a changing world. Application of this knowledge base supports clear vision, values, and goals to focus group energy.

Working Collaboratively

Collaboration is more than activities; it is about producing results through acting together. This theme focuses on how to work as equals with people of different resources to create positive results. Collaboration enables group members to focus on student learning, apply skill and repertoire in forms of professional talk, have effective meetings, and use conflict constructively. Collaborative group members see diversity as a necessary resource and help subcultures to connect with and value one another.

Managing Systems

As systems become more complex, the ability to think systematically and know when and how to set aside linear logic is important. Schools function as systems within systems. This theme helps readers to learn which interventions create the greatest change with the least effort. It explains how to strategically develop an organization's capacity for self-directed learning, understand teachers' professional knowledge bases, and develop professional capacities for adaptivity. This theme illuminates applications of rational and nonlinear principles from the new sciences to improve schooling.

Developing Groups

All ongoing groups face three simultaneous agendas: (a) task focus and accomplishment, (b) process skills development, and (c) group development. This theme presents principles and tools for assessing and developing effective groups. It offers strategies to build group strength in the short range (effective meetings) and in the long range (group maturity). Readers will find principles of intervention and methods to build and focus individual and group energy. This theme examines ways to improve the communication habits of groups as a means of increasing a group's effectiveness. It also explores principles of community development.

Adapting to Change

For groups to function effectively, they must constantly adapt to external environments. The more turbulent the environment, the more a group's energy must focus outward. This theme provides maps and tools for generating adaptivity, freeing trapped energy, coping intelligently with inter- and intragroup conflict and working with ordinary and unmanageable problems.

A Problem-Based User's Guide

This is a book of possibilities and tools for how adult interaction in schools can improve student learning. Many problems exist in such an endeavor. The user's guide is designed to assist you in locating information about some immediate challenges you might be facing. Table I-2 lists some of them.

Table I-2. Immediate Challenges

Problem Locator Topics

1. What to do about group members who:

(a) don't listen	PAG/PAU (78, 113), Numbered Heads (109), Attention First (112), Two Reflection Questions (178), Norms Inventory (278).
(b) are uncomfortable about speaking up	Paraphrasing (39), Gatekeeping (82), Grounding (107), A Pop-up Survey (107), Clock Partners (109), Limited Participation (132), Two Reflection Questions (178), Norms Inventory (278).
(c) dominate	Presuming Positive Intentions (45), Naive Questions (67, 71, 76, 82), "Cape" Comments (78), Stop, Redirect (79), Facilitator Moves to Balance Participation (80), Clock Partners (109), Multitask (111), Broken Record (132), Yes-But (133), Domination (133), Two Reflection Questions (178), Fogging (197).
(d) are unaware of the effects of their behaviors on others	Rate Your Group (65), Naive Questions (67, 71, 76, 82), Challenge Relevancy (78), Set & Test Working Agreements (82), Latecomer (132), Broken Record (132), Yes, but (133), Two Reflection Questions (178), Principles of Community (266), Norms Inventory (278), Team Development Survey (291).

2. What to do about groups that:

(a) are resisting	Focusing Questions (9), Reenergize (128), Group Groan (144), Value Tips (144), Behavioral Feedback (144), Clarify Conflicting Mental Models (202), Sea View School Low Scores (246), Change = A x B x C > X (248), William Bridges (248).
(b) don't stay on task on process	Task Process Rational (64), Naive Questions (67, 71, 76, 82), Planning, Deciding, Implementing (68), Multitask (111), Miring in Details (133), Is a Meeting Necessary (138), Never Meet to Pass Down Information Unless (139), Generic Agenda Planner (145), Final Planning Tips (151), Posted Outcomes (152).
(c) lack clear standards for collective performance and products	Rate Your Group (65), Naive Questions (67, 71, 76, 82), Develop Standards (76), Public Recording (84), Principles of Productive Transactions (93), Done–Yet To Do–Questions (116), Responsibility Charting (128), Activities Profile (130), Assessing Six Domains of Group Development (161), Contracting For Facilitation Services (285), Structuring Conversations About Data (296), Applying Principles of Nested Learning (170).
(d) have difficulty with decision making	Decide Who Decides (66), Naive Questions (67, 71, 76, 82), Force Field Analysis (120), Rule of One Third (124), Combine Opposites (125), Ranking (125), Forced Choice Stickers (126), Eliminate the Negative (126).
(e) have unproductive meetings	Task-Process Ratios (64), Decide Who Decides (66), Naive Questions (67, 71, 76, 82), Define the Sandbox (70), Design the Surround (71), PAG/PAU (78), Facilitator Moves to Balance Participation (80), Analogy (115), 1-2-6 (119), Is/Is Not (123), Miring in Details (133), Final Planning Tips (151), Two Reflection Questions (178).
(f) need help with problem finding and problem solving	Futures Wheel (121, 232), Spot analysis (122), Cluster (122), Fishbone (122), Mindmapping (123), Is/is Not (123), Solution Analysis (129), Curriculum Audit (130), Sensing Interviews (131), Issues Agenda (168), Causal-Loop Diagram (169), See the Big Picture (169), Fix What Shows, Not What Is Broken (192), Sensing Interview (201), Adaptive Responses (226), Question Brainstorm (229), Name the Elephants (230), Double-Loop Learning (231), Outcome Mapping (234), Action Planning (237), Dynamical Action Planning (238), Writing Skills Matrix (246), Facilitator's Contracting Conversation (289).

3. What to do about increasing your effectiveness in:

(a) influencing the thinking of others	Paraphrasing (39), Probing (41), Putting Ideas on the Table (44), Advocacy & Inquiry (46), Balcony View (56, 201), Choose Voice (112), Assumptions Wall (127), Principles Assessment (168), Values Challenge Seminar (168).
(b) managing your fear during conflict	Presuming Positive Intentions (45), Balcony View (56, 201), Ten Energy Traps (186), Joe Montana (199), Breathe (199), Self Talk (200), Monitor & Adjust Oxygen Levels (207), Respect Arousal States (208), Move Facial Muscles (212).
(c) fighting gracefully	Paying Attention to Self and Others (45), Advocacy & Inquiry (46, 198), Balcony View (56, 201), Confrontive Interchange (132), Ten Energy Traps (186), Instead of ... Say (195), Fogging (197), OSHA Example (197), Define Fairness (203), Address Values, Not Wants (206), Conflict Coping Moves (213), Conflict-Coping Moves (213).
(d) exercising your metacognitive skills as a group member	Capabilities (33), Know One's Intentions (34), Set Aside Unproductive Patterns (34), Know When to Self-Assert and When to Integrate (35), Support Group Purposes (36), Pausing (38), Suspension (54), Two Reflection Questions (178).
(e) maintaining your individuality while being a productive member of a group	Capabilities (33), Know When to Self-Assert and When to Integrate (35), Who Am I (98), Two Reflection Questions (178), Responsibilities-Dilemma of the Teacher-Facilitator Person (281), Facilitators Contracting Conversation (289).

Chapter 1   What Is an Adaptive School?

this chapter features:

Getting work done
Doing the right work
Working collaboratively
Managing systems
Developing groups
Adapting to change

I MAGINE a world where points of reference are not fixed and not predictable; a world in which north is constantly shifting and compasses twirl in their dials; a world in which the North Star becomes a meteor. How will you orient yourself in space and time? How will you find your way? How will you know where you are and where you are going? What will you cling to, pretending that it is permanent?

In many ways such a world surrounds the work of schools and schooling. Educators are caught between the tension of being guardians of the past and preparing students for an unknown and unknowable future. The great thinker and management consultant Peter Drucker observes that no era in recorded history has experienced as many radical social transformations as has the 20th century.

Work and workforce, society and polity, are all, in the last decade of the century, qualitatively and quantitatively different not only from what they were in the first years of this century but also from what existed at any other time in history: in their configurations, in their processes, in their problems, and in their structures.[1]

In response to uncertainty, parents, policy makers, and commentators simultaneously promote conflicting goals with calls for change and continuity, autonomy and accountability, and specialization and standardization.[2] It is no wonder that many administrators and teachers feel whiplash from such conflicting agendas.

Human brains and response systems were shaped by evolutionary forces to meet the demands of much earlier times. Were a saber-toothed tiger to bound through the door, these systems would immediately trigger a host of chemical, physical, and emotional reactions. Modern humans still possess automatic routines for Pleistocene-era problems.

Fast reflexes will not help educators to develop the types of schools and school systems needed in the next century.

These challenges require new minds and new mental models better equipped for the issues and obstacles of today. Most of all, educators need new sensitivities that can discern what is not readily apparent to the senses and help to shape new ways of improving schools for the journey ahead.

As educators, authors, and consultants, we are actively exploring new possibilities and developing ways of thinking about adult interaction in schools. Our own thinking is influenced by the emerging sciences of quantum mechanics, chaos theory, complexity theory, fractal geometry, and evolutionary biology as they apply to social organizations. We are also influenced by constructivist psychology, as it relates to learning and leadership, and our personal experiences in a variety of roles in education—teacher, curriculum consultant, staff developer, principal, superintendent, professor—and in our current work as consultants with schools, districts, and agencies throughout North America and with schools in Africa, Asia, Europe, and the Middle East.

Learning From the New Sciences

As we struggle to understand ways to improve schools, the new sciences reveal a world in which chaos and order are parts of the same system, existing simultaneously. We live not in a world of *either/or* but in the dawning of a world of *both/and*. We learn that schools are complex dynamical systems that are continually influenced by many variables, just as wind, temperature, and moisture affect a weather system and each other. Weather systems and the course of school improvement are both unpredictable in their details but not in their patterns.

Dynamical systems are governed by nonlinear relationships. They differ from mechanical systems like automobiles, in which direct cause-and-effect reasoning can be used to solve problems and isolate malfunctions. John Briggs describes this new world as follows:

> It appears that in dynamical systems chaos and order are different masks the system wears: in some circumstances the system shows one face; in different circumstances it shows another. These systems can appear to be complex; their simplicity and complexity lurk inside each other.[3]

Our premise is that information and metaphors from the new sciences can reframe and clarify challenges for educational leaders. These new challenges are not about working harder—there is hardly a profession in which people pour out as much energy and work—but about working in new ways within principles suggested to us by the new sciences. In adopting these lenses, however, we do not advocate refuting what has been learned in the past 70 years of research on school improvement.

The History of School Change

School improvement research parallels and intertwines with organizational development research and practice. As far back as the 1930s, education, government, and business thinkers developed lenses and tools for improving organizational focus and productivity.

Important findings endure from each decade. Efforts from the 1930s through the 1950s focused on innovation and diffusion of ideas. During the 1960s, parallel to the work in organizational development, school research emphasized organizational health and stages in the change processes. The 1970s saw increased attention to activities related to the whole organization: building mutual trust, removing barriers to communication, establishing positive climates, and encouraging participation in planning and decision making.

During the 1970s researchers increased their understanding of the processes of change in schools and the means of technical assistance for promoting it. The Concerns Based Adoption model, widely disseminated and applied, is a product of this era.[4] These findings are still successfully employed in school improvement efforts.

The Rand change-agent study in the late '70s brought to light fundamental principles of school change. These include: (a) the importance of staff efficacy, (b) the value of participation in decision making, and (c) the necessity for both bottom-up and top-down change efforts. These factors are now taken for granted in improvement efforts.

The 1980s and 1990s brought wide exposure to the effective schools research. Efforts to apply this were largely rationalistic, resulting in lists, inventories, and efforts to install various desirable characteristics in school life. Recent change efforts draw from the meta-analyses of school improvement designs by such authors as Michael Fullan, Larry Cuban, Mathew Miles, and Seymour Sarason, who are themselves working within the influence of the larger knowledge bases that are being developed in the field of organizational development.

An important current perspective on school change is that the sole issue is not innovation. Although it may start with that, it also includes implementation, fidelity, impact, institutionalization, maintenance, and replication.[5]

This growing knowledge base points to the influence of organizational culture on employee behavior. Change agents must learn how to focus attention on developing productive collective norms, mediating individual and collective belief systems, and enhancing interpersonal relationships inside the organization.[6]

From these decades of effort and research, three fundamental questions remain for school improvement efforts: (a) Are teachers and students doing things differently in classrooms? (b) Are these differences improving student learning? and (c) Are schools learning from experience so they can be increasingly effective in response to changing needs? It is to this last question that this book attempts to make a modest contribution in answering.

"Thing" and "Energy" Models of the World

Marshaling, focusing and developing energy, information and relationships becomes the role of leaders.

—Margaret Wheatley

Improving schools requires two ways of looking at the world. One view focuses on "things," the basic stuff of good management. "Thing" ways of seeing and working get the details handled, the bills paid, the buses running on time and making the right stops in the right neighborhoods. "Thing" thinking is the historical foundation of all management systems in modern organizations.

Another leadership perspective focuses on energy. Author Margaret Wheatley observes that the quality of human relationships creates the energy source that produces all organizational work.[7] This is the energy with which organization members commit, persevere, and relate. With the special lenses explored in this book, such energy can be discerned, modified, and focused.

The celebrated revolution in physics called quantum mechanics clarifies essential distinctions between matter and energy and simultaneously blurs the line between them. The very term *quantum mechanics* means bundles of energy (quantum) in motion (mechanics).[8] This book describes ways to shape this energy through collaborative norms, well-structured meetings, new frames for conflict, and communication practices that make a difference for student learning.

As Richard Elmore reminds us, the real work of changing schools lies in changing norms, knowledge, and skills (energy) at the individual and organizational level before we attempt to change the structure of schools (things). In fact, without new norms, knowledge, and skills, structural changes such as block scheduling, site-based decision making, multiage classrooms, and heterogeneous grouping will have little or no effect on student learning.[9]

In adaptive schools, leaders pay attention both to things and to the flow and interchange of energy. Energy becomes an avenue to attainment. We will expand on this idea with descriptions of four leadership roles in the next chapter and with an elaboration of one of the roles (facilitator) in chapter 6.

Adaptive, Not Adapted, Schools

Evolutionary biology is the source for a central notion in our work: adaptivity. To be *adaptive* means to change form in concert with clarifying identity. This is quite different from being *adapted,* which means to have evolved through specialization to fit specific conditions within tightly defined boundaries.

Monarch butterflies are a good example of an *adapted* species. Across North America, the summer fields sparkle with their flight. Monarchs, as most school children learn, lay their eggs only on milkweed plants. When the larvae hatch they feed on the milkweed leaves, growing and developing until it is time to spin a cocoon attached to the same milkweed plant. The larvae metamorphize into adult butterflies, and the cycle repeats. Without the milkweed there would be no monarchs. Monarchs' nutritional and habitat needs are firmly adapted to this one family of plants.

An example of adaptivity within a species lives on another continent. In southwest Africa, the leopards in parts of Namibia have developed new behaviors that radically change their ways of hiding recent kills. Their long-used practice was to drag the kill up into a tree to keep it away from other predators. Human hunters learned to check trees for signs of leopard and in that way to find and kill the cats that were damaging their livestock herds. Over time, the leopards have abandoned the tree-hiding strategy and now drag their kill into the tall grass where human hunters fear to track them.

Organizations, like species, also need to contend with issues and transitions of being adapted to existing environments and becoming adaptive to changing conditions. The Eastman Kodak Company is a prime example of a large organization struggling through form and identity tensions. Kodak, a Fortune 500 company,

In adaptive schools, leaders pay attention both to things and to the flow and interchange of energy.

derives most of its current revenue and profits from silver-based film and photo processing. From the snapshots of your daughter's birthday party to your x-rays at the dentist's office, *film* and *Kodak* are synonymous. The problem for Kodak is that the world is rapidly going digital. Its biggest rival in the future may not be the Fuji film company of Japan but computer and printer maker Hewlett-Packard of Silicon Valley, California.[10]

The central tension for Kodak is the change in focus from the form of film to the identity of image making. Images can be created with many different technologies. Film is a limited medium. Some forecasters are suggesting that in 10 years the only people using film will be artists. The rest of us will be happily snapping away with digital devices, uploading our images to the Internet and transmitting them to our friends and relatives all in less time than it would take to drive to the store to drop off our negatives.

Form and identity confusions are rampant in schools these days. At a seminar we were conducting, a woman stopped by at the break to share her struggles with these issues. As the head librarian for a medium-size school district, she remarked on all the professional changes she has experienced since completing her masters degree in library science in the early 1970s. As a supervisor, she is supporting several librarians struggling with similar changes. She noted that as librarians they are taught to be quality filters and to stock the shelves with reliable and authoritative reference materials. When students and teachers ask for resources, the librarians are then able to supply the best sources available and take professional pride in knowing and having these materials.

As students and teachers become increasingly computer savvy, the librarians are beginning to feel left out. The budget for reference materials is being questioned, and there is concern about the quality of information that students and teachers are accessing. Being a quality filter is a form that gave the librarians pride in their work. They now find that they must develop new ways of applying their knowledge and skills and become teachers of quality filtering. The deepest transition here is not a change in the knowledge base of librarians but in the ways that this knowledge is applied within their new identities.

All around us we see examples like this. As Internet-based courses continue to come on-line for students, what it means to be a teacher and to have a class will dramatically shift.[11] The very concept of the schoolhouse will increasingly be seen as historical artifact rather than current reality.

Voice-recognition software will dramatically change the teaching of foreign languages. It is not hard to imagine computer environments in which students interact with native speakers of the language they are learning. The scenes will come complete with full cultural settings, appropriate body language and nonverbal messages, and an oscilloscope readout displaying the voice inflections of the native speaker compared to the voice inflections of the novice learner. Conversations can be repeated until fully mastered. In such an environment the form of specialty teacher of one language is replaced by the identity of master of second-language learning. This identity is accompanied by the elements of designer, motivator, manager, and clinician. The number of languages to be taught is limited not by personnel but by the availability of software and hardware (Table 1-1).

Table 1-1. Form vs. Identity

Example	Form	Identity
Eastman Kodak	Film manufacturer	Image technology company
Reference Librarian	Quality filter	Teacher of quality filtering
Foreign Language Teacher	Specialist in one language	Specialist in second-language learning

The traditional North American high school serves as a striking example of an adapted, not an adaptive, system. Designed in another time for the purposes of that time, the typical high school often shows a remarkable lack of flexibility, with staff members clinging to tightly defined niches within increasingly fragile specialties.

The basic design of the "modern" high school dates to 1892, when an august body called the Committee of Ten met to develop uniform entrance requirements for colleges. Their goal was to create a smoother transition from high school to college for the elite students of the day. It is important to note that in 1890, only 360,000 students ages 14 to 17 attended high school in the United States. That was approximately 6.7% of the total age group. Of that number, only a small percentage was college-bound.[12]

The basic course structures that the Committee of Ten recommended are still in place today. In a rapidly changing world, we cling to the comfort of tradition and do not effectively question the roots of our institutions and norms. The students we serve and our expectations for them are substantially different from the structures that contain them. Our rapidly changing world is driven by demographic, technological, economic, social, and political pressures in many different directions. For many educators and parents, the solace of the past seems a greater surety than the vagueness of the future. Their response to change is the embrace of tradition. This may well turn out to be the equivalent of training Linotypists to work with hot lead in an era of digital design.

The great challenge for schools is to let go of the comforts of adapted behaviors and to develop the patterns and practices of adaptivity. This is especially true in climates in which the milkweed might not live forever. Adaptivity manifests in flexible responses interacting with changing environmental conditions. This is true for individuals, species, and organizations. It requires a clear identity and lack of attachment to form.

Schools Are Nonlinear Dynamical Systems

Schools change through different mechanisms than researchers have supposed. Schools are nonlinear dynamical systems in which cause and effect are not tightly linked. They are shaped by a blend of regularity and irregularity and patterns of stability and instability. Critical-choice points present new possibilities and new forms of order. Instability permits creative life in school systems. The self-organizing interactions between people develop feedback loops that recur and amplify across the scale of the organization.

Management thinker Ralph Stacey observes, "Top managers cannot control this, but through their interventions they powerfully influence it. It is their prime responsibility to understand the qualitative patterns of behavior that their interventions may produce. Order through installation by the designing minds is replaced by order emerging from instability through a process of self-organization."[13]

Self-organization develops through meaningful adult interactions about students, student work, and the purposes and processes of schooling. To be productive, such interactions must be infused with and guided by shared values and norms of collaboration. The environment must encourage reflection, inquiry, challenge, and deprivatization of practice. This in turn requires skills in dialogue, discussion, planning, and problem solving. At times, the work is messy and nonrational. Habitual, linear ways of thinking will work for some issues but not for the increasingly complex and ill-structured problems that beset many schools today.

Five guiding principles frame our thinking about schools as nonlinear dynamical systems:

1. More data does not lead to better predictions.

2. Everything influences everything else.

3. Tiny events create major disturbances.

4. You don't have to touch everyone in the system to make a difference.

5. Both things and energy matter.

In the chapters that follow, we describe these overarching, dynamical principles in action as they play out through new forms of positive adult interaction.

How Schools Become Adaptive

So far we have discussed the importance of adaptivity and the need to clarify identity, both as individuals and as organizations, without clinging to outmoded forms. We've suggested a rationale for why that is important by framing schools as nonlinear dynamical systems in which cause-and-effect linkages are not so easily drawn. We'd now like to briefly describe how schools might achieve this. The chapters that follow will expand, elaborate upon, and share many of the concrete tools we have learned to use from our work with successful schools.

A Short Course in Adaptivity: Focusing Questions

We encourage departments, committees, councils, and faculties to reflect frequently on three focusing questions. The by-product of this reflection is action for improving student learning.

1. Who are we?

2. Why are we doing this?

3. Why are we doing this, this way?

Who Are We?

Principal Kathy Dunton of Vine Hills Elementary School in California told us that these three questions transformed her school. She encourages teachers—and parents—to ask these frequently and to explore them in depth. The question "Who are we?" leads directly to the issue of identity. This issue forces the related questions of "About what do we care?" and "How much do we dare?" The form taken by a school, team, department, or teacher's assignment is less important than identity. Identity represents the story that a group tells itself to organize its values and beliefs. A group's beliefs determine its behavior. Collectively, its behavior affects student learning.[14]

Identity cannot be found in a mission statement. It displays itself in hallways, faculty lounges, meeting minutes, and student academic results. Identity reveals itself in periods of stress: What a group strives to preserve or fight to protect describes its identity. The very definitions of success, the awards and rewards for both students and staff members, symbolize driving values and beliefs.

Why Are We Doing This?

Folk wisdom, tradition, and unexamined habit rule much of what schools do. The agricultural calendar, factory schedules, and athletic practices continue to frame yearly and daily time use. Bus schedules and teacher contracts exert powerful and often unexamined influences on student learning. Yet these and other features of school life go unquestioned. "It's just the way we do things around here," one is told when bold enough to inquire.

A classic story captures the essence of this issue. A little girl, watching her mother prepare a ham for the oven, wanted to know why her mommy was cutting the end off before placing it in the roasting pan. "I don't really know," her mother replied. "That's the way my mommy did it."

So the little girl went to see her grandmother and asked her why *she* cut the end of the ham off before putting it in the roasting pan. "I don't really know," her grandmother replied. "That's the way my mommy did it."

So the little girl went to see her great-grandmother and asked her why *she* cut the end of the ham off before putting it in the roasting pan. "Well," the old woman exclaimed, stretching her arms wide, "I grew up on the prairie in a little sod house, and our hams were *this big*." Bringing her hands close together, she finished, "And our oven was *this big*. We had to cut the end off the ham to fit it in the oven."

In many settings, educators continue to cut the end off the ham long after the original rationale has passed. The deep structure of schooling is set on foundations of hams and end scraps from earlier eras. Unquestioned assumptions form the ovens in which they cook. Many current practices are rooted in beliefs about the need for power and control over others and over resources.[15] Interestingly, such beliefs were at the heart of the management literature during most of the 1800s and 1900s. They are the source of conflicts over curriculum and at the center of most tensions around any form of shared decision making. The question "Why are we doing this?" brings attention and choice to practices that may have become unquestioned habits.

Why Are We Doing This, This Way?

"This" might be grouping students for instruction, developing learning experiences, or deciding time allotments for activities. This last question, valued so highly by California principal Kathy Dunton, brings focus not to the *what* and *why* of the activity but to the *how*. Walk through any school with a notebook in hand. This question will have you scribbling rapidly.

The daily schedule is a good starting point. Anyone who has observed the sleeping and waking patterns of adolescents knows that 8:00 a.m. is not peak time for anything not conducted in a prone position, yet district schedules organized by transportation patterns typically have high schools starting around that hour. On the other hand, many 5- and 6-year-olds are up and bustling, ready to get on with the new day. Schools may, in fact, have the daily time schedule for the various levels of schooling in reverse order from what would be a better fit with physical development patterns.

The question "Why are we doing this, this way?" could be restated, "Who benefits from the current system?" Exploring this form of the question provides insight into the forces that keep current practices in place. As our principal friend found, these three focusing questions open up new ways of seeing school practices. Revealed, they can be acted upon and modified. Left unexamined, they keep the institutional drivers on autopilot and the map stuffed in the glove compartment.

This Book Teaches New Songs

All cultures have creation stories to explain the coming of the world and their place in it. The Aboriginal people of Australia believe that their land is covered with a web of invisible pathways. These "dreaming-tracks" or "songlines" first appeared during the *Tjukurpa* (djook-oor-pah) or "Dreamtime," when ancestral beings wandered over the featureless landscape singing the world into existence. These totemic ancestors sang out the name of everything that crossed their path. They sang out the names of plants, animals, rocks, rivers, saltpans, and waterholes, coding and wrapping the world in a web of song.[16]

When an Aboriginal mother is pregnant and feels the baby kick for the first time, she calls the shaman to identify that child's totemic spirit guide. Physical features at the site of the kick are then interpreted, and the spirit of the child—the child's "dreaming"—is thus identified. This dreaming can be one of any number of mammals, insects, birds, or reptiles. As the child grows, he or she learns the song of this spirit guide. Coded into the song are the features of the local landscape—where to find food, water, shelter, and safe travel routes. Song is the oldest mnemonic device, far easier for a nomad to carry than any road atlas.

An Aborigine who goes "walkabout" on a journey of discovery or on a hunting foray calls on this song to guide him or her. Along one's "songline," one has safe passage, meeting others who share the dreaming along the way. Memory carries the traveler to the limits of the song. At the boundaries Aborigines meet and, through ritual, swap songs. This sharing relationship extends the territory of each and binds one to another through song.

To find new territory and new routes, we all need to learn new songs. This earth and its workings are not as we were once taught. At the limits of our songs, we need each other so that we can be adaptive in a world made of bundles of energy in motion.

End Notes

[1] Drucker, P. (1994, November). The age of social transformation. *Atlantic Monthly*, 53.

[2] Hargreaves, A. (1995). Renewal in the age of paradox. *Educational Leadership*, 52 (7), 14–19.

[3] Briggs, J. (1992). *Fractals: The pattern of chaos*. New York: Touchstone, p. 20.

[4] Hall, G., & Hord, S. (1987). *Change in schools: Facilitating the process*. Albany, NY: State University of New York Press.

[5] Louis, K. S., Toole, J., & Hargreaves, A. (in press). Rethinking school improvement. In J. Murphy and K. S. Louis (Eds.). *Handbook of educational administration*. San Francisco: Jossey-Bass.

[6] Hall, G., & Shieh, W. H. (1998). Supervision and organizational development. In G. Firth & E. Pajak (Eds.), *Handbook of research on school supervision* (pp. 842–865). New York: MacMillan.

[7] Wheatley, M. (1992). *Leadership and the new science: Learning about organizations from an orderly universe*. San Francisco: Berrett-Koehler.

[8] Capra, F. (1991). *The tao of physics*. Boston: Shambhala.

[9] Elmore, R. (1995). Structural reform and educational practice. *Educational Researcher*, 24 (9), 23–26.

[10] Burrows, P., Smith, G., & Brull, S. (1997, July 7). HP pictures the future. *Business Week*, 100–109.

[11] Berman, S., & Tinker, R. (1997, November). The world's the limit in the virtual high school. *Educational Leadership*, 55 (3), 52–54; and Goodham, M. (1997, August 26). Students stay home for

cyber-school. *The Globe and Mail*, C1–C2.

[12] DeBoer, G. E. (1991). *A history of ideas in science education.* New York: Teachers College Press.

[13] Stacey, R. (1992). *Managing the unknowable: Strategic boundaries between order and chaos in organizations.* San Francisco: Jossey-Bass, p. 13.

[14] Dilts, R. (1994). *Effective presentation skills.* Capitola, CA: Meta.

[15] Sarason, S. (1990). *The predictable failure of educational reform.* San Francisco: Jossey-Bass.

[16] Chatwin, B. (1987). *The songlines.* New York: Penguin Books.

Chapter 2   The Importance
of Professional
Community

TEACHERS in successful schools are undeniably
interdependent. Professionals working in concert
produce cumulative effects in student learning.
As more schools, districts, states, and provinces develop
and attempt to implement clear standards and high expectations, the need for collaborative energy becomes increasingly clear.

this chapter features:

Getting work done
Doing the right work
Working collaboratively
Managing systems
Developing groups
Adapting to change

Academic standards
are an example of policy makers
operating with "thing" models of
the world. While clarity and
explicitness in detailing the
knowledge and skills that
students will develop is necessary and difficult to achieve, it is
equally necessary to rethink and
develop the support systems
among educators that will
produce such achievement.
Equal attention must be given to
"energy models" for making
standards real in classrooms and
schools. Central to this notion is
the idea of adults operating in
professional communities to
release the energy trapped by
existing organizational patterns.

It is important to
remember that the current
system and ways of running
schools produce the current
results. The deep structure of
North American schools and the
ways of organizing and operating them has remained fairly

stable throughout this century.
Students, parents, educators, and
the greater public all seem to
know what a "real school" is.
This cultural template provides
stability and legitimacy to the
school as an institution in society
and support for many of the
practices that occur within the
institution.[1]

One of the most stable
factors in schools over the years
has been the relative isolation of
teachers from each other
throughout their workday and
work year. What sociologist Dan
Lortie described in his
groundbreaking 1975 study is
still true in many schools today.
In these "egg-crate" schools, he
observed a work life in which
autonomous teachers were
organized by a culture of
presentism, individualism, and
conservatism.[2] These teachers
lived from moment to moment in
their classrooms and sought
routines that were efficient and

energy conserving. They were careful not to tread on the territory of others and were proactively conservative about changes in curriculum and instruction. Such behaviors and attitudes are still deeply embedded in many schools today yet do not contribute to building the kinds of schools that will be flexible and adaptive to meeting the challenges of changing demographics and increased academic demands and serving the learning needs of a society in rapid transition.

Professional Community and Student Learning

In our work, we have not discovered a magic elixir that will improve schools once and for all. Our intent in this book is to share what we are learning about ways in which staffs can better interact to improve results for all students. We will offer ways to build professional communities in schools where difficult things can be talked about, where hard questions about teaching and learning get asked, and where adults actively learn from one another.

An emerging research base supports these goals. Images of improving schools detail both the promise and practicality of these ideas. Karen Seashore Louis, Helen Marks, and Sharon Kruse have identified five elements of teachers' professional community that produce a collective sense of responsibility for student learning in restructured schools:[3]

1. Shared norms and values

2. Collective focus on student learning

3. Collaboration

4. Deprivatized practice

5. Reflective dialogue

This shared effort develops schoolwide gains in student achievement. When teachers take collective responsibility for students they conceive their work to be a joint enterprise.[4] They have a higher sense of personal and collective efficacy and assume that learning is a result of school rather than nonschool factors.[5] In high schools where this sense of collective responsibility was strong, students made larger gains in mathematics, reading, history, and science than in schools where the collective sense was weaker. These outcomes were especially true for minority students and students from low socioeconomic backgrounds.

Elements of Professional Community

Shared Norms and Values

Communities come into existence and thrive because of common values and ways of working together. Norms and values are the grains of sand that become pearls in the oyster of true community. How people treat one another, their social taboos, and the whys and hows of celebrations are manifestations of norms and values in action. Shared norms and values establish reciprocal expectations for community members. Louis, Marks, and Kruse assert that teachers' professional communities operate with a sense of moral authority and moral responsibility for making a difference in the lives of students.

Developing consciousness about norms and values is central to the community-building process. Leaders at all levels of the school teach in two ways: by example and by calibrating their actions and responses to others against clearly articulated values and explicit norms of interaction.

In chapter 3 we elaborate on seven norms of collaboration that, when consciously attended to over time, produce skilled communication and increased clarity and cohesion within working groups.

Collective Focus on Student Learning

Professional communities focus on student learning as the end and teaching as the means. In too many school teams and departments, professional sharing consists of little more than swapping activities and exchanging materials.

"What is good work? Do all students have ample opportunities to learn important material? How can instruction be differentiated to meet the needs of diverse learners?" are a few of the questions asked in schools with professional communities. Such conversations focus on the output of teaching, not the input. To achieve the goal of cumulative effect, departments in secondary schools and teams in elementary and middle schools clarify among themselves the standards for quality student performance.

As an example, the social studies department members and the English department members develop consensus on the qualities of good writing and on the types of writing products that students must master. They then agree on developmental schemes and feedback systems that are coherent and consistent across classrooms. They engage in periodic checks and round-table examinations of actual student work from various classrooms as one way to ground these conversations.

Collaboration

Who teachers are to one another is as important as who they are to their students. In high-performing and improving schools in numerous studies, collaboration is the norm.[6] We are not talking here about project-based collaboration or the "contrived collegiality" described by Hargreaves and Dawe in which administrators create tasks and agendas to occupy teachers' collective energies.[7] Rather, we are referring to sharing expertise and perspectives on teaching and learning processes, examining data about students, and developing a sense of mutual support and shared responsibility for effective instruction.

Collaboration and collegiality in this way is part of one's professional identity. It does not happen by chance; it needs to be structured, taught, and learned. Developing collaborative cultures is the work of leaders who realize that a collection of superstar teachers working in isolation cannot produce the same results as interdependent colleagues who share and develop professional practices together. From such interactions come growth and learning for teachers, teams, and schools as adaptive organizations.

Deprivatized Practice

In his speeches and articles, researcher and author Bruce Joyce refers to teaching as the second most private act. In professional communities, teaching comes out into the open so that teachers can learn with and from one another. This may be one of the most countercultural practices that both supports and enhances professional communities in schools.

The norms of privacy have deep roots in "real schools." Once the classroom door is closed, the teacher is God. In this sphere of autonomy lies both greatness and sorrow. Within the zone of isolation, some teachers still find ways to develop craft knowledge, content knowledge, and compassion for their students. These extraordinary individuals manage to stimulate their teaching and continually renew their passion for daily interactions with young minds.

All too often, though, this same isolation buffers mediocrity and hides high performers from those who might learn from their modeling, consultation, and coaching. When practice is deprivatized, teachers visit one another's classrooms to observe master teaching, to coach each other, to mentor, and to problem solve in the living laboratory of instructional space.

Schoolwide action research, practiced at schools with membership in the League of Professional Schools, collides with norms of isolation and can be an effective approach to deprivatization.[8]

Reflective Dialogue

The work of professional communities in schools is a melding of the private and the public and of autonomy and interdependence. Reflective dialogue is a key leavening agent in this process. By dialogue we mean developing shared understandings of such things as the purposes of and processes for learning. In chapter 4 we make distinctions between this type of teacher talk and talk organized as discussions that lead to decisions.

Shared understandings bind communities together and bind members to shared goals and shared work. Through reflective dialogue, group members gain perspective on who and how they are to each other and to those they serve. Reflective dialogue is the catalyst for reflective practice. It helps participants develop self-awareness and collective awareness of personal and shared work.

It is one thing to note that professional communities are characterized by shared norms and values, a collective focus on student learning, collaboration, deprivatized practice and reflective dialogue. How they get that way remains the educational leader's most pressing question.

Developing Teachers' Professional Communities

Despite the existence of these descriptors of schools making a difference for students, the question of how we get there remains. Schools need frameworks, role clarity, and self-renewing tool kits for collaborative practice. Based on our understanding of the literature on school change, organizational development, teaching and learning, and our experiences with schools these past several years, we offer the following frameworks as organizers for this journey.

Leaders in adaptive schools pay attention to twin goals, four hats of shared leadership, five energy sources, and seven norms of collaboration. We will briefly describe the first three frameworks here (Fig. 2-1) and elaborate on the collaborative norms in chapter 3.

To address problems in low-performing schools (see sidebar), districts and schools continually apply energy and resources to both production and production capacities. Leaders of adaptive schools simultaneously develop two goals related to the organization's

The Adaptive School

Twin goals
- developing organiza-
  tional capacities
- developing profes-
  sional capacities

Four Hats
- coaching
- consulting
- facilitating
- presenting

Energy Sources
- efficacy
- craftsmanship
- flexibility
- consciousness
- interdependence

Figure 2-1 Adaptive Schools

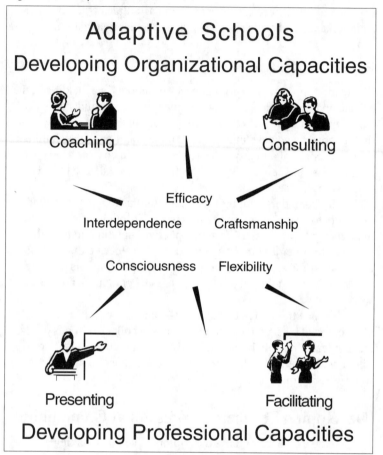

ongoing need for self-improvement. The first goal expands six organizational capacities for adaptivity. The second goal strengthens six professional capacities for adaptivity. We will provide brief descriptions here and elaborate on them in chapter 11.

Organizational Capacities for Adaptivity

Vision, Values, and Goal Focus

Clarity in this area is a hallmark of successful schools. The most important goals are the academic goals for students. These in turn are an expression of the value system that governs the organization. Healthy schools and organizations hold a vision for themselves of how they wish to operate in the world. This is a vision of values and

The Low-Performing High School

At the low-performing high school, many students proactively disengage from learning. They slump in their seats on the days that they bother to come to class. Students ignore homework assignments, and remediation needs outweigh coverage of new material. External rewards such as grades, honor rolls, and college admissions requirements hold little or no motivational power.

Teachers are attempting to deal with this situation by embracing tradition, enforcing standards, and struggling to maintain the integrity of teaching methods and materials.

The net result of all these interactions includes departments with abnormally high failure rates, decreased enrollments in advanced courses, falling attendance, and increased dropout rates. Staff morale and teacher efficacy are plummeting.

This is a classic situation in which the five principles of dynamical systems are at work.

1. More data does not lead to better predictions. Additional surveys and reports about attendance, dropout rates, test scores, and staff attitudes will not improve this school.

2. Everything influences everything else. Tough standards only raise the bar higher for students who lack basic jumping skills. Poor student performance lowers expectations and teachers' professional pride and sense of purpose. Parental concerns and complaints cause defensiveness and withdrawal.

3. Tiny events create major disturbances. Student expulsions, a dropped section of an honors course, and half-full classes create ripple effects throughout life in the school.

4. You don't have to touch everyone in the system to make a difference. A belief that everyone in the school needs to be ready for change before any action can be taken blocks movement and innovation.

5. Both things and energy matter. Rules, routines, and procedures will count for little without also attending to the qualities of human relationships in the school.

---

goals in action. Such a vision is informed by real-world measures of student achievement and other goal accomplishments.

At the low-performing high school, vision, values, and goals require rethinking and refocusing. English literature may not be the most appropriate course to teach students with fundamental literacy needs.

Systems Thinking

This capacity and vision, values, and goal focus are the major organizers of adaptivity. Helping others to see systems places the work of schools and within schools in larger contexts. This framework reveals influencing interactions and helps to answer the question "What part of the system can we influence to get positive change?"

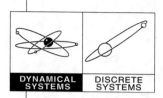

One major concept in systems work is the idea of feedback loops. These can be either negative or positive. School systems governed by punishment and reward systems based on test scores operate with negative feedback loops that attempt to keep test scores within acceptable parameters, which are usually calibrated by political pressures.

Positive feedback loops work the other way—the more there is, the more develops. How people talk to one another is an example of a positive feedback loop illustrating the dynamical principle of how a little input can have a major influence. In the next chapter we will discuss seven norms of collaboration as examples of positive feedback loops within organizations.

Systems thinking, whether explicitly labeled as such or not, is what professional communities do. This would be an essential entry point at the low-performing high school. Administrators and teachers would gain much perspective by stepping back and looking at the interactions of the parts of the system in which they are involved.

Initiating and Managing Adaptation

This is the work of leaders at all levels of the school and professional community. Inquiry is an essential tool of adaptation. The three focusing questions offered in chapter 1 are resources: "Who are we?" "Why are we doing this?" and "Why are we doing this, this way?"

Adaptation is not limited to external events. Adaptive schools help all players to learn how to cope with the psychological transition related to change.

The three focusing questions do not seem to be asked at the low-performing high school. The questions, if asked persistently by all players, would positively perturb the system and produce enough shared dissatisfaction to create a willingness to consider changing entrenched patterns and practices.

Interpreting and Using Data

Data has no meaning on its own. Meaning is a result of human interaction with data. Many schools are data rich and meaning poor. Adaptive groups develop the capacity to discern what data are worth paying attention to and what collaborative practices help people to engage with data in ways that increase ownership and willingness to act on conclusions.

Data can be quantitative or qualitative. Schools are difficult places to motivate and govern with numbers. A 6% rise in student reading scores is often not as compelling as a teacher's tale of the

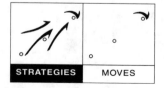

slow reader who makes a breakthrough. Reasoning by anecdote is often more common than reasoning with data. Interpreting and using data is a learned skill that takes time and practice to develop.

The low-performing high school usually has enough data about the system but little knowledge. Knowledge, meaning, and commitment result from dialogue and discussion about what story is told by the data. Without organized story making, people in organizations make up their own explanations for events. Part of the reason for this is protection from unwanted truths.

Developing and Maintaining Collaborative Cultures

This is the essence of teachers' professional community in schools. Collaborative and group development work hand in hand. In chapter 8 we discuss ways to help groups become more interdependent and cohesive.

Collaboration operates within and between groups. When students work with units of measure as they quantify lab materials, interdependence connects the math teachers to the science teachers. Success in the lab builds on math skills learned in other settings. Laboratory applications further reinforce the practical nature of algorithms learned in math class.

Collaboration fuels group development when individual members envision (a) the potential of the group as a collective force in the school and (b) the expanding capacity of the group for accomplishing important work that individuals working in isolation would not be able to achieve.

A sense of collaboration is lacking at the low-performing high school. Teachers and departments feel besieged, hunkering down and fighting their own fights for some sense of accomplishment and dignity. Students and teachers do not see themselves aligned in a shared task. Each sees the other as an adversary, with small victories and losses accumulating on a daily basis.

Gathering and Focusing Resources

Time, money, and human energy are some of the resources that support goal accomplishment in schools. Overload and fragmentation are the enemies of success. Resources need to be focused where they will make the greatest difference. Ultimately this leads to some hard decisions in schools. Resource allocation and goal accomplishment are directly linked. What receives attention gets done.

This last organizational capacity for adaptivity cannot work without clarity in the other frames. Values and goals point out resource needs. Systems thinking frames where to target resources.

Overload and fragmentation are the enemies of success.

To initiate and manage adaptation means applying and managing resources. Data use and interpretation sets up essential feedback loops that reflect whether and how goals are being achieved. Collaboration is the glue that allows groups to both agree upon and work toward the goals.

All of this is missing at the low-performing high school. Energy, time, and money are thrown at problems to fix the most visible ones. Doing anything is considered good enough. The goal is to protect individuals and the organization from the accusation of not working hard enough. Without a clear focus and without honest feedback systems, however, this only saps resources and increases the magnitude of the problems.

Professional Capacities for Adaptivity

Collegial Interaction

In many respects, collaboration needs to be taught. Past practices and workplace culture influence the capacity for collaboration. So does gender and school organization (elementary, middle, or high). Attitudes, knowledge, skills, and practices can be taught; these are the focus of chapters 3, 4, 5, 6, 7, and 9. The capacity to be a colleague is different from other capacities of good teaching. It draws upon craft knowledge, self-knowledge, and interpersonal skills to form a web of reciprocal relationships and services.

Norms of privatism are strong at the low-performing high school. Each teacher operates as an independent artisan. There is no craft guild with which to share professional knowledge and concerns. Small breakthroughs with students are personal victories to be savored and fleetingly enjoyed in quiet moments.

Cognitive Processes of Instruction

Instructional thinking occurs in four phases: planning, teaching, analyzing and evaluating, and applying what has been learned to future work.[9]

The more cognitively adept a teacher is, the better the results in classrooms and with colleagues. This capacity includes the abilities to manage multiple goals simultaneously, to align one's work with that of one's colleagues, and to learn from experience in the classroom.

Teachers in the low-performing high school feel that they have no time to reflect. The pace of survival puts action ahead of reflection on most personal and collective agendas. Peer coaching programs sputtered out in the press for time. Formal supervision is pro forma and ritualized. Administrators are mostly satisfied with teachers who keep the lid on in a classroom and keep kids out of the office.

Knowledge of the Structure of the Discipline

This moves beyond content knowledge, which is necessary but not sufficient for good teaching. Knowledge of the structure of the discipline is informed by knowing the organizing schema of the field, including the significant ideas in the discipline and how they relate to one another. Anticipating major misconceptions and barriers to learning and understanding the significant ideas are also important here. These inform curricular choices and the selection and use of resource materials.

This area is looming as an important entry point for instructional improvement. In chapter 11 we will elaborate on the connections between teacher knowledge of the structure of the discipline and student achievement. Just as there are no teacher-proof curricula, there are no knowledge-free curricula. To interact flexibly with students in the flow of instruction, teachers need to deeply know their content and the organizing principles of that content.

Little attention has been given to matters of curriculum at the low-performing high school beyond periodic textbook adoptions. Teachers' knowledge of their fields is not always up to date. In fact, more than a quarter of the staff may be teaching outside their areas of certification or in areas in which they did not major in college.

Self-Knowledge, Values, Standards, and Beliefs

A teacher's self-knowledge of what he or she stands for is the most important gyroscope a professional educator has to maintain a steady course through the bumpy shoals of life in schools. Having clarity about personal standards for good work and good behavior and effectively communicating these standards to students is a basic skill of all good teachers.

Such clarity is not bestowed with teaching credentials. It is the result of trial and error, reflection and experimentation, and dialogue and iteration with colleagues. Values and beliefs about learning, collegiality, and relating to students and parents are all shaped by personal reflection and interaction with other professionals. Reflective dialogue serves the dual purpose of developing shared understanding and helping individuals to clarify personal thinking to ground their actions.

A lack of deep professional interaction does not serve the teachers in the low-performing high school. Many are unsure of themselves and insecure in the changing world in which they find themselves. Old touchstones, such as grades, course syllabuses, and school traditions no longer provide comfort and a sense of purpose in the world. Some cling tightly to known elements even in the face of evidence of their negative effects. The comforts of the past hold memories of the way things are supposed to be.

Repertoire of Teaching Skills

In chess, the queen is the most powerful piece on the board because she has the most moves: She can move forward or backward, to one side or the other, and diagonally, any number of spaces. Like a chess queen, teachers with an expanded repertoire of teaching skills have the most moves and the most options.

No one knows it all in the classroom. This important craft knowledge is a lifetime in the making. There is always something new to learn as research, technology, and professional practice continually expand both the knowledge base of teaching and the answers to the questions about what works and why. The revolution in brain biology that is driving new understandings of cognitive psychology and pedagogy will continue to push the need for repertoire building for all practicing professional educators throughout their careers.

Teachers at low-performing schools cling to old ways.

Teachers at the low-performing high school cling to old ways of doing business in the classroom. Lectures, videos, reading from textbooks, note taking, and quizzes prevail. Students play out their part of the ritual, minimally complying with this production. Alternative teaching techniques such as simulations and cooperative learning are usually rejected as being "not my style."

Knowing About Students and How They Learn

Just as educators can never know enough about the structure of their disciplines, themselves, and their teaching repertoire, they can never know all there is to know about their students and how they learn. This capacity is divided into two parts. The first, knowing about students, means knowing them as people—who they are and where they come from. This is the stuff of genuine relationships that nurture and motivate learning. The second part, knowing how students learn, is informed by knowledge of learning styles, developmental stages of intellectual growth, cultural differences, and gender differences.

Students in the low-performing high school are often viewed as problems to overcome. They are the objects of instruction, not the constructors of meaning. All too often, relationships between teachers and students are strained in the battle for power and control.

Each side needs the other but does not always know how to cross the gap that divides them.

The 12 capacities for organizational and professional adaptivity are the source of and focus for reflective dialogue in professional communities. Exploration of these 12 areas helps communities to focus their work and strengthen their ties to one another. We offer them here as lenses for examining schools and teaching practice in the hope that they will become focal points for important dialogues and discussions in schools, departments, teams, and governing councils.

Four Hats of Shared Leadership

In adaptive schools, all players learn to wear four hats. By all players we mean administrators, teachers, support staff, students, and, where appropriate, parents. In such schools all the players must have the knowledge and skills to manage themselves and influence and lead others.

Leadership is a shared function in meetings, staff development activities, action research, and classrooms. Recognizing the hats and knowing when and how to change them is shared knowledge within the organization. When values, roles, and work relationships are clear, decisions about appropriate behavior are easy. We offer definitions to illustrate the major functions of four leadership roles and the distinctions among the roles.

In adaptive schools all players learn to wear four hats.

Facilitating

To facilitate means "to make easier." A facilitator is one who conducts a meeting in which the purpose is dialogue, shared decision making, planning, or problem solving. The facilitator directs the processes used in the meeting, choreographs the energy within the group, and maintains a focus on one content and one process at a time. The facilitator should never be the person with role or knowledge authority. (See chapter 6 for details on this role.) The role of facilitator is central to the ideas in this book. Many of the templates, tools, and strategies provided here apply to it. We have therefore elaborated on this role in chapter 6.

Presenting

To present is to teach. A presenter's goals are to extend and enrich knowledge, skills, or attitudes and to enable these to be applied in people's work. A presenter may adopt many stances—expert, colleague, novice, or friend—and use many strategies of presentation—lectures, cooperative learning, study groups, or simulations. Touchstones of effective presentations include clarity of instructional outcomes, standards for success, and ways to assess learning.[10]

Coaching

To coach is to help another take action toward his or her own goals. Simultaneously, the coach supports the colleague in developing his or her expertise in planning, reflecting, problem solving, and decision making. The coach takes a nonjudgmental stance and uses tools of paraphrasing, pausing, mediational questions, and probing for specificity. By focusing on the perceptions, thinking, and decision-making processes of the other person, the skillful coach develops the colleague's resources for self-directed learning.[11]

Consulting

To consult is to have your expertise be used by others. A consultant can be an information specialist or an advocate for content and or process. As an information specialist, the consultant delivers technical knowledge to another person or group. As a content advocate, the consultant encourages the other party to use a certain instructional strategy, adopt a particular curriculum, or purchase a specific brand of computer. As a process advocate, the consultant influences the client's methodology, such as by recommending an open rather than a closed meeting to increase trust in the system. To effectively consult, one must have trust, commonly defined goals, and the client's desired outcomes clearly in mind.[12]

Marshalling the Energy for Changing Schools

Carl Glickman writes that without the will to change for the better, all resources and management schemes will have little effect. "This issue of will—wanting to be better—is critical to understanding how long-term policies, allocation of resources, and work conditions can or cannot work."[13]

Two major problems related to change confront all groups. One is adapting to and surviving in the external environment. The other is developing internally to support daily functioning and increase the capacity to adapt.[14] Groups either develop toward greater inclusion and effectiveness or dissolve through fragmentation and disarray. Changing the structure of the group or teaching group members skills does not guarantee growth toward increased group performance. Helping members pay attention to basic energy sources within the group encourages the development of these resources and permits learned skills to be applied and structures to be reinvented for greater impact.

Group development is accelerated by five intervention approaches, which we will elaborate on in chapter 8:

1.   Structure the environment to release and enhance energy sources.

2.   Teach about the five energy sources of high-performing groups.

3.   Mediate selected intervention points.

4.   Model five energy sources.

5.   Monitor evidence and artifacts of selected energy sources.

The five energy sources, drawn from the work of Costa and Garmston[15] and members of the Institute for Intelligent Behavior, are discussed below.

Efficacy

The group believes in its capacity to produce results and stays the course through internal and external difficulties to achieve goals. The group aligns energies within itself in pursuit of its outcomes.

Flexibility

The group regards situations from multiple perspectives, works creatively with uncertainty and ambiguity, and values and utilizes differences within itself and the larger community of which it is part. The group attends to rational and intuitive ways of working.

Craftsmanship

The group strives for clarity in its values, goals, and standards. It applies these as criteria for its planning, actions, reflections, and refinements. It attends to both short- and long-term time perspectives. It continually refines communication processes within and beyond the group.

Consciousness

The group monitors its decisions, actions, and reflections based on its values, norms, and common goals. Members are aware of the impact of their actions on each other, the entire group, and outside individuals and groups.

Interdependence

The group values its internal and external relationships. It seeks reciprocal influence and learning. Members treat conflict as an

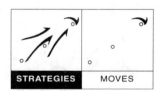

STRATEGIES   MOVES

opportunity to learn about themselves, their own group, and other groups. The group trusts its interactions and the processes of dialogue and discussion.

Simple Rules Govern Complex Behavior

In this book we are attempting to frame the complex work of developing and facilitating collaborative groups. While the frameworks, lenses, and tools we offer may seem a bit overwhelming at first, underneath them are some simple principles that guide our work.

This simplicity is caught in a story related by M. Mitchell Waldrop in his book, *Complexity: The Emerging Science at the Edge of Order and Chaos.*[16]

Complexity is the study of intricate dynamical systems. It is an integrative science in which economists, biologists, ecologists, meteorologists, and specialists from other fields connect to explore the underlying principles that govern natural and human systems. Much of the work is done using high-powered computers to simulate natural and designed systems.

Craig Reynolds of the Symbolics Corporation in Los Angeles is one such researcher. He designed a computer program that captures the essence of the flocking behavior of birds, the herding behavior of sheep, and the schooling behavior of fish. The elegance of his design was in not trying to build rules into the group. Instead the rules resided within individuals. He created a collection of autonomous, birdlike agents he called "boids." Each "boid" was programmed with three simple rules:

1. Maintain a minimum distance from other objects in the environment, including other "boids."

2. Match the velocity of other "boids" in your vicinity.

3. Move toward the perceived center of the mass of other "boids" in your vicinity.

There was no superintendent of "boids." None of these rules said to form a flock, yet flocks formed every time the program ran. "Boids" would at first be scattered around the computer screen but would soon flock up. Flocks were able to fly around obstacles or break into subflocks to flow around objects, re-forming on the other side. On one occasion a "boid" banged into a pole, lost its bearings momentarily, then darted forward to rejoin the flock.

If simple rules govern complex behavior in groups, what might be some simple rules for group members to follow? We propose the following.

1. *Take care of me.* It is each group member's groundedness, resourcefulness, and energy that develops the synergy that makes high-performing groups possible.

2. *Take care of us.* It is our interdependence, interactions, and caring for each other and the group that motivates us to want to continue to work together.

3. *Take care of our values.* It is our values that drive our goal clarity about who we are, how we want to be together, and what we will accomplish for students.

In the chapters 3 and 4 we explore these simple rules in action as we frame group-member capabilities, seven norms of collaboration, and two ways of talking in groups.

End Notes

[1] Tyack, D., & Cuban, L. (1995). *Tinkering toward utopia: A century of public school reform.* Cambridge, MA: Harvard University Press.

[2] Lortie, D. (1975). *Schoolteacher: A sociological study.* Chicago: University of Chicago Press.

[3] Louis, K. S., Marks, H. M., & Kruse, S. (1996). Teachers' professional community in restructuring schools. *American Educational Research Journal, 33* (4), 757–798.

[4] Little, J. W. (1990). The persistence of privacy: Autonomy and initiative in teachers' professional relations. *Teachers College Record, 91*, 509–536.

[5] Lee, V. E., & Smith, J. (1996). Collective responsibility for learning and its effects on gains in achievement and engagement for early secondary students. *American Journal of Education, 104*, 103–147.

[6] Little, J. W. (1982). Norms of collegiality and experimentation: Workplace conditions of school success. *American Educational Research Journal, 19,* 325–340; Little, J. W. (1993). Professional community in comprehensive high schools: The two worlds of academic and vocational teachers. In J. W. Little and M. McLaughlin (Eds.), *Teacher's work: Individuals, colleagues and contexts* (pp. 137–163). New York: Teachers College Press; and Newmann, F., et al. (1997). *Authentic achievement.* San Francisco: Jossey-Bass.

[7] Hargreaves, A., & Dawe, R. (1990). Paths of professional development: Contrived collegiality, collaborative culture, and the case of peer coaching. *Teaching and Teacher Education, 6,* 277–241.

[8] Allen, L., & Calhoun, E. F. (1998). Schoolwide action research: Findings from six years of study. *Phi Delta Kappan, 79* (9), 706–710.

[9] Costa, A., & Garmston R. (1994). *Cognitive coaching: A foundation for renaissance schools.* Norwood, MA: Christopher-Gordon.

[10] Garmston, R. (1997). *The presenter's fieldbook: A practical guide.* Norwood, MA: Christopher-Gordon, and Garmston, R. & Wellman B. (1992) *How to make presentations teach and transform.* Alexandria, VA: Association for Supervision and Curriculum Development.

[11] Costa & Garmston, op. cit.

[12] Block, P. (1981) *Flawless consulting: A guide to getting your expertise used.* San Diego, CA: University Associates.

[13] Glickman, C. (1998). Human will, school charters and choice: A new centralized policy for public education. Unpublished paper, University of Georgia, Athens, p. 3.

[14] Schein, E. H. (1992). *Organizational culture and leadership.* San Francisco: Jossey-Bass.

[15] Costa & Garmston, op. cit.

[16] Waldrop, M. M. (1992). *Complexity: The emerging science at the edge of order and chaos.* New York: Simon and Schuster.

Chapter 3   Developing Collaborative Norms

T HERE is no such thing as group behavior. All "group behavior" results from the decisions and actions of individuals. When individual choices align in productive patterns, the group produces positive results.

Group work would seem to be a natural condition of human life. Since the dawn of humanity on the plains of Africa, bands, clans, tribes, and teams have collaborated for defense, food gathering, and ceremonial purposes. Yet work in groups is often difficult, full of conflicts and tensions, but at the same time is absolutely necessary for producing results in modern organizations.

this chapter features:

Getting work done
Doing the right work
Working collaboratively
Managing systems
Developing groups
Adapting to change

The tensions between part and whole are not easily resolved. Each group member must balance personal goals with collective goals, acquire resources for his or her own work, and share those resources to support the work of others.

Many organizations try to control these tensions by using facilitators to shape and mold group energy and task focus. While a person in such a role can often make a difference in group performance, a skilled facilitator is only one ingredient for group success. (See chapter 6 for more on the role and skills of the facilitator.) Individual group members need consciousness and lenses for shaping personal decisions and behaviors in meetings. Four capabilities shape the self-monitoring system of high-performing group members. These in turn organize and drive seven norms of collaboration.

Four Group-Member Capabilities

We first realized the special power of focusing on capabilities as part of a group developing cognitive coaching with Art Costa and other colleagues[1] from the Institute for Intelligent Behavior. A *capability* names what a person is able to do. It is different than *capacity*, which refers to how much one can hold. Capabilities are the metacognitive awarenesses with which people determine when to use, how to use, or not to use certain skills. Capabilities therefore organize and direct the use of skills; they influence the application and effectiveness of knowledge and skills.

The four group-member capabilities are as follows:

1. To know one's intentions and choose congruent behaviors

2. To set aside unproductive patterns of listening, responding, and inquiring

3. To know when to self-assert and when to integrate

4. To know and support the group's purposes, topics, processes, and development

To Know One's Intentions and Choose Congruent Behaviors

Clarity of intention in the moment and over time drives attention, which in turn drives the *what* and *how* of a group member's meeting participation. This clarity precedes and influences the three other capabilities. It is the source of impulse control, patience, strategic listening, and strategic speaking.

This capability is the foundation for flexible and effective behavior. If, for example, a person's intention is to positively influence the thinking of others, various behaviors can be used congruently with that intention: Under some circumstances, a paraphrase will convey an attempt to understand and open the door for reciprocal understanding; in some situations, direct advocacy will be more persuasive; in other cases, an inquiry into the thinking of another speaker may be more effective.

To Set Aside Unproductive Patterns of Listening, Responding, and Inquiring

For each meeting participant, there are two audiences. One is external, made up of the other group members. The other is internal, made up of the feelings, pictures, and talk going on inside each individual. Group members need to continually decide which audience to serve. Three major set-aside areas focus this choice and allow fuller and more nonjudgmental participation. They are as follows:

1. To set aside autobiographical listening, responding, and inquiring.

"ME TOO!"

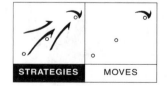

STRATEGIES MOVES

2.   To set aside inquisitive listening, responding, and inquiring.
     "TELL ME MORE!"

3.   To set aside solution listening, responding, and inquiring.
     "I KNOW WHAT TO DO!"

The autobiographical frame leads to several problems in group work. The first is the filtering process that goes on when individuals try to hear another's story through the lens of their own experiences. Although this can be a source of empathy, it can also lead to distortion and miscommunication.

This type of listening, responding, and inquiring is a major source of wasted time in meetings. It can lead to endless storytelling in which everyone around the table shares a related anecdote. This is dinner party conversation, not productive meeting talk. Each member of the eighth-grade team does not have to relate a discipline horror story. The team should explore a collective understanding of these students and their needs and develop appropriate response patterns that elicit desired behaviors.

The inquisitive frame is sometimes triggered by the autobiographical. People inquire to see how others' stories compare to their own. Pure curiosity also motivates inquisitive listening, responding, and inquiring. A critical question at this juncture is "How much detail do we need to move this item?" This is an example of what we call a "naive question." (See Appendix A for other examples of naive questions.) Such questions can be asked by any group member. The purpose is to focus attention on critical matters and avoid unnecessary specificity.

The solution frame is deeply embedded in the psyche of educators. Status, rewards, and identity are all tied up in being a good problem solver. The pressure of time in schools pushes people toward action and away from reflection. The down side of this pattern is that groups and group members get trapped in situations and action plans before they have time to fully understand the perspectives of others.

The solution frame also stifles the generation of new possibilities. It gets in the way of developing alternative ways of framing issues and problems, and it pushes groups toward action before creating clear outcomes.

To Know When to Self-Assert and When to Integrate

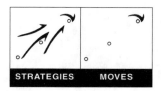

In productive groups, each member must decide when to self-assert and when to integrate with the group. In one group, a member confided to us that she was concerned about the autocratic disposition of the new chairman. While she valued the directness that he brought to the group's work, she was concerned that a collective ownership would gradually be lost if he were not sometimes challenged. Her issue, and the tension for each group member, is when to challenge and when to go with the flow. Self-assertion and integration are conscious choices only when group members have personal clarity about their own intentions and knowledge of and a willingness to support the group's outcomes and methods.

Self-assertion does not necessarily mean self-focus. It can mean asserting oneself into the flow of group interactions to refocus the group on a topic or on a process. It can mean reminding others of the purpose of the meeting when the conversation strays off course. It can also mean speaking up and advocating for topics and processes.

When individual group members integrate, they align their energy with the content and processes of the meeting. During dialogue they suspend judgments and counter arguments in an attempt to understand viewpoints different from their own. During discussions, they follow the flow of logic and reasoning as it emerges. In this way, solutions satisfying to the group as a whole are more likely to emerge.

Consensus decision making is the ultimate test of this capability. This procedure assumes that participants know when and how to self-assert and when and how to integrate, both during and after the decision-making process.

The next two chapters describe ways of talking in groups and principles and practices for successful meetings. In these chapters you will find many ideas and examples of places for self-assertion and for integration.

To Know and Support the Group's Purposes, Topics, Processes, and Development

All ongoing groups need to balance three simultaneous agendas. The first is *task focus,* which is the ultimate expression of the group's purpose. The second agenda is *process skills development.* Without continued attention to expanded repertoire and expanded skills, the group stagnates and does not expand its capacity for handling more complex work in the future. The third agenda is *group development.* All groups exist on a continuum from novice to expert performance. Experience alone is an insufficient teacher. Many longstanding groups operate at novice levels of performance. In chapter 8 we elaborate on our concepts of group development.

High-performing groups are adaptive groups. They learn from experience and improve the way they work. In supporting the group's purposes, topics, processes, and development, individual group members make a commitment to this shared learning and to personal learning.

Seven Norms of Collaboration

The paradoxes of work in groups establish the essential tensions that groups and their individuals must continually resolve. The four group-member capabilities supply metacognitive and emotional filters for decisions, choices, and behaviors. All of this requires a tool kit for productive group work.

Several years ago our friend and colleague Bill Baker commented that organizations have been training the wrong people. Instead of spending time and energy developing more skilled facilitators, he said, they should develop group members' skills as the way to improve practice and success. Our experience bears out the wisdom of this approach. When group members are knowledgeable and skilled, anyone with simple knowledge of facilitation principles and moves can facilitate constructive group work.

Drawing from the cognitive coaching model[2] and from the work of Peter Senge,[3] Baker and his colleagues enumerated a set of norms of collaboration as the tools for productive communication between group members. These are as follows:

1. Pausing
2. Paraphrasing
3. Probing for specificity
4. Putting ideas on the table
5. Paying attention to self and others
6. Presuming positive intentions
7. Pursuing a balance between advocacy and inquiry

There is a marked difference between skills and norms. A *skill* is something that someone knows how to do. A skill becomes a *norm* when it is "normal" behavior in the group. When this occurs, the behavior becomes "normative" for new group members, who model their own behavior on the standards tacitly set by the veterans.

When the seven norms of collaborative work become an established part of group life and group work, cohesion, energy, and commitment to shared work and to the group increase dramatically.

Intention, Attention, Linguistics

The norms of collaboration are driven by the following:

1. Intention to support thinking, problem solving, and group development

2. Attention of each group member, who attends fully with ears and eyes for the essence of others' messages.

3. Linguistic skills of the listener and/or responder

In our follow-up work with clients, this is reported time and again. An assistant superintendent recently shared with us that when one or two people in a meeting practice the norms, the behaviors of other group members becomes more effective.

A major tension is that all groups have more tasks to accomplish than time in which to do them. Yet any group that is too busy to reflect on process is too busy to improve. The seven norms become goals for collective growth. In adaptive schools, individuals and groups select goals from among the seven norms. They practice, monitor, and reflect upon the impact of the norms for themselves and for the group.

Each norm is deceptively simple. Most are skills that people regularly apply in one-to-one communications. The irony is that these seemingly simple behaviors are rare in many meetings. Pausing and paraphrasing are often missing, especially when things get tense. Probing for details is forgotten when members presume to understand others' meanings. This can lead to later confusion and complication. Presuming positive intentions prevents members from judging others. Interpersonal judgments spawn blocked thinking and negative presuppositions. Advocating and inquiring into the ideas of others increases the capacity for group members to influence each other.

We offer the following explanation of each of the norms as a rationale for their importance.

Pausing

There is a vast research base on the positive effects of teacher pausing and silence on student thinking. The "wait time" research of Mary Budd Rowe has been replicated around the world.[5] Thinking takes time. Higher level thinking takes even longer. This research indicates that it takes from 3 to 5 seconds for most human brains to process higher level thoughts.

Not all brains work the same way. This is especially evident in meetings and group work. Some people prefer to think out loud and construct their ideas externally; others prefer to process ideas internally and reflect and analyze before speaking. The external processors often get in the way of the internal processors. This can be an alienating experience for deliberate, internal thinkers. The meeting topics move by before they have a chance to contribute.

One middle-school team with whom we worked began to laugh at themselves after completing the Norms of Collaboration Inventory (Appendix B). When we inquired, they said they'd been working

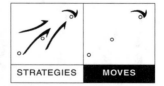

STRATEGIES   MOVES

together for more than 2 years and had yet to make a decision. In their group, if you stopped to breathe while speaking, you lost the floor. Consequently, they all had tremendous lung power and claimed they could each talk for hours on a single inhalation. What they recognized was that without a norm of pausing, meetings became a competition for air space. They soon learned to monitor several types of pauses to increase their productivity and satisfaction.

Groups become skilled at four types of pauses. The first type occurs after a question is asked. This allows initial processing time for those being asked the question. The second type occurs after someone speaks. Human beings think and speak in bursts. With additional processing time, more thoughts are organized into coherent speech.

In the original wait time research with students, when teachers paused after asking questions and after students' initial responses, the length of those responses increased from 300% to 700% depending on the socioeconomic status (SES) of the child. The lower SES children had the greatest gains.

The first two types of pauses require the questioner and other group members to monitor and control their own behavior. These are pauses to give other people time to think. A third type is under the control of each individual who is asked a question. This is personal reflection time in which that person waits before answering. Sometimes they say, "Give me a moment to think about that before answering." At other times they acknowledge the question nonverbally, go inside themselves to think, and then respond to the question. This is also a nice way to model thoughtfulness for others and can be an important normative behavior in groups.

A fourth type of pause in meetings is a collective pause. This can be formally structured or can occur spontaneously. These shared pauses allow ideas and questions to settle in and allow time for note taking and reflection. The intent of these breaks in the action is to create shared cognitive space for the group and its members.

Pausing begins a pattern that is followed by paraphrasing and questioning. Groups give themselves a powerful gift when they establish this pattern as a norm; pause, paraphrase, and probe for details; pause, paraphrase, and inquire for a wider range of thoughts; and pause, paraphrase, and inquire about feelings.

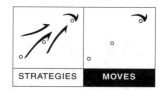

STRATEGIES   MOVES

Paraphrasing

Paraphrasing is one of the most valuable and least used communication tools in meetings. Even people who naturally and skillfully paraphrase in one-to-one settings often neglect this vital behavior in group settings. Groups that develop consciousness about paraphrasing and give themselves permission to use this reflected tool become clearer and more cohesive about their work.

Try this experiment. Paraphrase, then ask a question. Do this several times. Now ask questions without preceding them with paraphrases. Since a well-crafted paraphrase communicates "I am trying to understand you—and therefore, I value what you have to say" and establishes a relationship between people and ideas, questions preceded by paraphrases will be perceived similarly. Questions by themselves, no matter how artfully constructed, put a degree of psychological distance between the asker and the asked. Paraphrasing aligns the parties and creates a safe environment for thinking.[6]

Mediational paraphrases reflect the speaker's content and the speaker's emotions about the content and frame a logical level for holding the content. The paraphrase reflects content back to the speaker for further consideration and connects that response to the flow of discourse emerging within the group. Such paraphrasing creates permission to probe for details and elaboration. Without the paraphrase, probing may be perceived as interrogation.

The Structure and Flow of Effective Paraphrasing

Listen and observe carefully to calibrate the content and emotions of the speaker.

Signal your intention to paraphrase. This is done by modulating intonation with the use of an approachable voice and by opening with a reflective stem. Such stems put the focus and emphasis on the speaker's ideas, not on the paraphraser's interpretation of those ideas.

For example, reflective paraphrases should not use the pronoun "I." The phrase "What I think I hear you saying . . ." signals to many speakers that their thoughts no longer matter and that the paraphraser is now going to insert his or her own ideas into the conversation.

The following paraphrase stems signal that a paraphrase is coming:

> You're suggesting . . .
>
> You're proposing . . .
>
> So, what you're wondering is . . .
>
> So, you are thinking that . . .
>
> Um, you're pondering on the effects of . . .
>
> So, your hunch is that . . .

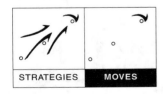

STRATEGIES   MOVES

Choose a logical level with which to respond. There are three broad categories of logical levels.[7]

1. Acknowledge and clarify content and emotion. If the paraphrase is not completely accurate, the speaker will offer corrections: "So, you're concerned about the budgeting process and ways to get input early on."

2. Summarize and organize by offering themes and containers to organize several statements or separate jumbled issues. This is an especially important type of paraphrase to use when multiple speakers contribute to a topic: "We all seem to be concerned about two issues here. One is resource allocation and the other is the impact of those decisions on student learning."

3. Shift focus to a higher or lower logical level. Paraphrasing within a flow of discourse often moves through a sequence of acknowledging, summarizing, and shifting focus to a higher or lower logical level. Paraphrases move to a higher logical level when they name concepts, goals, values, and assumptions: "So a major goal here is to define fairness in the budgeting processes and compare those criteria to the operating values of the school." Paraphrases move to a lower logical level when abstractions and concepts need grounding in details: "So 'fair' might mean that we construct a needs assessment form for each department to fill out and submit to the site council for public consideration."

Learning Styles and Paraphrasing

Paraphrases that summarize or shift the logical level of discourse support and stretch the thinking styles of different group members. Global thinkers appreciate paraphrases that separate and organize "thinking in progress." At other times the shift down in logical levels grounds global thinkers in specific examples and concrete details.

Concrete, highly sequential thinkers learn from the shift up to higher logical levels. This helps them to explore a bigger picture and creates a wider context for thinking.

Probing for Specificity

Human brains are not designed for specificity. In a world swimming in details, brains form quick generalizations from fragments of information. Brains delete particulars from streams of data and

STRATEGIES   MOVES

Generalizations, deletions, and distortions are survival patterns hardwired into the human brain.

distort incoming and outgoing messages to fit deeply embedded models of reality.[8] These are all natural processes; they do not willfully occur. Generalizations, deletions, and distortions are survival patterns hardwired into the human brain. They are adaptations for the challenges faced by our hunting and gathering ancestors who needed to make quick decisions for survival.

In more modern times these same traits cause difficulties in human communication. Conversations go haywire when the various parties make different assumptions about the meaning of words and concepts and neglect to verify or correct those assumptions. Problem definition, problem solving, and solution generation all rely on specificity for success.

Five categories of vagueness inhabit human speech:

1. Vague nouns and pronouns

2. Vague action words

3. Comparators

4. Rule words

5. Universal quantifiers

Vague Nouns and Pronouns

Someone named "they" makes most of the decisions in organizations. "They" are joined by "the central office," "the administrators," "the union," "the parents," "the students," and a host of others as the source of mysterious messages, concerns, and directives. Unless group members know who "they" are, communication takes longer and people do not always know how to treat the information.

When a speaker in a meeting says our students can't write, someone in the group needs to probe for specificity by paraphrasing and asking for details. It might sound like this: "So, you're concerned about student writing. What's your hunch about how many of our students have writing difficulties?"

After the speaker answers, the logical follow-up question would be about which areas of writing are of most concern. If the group discovers that a small number of students have specific skill gaps, they can develop a remediation plan for this targeted audience. If the group discovers that a large number of students have fundamental issues as writers, this calls for a more in-depth look at the patterns of curriculum and instruction in the school. Without the details, the group does not know which problem to solve.

STRATEGIES   MOVES

Vague Action Words

Planning and problem-solving sessions require specificity for targeted action. The verb *plan* itself means very different things to different people. Some think it means scratching ideas on a napkin; others imagine timelines and flowcharts with names and dates attached. Groups need to define their action words. Words like *improve, enhance, design, modify,* and *understand* are all examples of vague action words used by working groups. Someone should serve the group by probing for specificity in order for the team to agree upon concepts, plan for change, and act in concert.

Vague nouns and pronouns and vague action words often go hand in hand. "We want our students to be on time and prepared for class." This simple statement easily produces surface agreement in most groups of educators. It is only when we probe for which students are not yet meeting these requirements and what the meanings of "on time" and "prepared" are that the issue can even be discussed rationally.

Comparators

"This meeting was much better than last month's session." Unless the group discovers the speaker's criteria for "better," members do not know how to repeat the improvement or, for that matter, whether the speaker's "better" is desirable. Words like *best, larger, slower, more,* and *least* leave out the point of comparison and the standard for the comparison.

When undefined comparators are used, a group member should probe for criteria. "So you've enjoyed this meeting. What were some of the ways this was better for you?" The respondent has been careful here to ask the speaker for his or her criteria ("better for you"), which might not be important criteria to other group members. The intention is to draw the speaker out and expand the meaning of the statement.

Rule Words

People operate with conscious and unconscious rules about how the world works and how they are supposed to operate in it. These rules appear in language when people say things like, "We have to," "We must," "You shouldn't," and "I can't."

To clarify these rules and the ways that they govern behavior, other group members should probe for the rules behind the statements. "What would happen if we didn't?" "Who or what says we must?" "Shouldn't? Who made up that rule?" "What stops you?" Intonation is important here. The voice carrying the

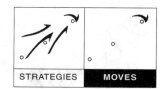

STRATEGIES   MOVES

response needs to be well modulated, friendly and non-threatening.

Universal Quantifiers

"Everyone knows that this program is great." Words and phrases like *everyone, all, no one, never,* and *always* are examples of universal quantifiers. Linguists use the term *deity voice* to describe this type of language. It is spoken as if the statement contains a universal truth of which "everyone" must be aware.

As most parents and middle-school teachers know, universal quantifiers are the lingua franca of teenagers. "I need to go to the mall; all my friends will be there." The typical response pattern is, "All your friends? I can't imagine that all your friends' parents would permit them to go."

By qualifying and clarifying a universal quantifier, group members ground their conversations in data and measurable details. When someone makes the statement that "These students never understand the assignments the first time," another participant can probe for "never": "Has there ever been a time when students understood the first time around?" This can be followed up with an inquiry into the qualities and conditions of the assignments that are an exception to the initial statement.

Putting Ideas on the Table

Ideas are the heart of group work. In order to be effective, they must be released to the group. "Here is an idea for consideration. One possible approach to this issue might be . . ." When ideas are owned by individuals, other group members tend to interact with the speaker out of their feelings for and relationship to the speaker rather than with the ideas presented. This is especially true when the speakers have role or knowledge authority related to the topic at hand. To have an idea be received in the spirit in which you tell it, label your intentions, "This is one idea . . ." or "Here is a thought . . ." or "This is *not* an advocacy, I am just thinking out loud."

Knowing when to pull ideas off the table is equally important. "I think this idea is blocking us; let's set it aside and move on to other possibilities." In this case, continued advocacy for the idea is not influencing other group members' thinking. This is a signal to pull back and reconsider approaches.

Productive group work is driven by data, both qualitative and quantitative. Data about student learning, school climate, teacher satisfaction, parent satisfaction, and the like are important grounded

STRATEGIES   MOVES

"ideas" to put on the table. Collaborative work in schools requires data as well as impressions. In fact, important learnings are possible when the data does and does not align with the impressions of group members.

Paying Attention to Self and Others

Meaningful dialogue and discussion is facilitated when each group member is conscious of oneself and of others. Skilled group members are aware of what they are saying, how they are saying it, and how others are receiving and responding to their ideas. This includes paying attention to both physical and verbal cues in oneself and others. Since the greatest part of communication occurs nonverbally, group members need consciousness about their total communication package.[9] This includes posture, gesture, proximity, muscle tension, facial expression, and the pitch, pace, volume, and inflection in their voices.

One important skill to develop is paying attention to and responding to the learning styles of others. The earlier section on paraphrasing offers some tips for communicating with global and concrete thinkers. In addition to using those ideas, skilled group members should try to match the language forms of others. This occurs when the respondent joins in a metaphor offered by another. It also occurs when the respondent matches the representation system of the speaker by using visual, kinesthetic, or auditory words in response to hearing the speaker operate within one or more of those categories.[10]

Speaker: "I'd like to *see* us develop a workable action plan."

Respondent: "So, you have an *image* of practical process that we can apply to our work. What are some of the features you'd like to *have on view* before us?"

Presuming Positive Intentions

Assuming that others' intentions are positive encourages honest conversations about important matters. This is both an operating stance that group members need to take if dialogue and discussion are to flourish and a linguistic act as speakers frame their paraphrases and inquiries within positive presuppositions.

Positive presuppositions reduce the possibility of the listener perceiving threats or challenges in a paraphrase or question. Instead of asking, "Does anybody here know why these kids aren't learning?", the skilled group member might say, "Given our shared

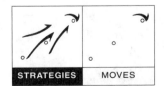

STRATEGIES   MOVES

concern about student achievement, I'd like to surface our assumptions about what might be causing gaps in learning."

The first question is likely to trigger defensiveness. The second approach will most likely lead to speculation, exploration, and collective understanding. This is especially true when a speaker has strong emotions about a topic and even more important when the respondent initially disagrees with the speaker. For example:

Speaker: "I'm really ticked off about the lack of communication in this school. We never find out about the important things until everyone else knows about them. In fact, I get more district news from the local paper than I do from internal sources."

Respondent: "So, as a committed professional, you'd like useful information about our organization in a timely fashion and in a means convenient for you. As you think about such a system, what might be some important components?"

In the example above, the respondent presumes that the speaker is a committed professional who wants to solve a real problem. People tend to act as if such presuppositions are true. The emotional processors in the brain hear the positive intention and open up access to higher level thinking.[11]

Pursuing a Balance Between Advocacy and Inquiry

This last norm of collaboration is based on the work of Peter Senge and his colleagues at the Massachusetts Institute of Technology's Center for Organizational Learning.[12] We have extended the concept and refined specific language patterns for operating within this norm.

The balance of advocacy and inquiry requires both emotional and cognitive resources. The balance is most necessary at the exact point when many group members are least likely to want to inquire into the ideas of others. It is at the moment of greatest disagreement and discomfort that this norm makes the biggest difference.

To balance means to spend equal amounts of time and energy advocating for one's own ideas and inquiring into the ideas of others. To do both equally requires the resources of the other six norms of collaboration. Advocacy and inquiry are built on the linguistic and perceptual foundation described earlier in this chapter.

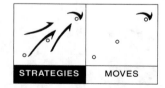

STRATEGIES   MOVES

The power of this norm became apparent to us in an experience related to us by our friend and colleague Diane Zimmerman, who was enrolled in a doctoral program in organizational development. At the time she was also a principal in Davis, California. Diane and her staff had taken on the norms of collaboration as a shared learning goal. As a skilled and congruent leader, Diane knew that she needed to apply the norms in her interactions with adults and students. To support her own learning, she continually sought opportunities to master and integrate these communication skills.

At an early stage in her graduate program, the professors organized a small-group learning experience. The students were placed in small groups and given a controversial topic to discuss. Most of the groups were soon at each other's throats with rising emotions, much heated talk, and little listening. Diane's group took a much different course. After a time, the professors gathered around in surprise, since the activity normally evoked the responses present in the other groups. Unable to resist their curiosity, they asked her group what was going on. At this point, Diane confessed that she had been practicing the norm of balancing advocacy for her ideas with pausing, paraphrasing, and inquiring into the ideas of others. Her behavior established this norm, solely by example, within her group.

The intention of advocacy is to influence the thinking of others.

The intention of advocacy is to influence the thinking of others. Group members sometimes attempt to influence with volume and passion. Advocacy works through revealing logic and the chain of reasoning that supports assumptions and conclusions.

The power of advocacy increases when it is structured to influence multiple audiences. Global reasoners increase their impact when they learn to frame issues for concrete and sequential thinkers. Those driven by logic and facts increase their influence when they learn to frame their ideas within feelings and emotions. It is this ability to stretch one's own thinking preferences that often makes the difference in group members being able to hear one another and be persuaded by the positions and stances of others (Table 3-1).

Developing Groups

Ballet dancers practice in mirrored studios to monitor posture and the subtleties of their movements. Groups also improve by reflection. The Norms of Collaboration Inventory (Appendix B) serves this purpose.

With groups in the early stages of development, the inventory can be filled out by individuals. Once completed, the form becomes the basis for dialogue about skills development and baseline data for goal setting for individuals and groups. We encourage groups to master one or two of the norms at a time rather than attempt to take them all on at once.

For intact groups with some history of working together, the form is best completed by subsets of the group. In twos and threes,

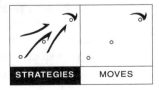

STRATEGIES   MOVES

Table 3-1. Balancing Advocacy and Inquiry

The Structure of Advocacy

Make your thinking and reasoning visible.

State your assumptions. "Here is what I assume are the causes of . . ."

Describe your reasoning. "I came to this conclusion because . . ."

Describe your feelings. "I feel _____ about this because . . ."

Distinguish data from interpretation. "This is the data I have. I'll share it as objectively as possible. Now here is what I think the data means . . ."

Reveal your perspective. "I'm seeing this from the viewpoint of _____."

Frame the wider context that surrounds this issue. "Several groups would be affected by what I propose."

Give concrete examples. "To get a clear picture, imagine that you are in a new school and . . ."

Test your assumptions and conclusions.

Encourage others to explore your model, assumptions, and data. "What do you think about what I have just said? Do you see any flaws in my reasoning? What might you add?"

Reveal where you are least clear. "Here's one area that you might help me think through . . ."

Stay open. Encourage others to provide different points of view. "In what ways do you see it differently?"

Search for generalizations, deletions, and distortions. "In what I've presented, do any of you believe that I might have overgeneralized, left out data, or reported data incorrectly?"

The Structure of Inquiry

Ask others to make their thinking visible.

Use nonaggressive language and an approachable voice. "Can you help me understand your thinking here?"

Use a pattern of pause, paraphrase, and probe or inquire.

Use tentative language. "What are some of . . . How might you . . . What are your hunches about . . .?"

Inquire for values, beliefs, goals, assumptions, examples, or significance. "How does this relate to your (values, beliefs, goals or assumptions)?" "What are some examples of what you think might happen if we act on your proposal?" "In what ways does this relate to your other concerns?"

Explain your reasons for inquiring. "I'm asking about your assumptions here because . . ."

Invite introspection. "What questions do you have about your own thinking?"

Compare your assumptions to theirs.

Investigate other assumptions. "Would you be willing to have each of us list our assumptions, compare them, and explore if there might be other assumptions surrounding this issue?"

Check your understanding of what is being said by pausing, paraphrasing, and inquiring. "So, your main concern is the way our team is interacting and you'd like to see more cohesion and focused energy. What are some of your thoughts about how this might look and sound in action?"

Test what others say by asking for broader contexts and examples. "How might your proposal affect . . . In what ways is this similar to . . . Please share a typical example of . . ."

Reveal your listening processes. "I have been listening for themes. So far I've heard two. Are there others?"

they can work through the form rating the full group's use of each norm. Each subset then compares its assessments with the other subgroups. Most groups discover that all members do not perceive meeting behaviors in the same way. This conversation leads to goal setting for individuals and groups.

The Likert scale (Appendix C) provides a useful vehicle for ongoing self- and group assessment. Regular monitoring with reflective processing keeps the norms alive and motivates steady improvement. In addition, the round-robin reflection pattern described in chapter 8 is a powerful tool for increasing personal and group consciousness and skills.

The four group-member capabilities and the seven norms of collaboration are essential capacities and skills for high-performing groups. They operate within several practical frameworks that help groups to develop shared meaning and gracefully reach decisions. In the next chapter we describe two ways of talking among adults that make a difference for student learning. Both ways, dialogue and discussion, draw on the group-member capabilities and norms.

End Notes

[1] William Baker, John Dyer, Laura Lipton, Peg Luidens, and Marilyn Tabor.

[2] Costa, A. L., & Garmston, R. J. (1994). *Cognitive coaching: A foundation for renaissance schools*. Norwood, MA: Christopher-Gordon.

[3] Senge, P. M. (1990). *The fifth discipline: The art and practice of the learning organization*. New York: Doubleday.

STRATEGIES   MOVES

[4] Baker, W., Costa, A. L., & Shalit, A. (1997). The norms of collaboration: Attaining communicative competence. In A. L. Costa & R. M. Liebmann (Eds.), *The process-centered school: Sustaining a renaissance community*. Thousand Oaks, CA: Corwin Press.

[5] Rowe, M. B. (1986, January–February). Wait time: Slowing down may be a way of speeding up! *Journal of Teacher Education*, 43–49.

[6] Lipton. L., & Wellman, B. (1998). *Pathways to understanding: Patterns and practices in the learning-focused classroom*. Guilford, VT: Pathways.

[7] Ibid.

[8] Bandler, R., & Grinder, J. (1971). *The structure of magic*. Palo Alto, CA: Science and Behavior Books.

[9] Burgoon, J. K., Buller, D. B., & Woodall, W. G. (1989). *Nonverbal communication: The unspoken dialogue*. New York: Harper & Row.

[10] Lankton, S. (1980). *Practical magic: A translation of basic neurolinguistic proramming into clinical psychotherapy*. Capitola, CA: Meta.

[11] Ledoux, J. (1996). *The emotional brain: The mysterous underpinnings of emotional life*. New York: Simon and Schuster.

[12] Senge, P. M., et al. (1994). *The fifth discipline fieldbook*. New York: Doubleday.

Chapter 4 Two Ways of Talking That Make a Difference for Student Learning

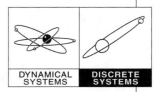

HOW TEACHERS talk to each other is an essential resource of strong schools. Skillful talk creates professional communities that reinvent instruction to match today's students with today's curriculum and today's conceptions of learning.

Group talk is the organizing ingredient of shared learning, yet it is dangerous and often counterproductive to put adults in a room without frameworks and tools for skilled interaction. The group-member capabilities and norms of collaboration described in the previous chapter supply part of the equation. What is missing is a map for two kinds of talking that make a difference for student learning.

An elementary school staff was struggling with the problem of reduced money for instructional aides. Although consensus and fairness were their goals, they reported that they felt like turkeys being asked to vote on the merits of Thanksgiving. No one really wanted his or her aide time cut. One first-grade teacher was adamant: She would agree to lose aide time "over my dead body." Six months later, as part of a schoolwide effort to support development of literacy and reading skills, this same teacher volunteered to share her classroom aide with a third-grade tutoring program "if it will really make a difference in helping those students learn to read."

What happened? In six months these teachers learned to distinguish and practice two different ways of talking—*dialogue* and *discussion*. They adopted the seven norms of collaboration, and individually they focused on their capabilities for professional discourse and openly reflected upon these in order to improve personal and collective practice.

These capabilities form the core of a professional community. Such communities talk about hard issues; they honor cognitive conflict and minimize affective conflict;[1] and they make decisions based on objective data, shared values, and deep examination of mental models. They measure success by increased student learning and adults' satisfaction with their work.

Developing a staff's capabilities for talking together professionally is no panacea, but it may represent one of the single most significant investments that faculties can make for student learning.

This chapter presents dialogue and discussion as two ways of talking that influence changes in teaching practice and student learning. Both forms of professional discourse use common tools. The four capabilities described in chapter 3 guide group members in selecting tools and help them to monitor the effectiveness of their participation.

Figure 4-1 shows the pathways of dialogue and discussion. First we will define the terms in the diagram. Then we will describe how groups use these concepts to guide their interactions. Finally, we will report ways that we introduce groups to these maps, tools, and capabilities.

Figure 4-1. Ways of Talking

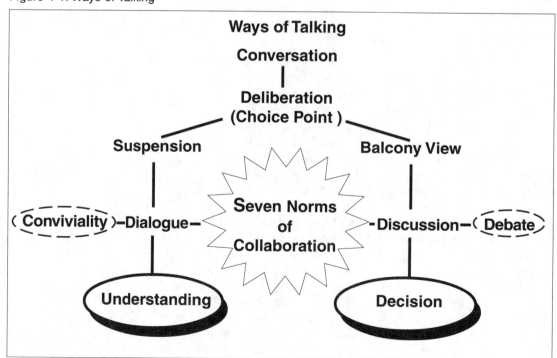

To take collective action, working groups need knowledge and skill in both ways of talking. One way of talking, dialogue, leads to collective meaning making and shared understanding. Dialogue honors the emotional brain, building a sense of connection, belonging, and safety. As a shape for conversation, it connects individuals to their underlying motivations and mental models. This form is the foundation for coherent sustained effort and community building. In dialogue we hear phrases like "An assumption I have is . . ."

The other way of talking, discussion, leads to decisions that stay made. Rigorous critical thinking infuses skillful discussions. Mutual respect, weighing options, and decision making then serves the group's and school's vision, values, and goals. In a discussion we might hear comments like "We need to clarify our goals before talking about solutions."

Definition of Terms

To converse means to turn together, to exchange information, ideas, opinions, or feelings. *Conversation* is informal talking in which participants can learn from one another or simply enjoy each other's company. When conversation begins to take on a consciously organized purpose—that is, the group must now either deepen understanding or decide—a choice point, *deliberation,* sends the group to either *dialogue* or *discussion.*

Without consciousness and maps, groups do not have choice. Most groups slide or tumble into a culturally embedded habit of discussion and debate. Our media-saturated world bombards us with arguments framed by commentators as point-counterpoint, pro and con, left versus right, and other polarities. These images carry into conversations. They frame how participants listen to others and how they speak. If people are not careful, they listen not to understand but to hear logical gaps in others' presentations, or they jump in to make a point. Conversations then break down into verbal combat with winners and losers. All too often, valued colleagues become conscientious objectors, choosing not to participate. The group then loses perspective and alternative viewpoints. The loudest and most persistent voices become the policy makers, and in the worst cases, the process sows seeds of passive noncompliance or sabotage in those who feel excluded.

When groups understand that they have alternate ways of talking, they consciously decide to pursue dialogue or discussion. They may explicitly mark agenda items as one or the other; important matters require both. For really important issues, the two ways of talking may occur in separate sessions. This option is especially valuable when personal reflection will add to the quality of the decision.

As group members become more sophisticated with ways of talking, the pathways become more malleable. For example, during a dialogue, someone senses an emerging consensus on an issue. He or she then inquires if this is so and frames a proposal to move the item. In another case (Table 4-1), during a discussion, emotions rise and the facts become muddied. Someone then proposes that the group switch to a dialogue format for a set period of time to explore the feelings and underlying issues that are present.

Table 4-1. Moving From Discussion to Dialogue

Discussion

"These test data point to a need to change our spelling program."

"I don't think it's the program; I think it's the test."

"I don't think it's either one; I think it's attitude."

Transition

"Wait a minute. This is sounding messier than it first looked. Can we shift to dialogue and explore our assumptions about what is going on with our kids and spelling?"

Dialogue

"We seem to have three areas before us; the test scores, kids' skills, and kids' attitudes. I'm wondering if there are other elements in this mix?"

"Help us to understand what you think some of these other elements might be."

The Path of Dialogue

Suspension

Suspension is the essential internal skill in dialogue. To suspend judgment, group members set aside for a time their perceptions, feelings, and impulses and carefully monitor their internal experience. Suspension requires being alert to ways of listening and doing

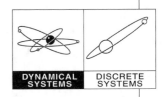

something about thinking in the moment. Points of personal conflict can easily emerge; people feel that others are not hearing them or that others are distorting their point of view. They may barely be aware of their anger or uneasiness, yet discomfort influences listening and can influence responses, which in turn can influence other group members.

Suspension also involves becoming aware of assumptions and hanging them from the ceiling—suspended in front of the group so that all can examine them.[2] Assumptions are beliefs—often unexamined—of why things work as they do. They drive perceptions, simultaneously opening and blinding us to certain awarenesses.

Peter Senge reports that managers exposed to a "thinking about thinking" training program discover that "all we ever have are assumptions, never 'truths.' We always see the world through our mental models and our mental models are always incomplete, and especially in Western culture, chronically nonsystemic."[3]

Dialogue

Dialogue is a reflective learning process in which group members seek to understand each other's viewpoints and deeply held assumptions. The word dialogue comes from the Greek *dialogos*. *Dia* means "through" and *logos* means "the word." In this "meaning making through words," group members inquire into their own and others' beliefs, values, and mental models to better understand how things work in their world. Each group member does much of the deepest work internally.

Physicist and philosopher David Bohm described dialogue as a process of surfacing and altering the "tacit infrastructure of thought."[4] As a quantum physicist, Bohm draws an analogy between dialogue and superconductivity. Electrons cooled to extremely low temperatures dramatically change their behavior, operating more as a coherent whole and less as separate parts. In supercool environments, electrons flow around barriers and each other without resistance, creating very high energy. The same electrons radically change behavior in a new environment. At higher temperatures they operate as separate entities with random movement and loss of momentum.[5]

Dialogue creates an emotional and cognitive safety zone in which ideas flow for examination without judgment. While many of the capabilities and tools of dialogue and skilled discussion are the same, their core intentions are quite different. Much of the work in dialogue is done internally by each participant as he or she reflects and suspends.

Conviviality

Meetings should be safe but not necessarily comfortable. When a group confuses safety with comfort, it sacrifices productive tension for the ease of conviviality. Humor and banter can be avoidance strategies as much as they can be social lubricants. A lack of comfort with discomfort weakens dialogue and undermines the learning possibilities in that moment.

Understanding

Well-crafted dialogue leads to understanding. This is the foundation for conflict resolution, consensus, and community. Decisions that don't stay made are often the result of group members feeling left out and or having their ideas discounted by the group. Dialogue gives voice to all parties and all viewpoints.

Misunderstanding lies beneath most intra- and intergroup conflict. Dialogue illuminates and clarifies misunderstandings when the underlying values and beliefs surface for examination. Often there is alignment at this level. It is at the solution level that opinions differ. Working from a foundation of shared understanding, group members can more easily and rationally resolve differences, generate options, and make wise choices when they move to the discussion side of the journey.

The Path of Discussion

Balcony View

While suspension has been extensively described as an internal skill necessary for dialogue, not much has been written about a parallel set of mental tools for skillful discussion. We call this the balcony view, a perceptual position that is neither *egocentric* (I am intensely aware of my thoughts, feelings, and intentions and know my own boundaries) nor *allocentric* (I am aware of how something looks, feels, and sounds from the point of view of another). The balcony view is a third perceptual position, a *macrocentric* view, in which with compassion and detachment a group member tries to understand the nature of the situation the group is in at that moment. It is with this view, looking down on the group, that members can gain the most knowledge about themselves, the group, and the group's interactions. From the balcony they can make the most strategic decisions about how and when to participate. At what points do they press? When should they probe for detail or let it go? How do they phrase an idea for greatest influence? This is the same internal skill that teachers employ when they "monitor and adjust" in their classrooms.

Discussion

Groups skilled in discussion employ many rigorous cognitive operations. There is no set sequence to these efforts. The task before the group determines the intellectual tool kit. Thinking skills expert Barry Beyer lists 10 critical thinking skills that individuals and groups need.[6]

1. Distinguishing between verifiable facts and value claims
2. Distinguishing relevant from irrelevant information, claims, or reasons
3. Determining the factual accuracy of a statement
4. Determining the credibility of a source
5. Identifying ambiguous claims or arguments
6. Identifying unstated assumptions
7. Detecting bias
8. Identifying logical fallacies
9. Recognizing logical inconsistencies in a line of reasoning
10. Determining the strength of an argument or claim

The term *discussion* shares linguistic roots with words such as *percussion, concussion,* and *discus.* At its most ineffective, discussion is a hurling of ideas at one another. Often it takes the form of serial sharing and serial advocacy. Participants attempt to reach decisions through a variety of voting or consensus techniques. When discussion is unskilled and dialogue is absent, decisions are often of poor quality, represent the opinions of the most vocal members or the leader, lack group commitment, and do not stay made.

Skilled discussions take place within a shape known to participants. Three elements help to form this shape: (a) clarity about decision-making processes and authority, (b) knowledge of the boundaries surrounding the topics open to the group's decision-making authority, and (c) standards for orderly decision-making meetings. These elements are elaborated in the next chapter on principles and practices of successful meetings. Most meetings are, in fact, structured discussions.

Debate

When working groups stray from skilled discussion, they may move to an unskilled use of debate. This appears in Figure 4-1 within a dotted-line circle to indicate that a group has overshot useful advocacy for ideas and entered a space of listening only for logical fallacy and argument. The Latin origins of the word *debate* mean "to beat down" the ideas of others.

By debate, we mean street debate, not academic debate. Scoring points is the goal of street debate. Winning comes from intimidation and intonation as much as from logic and reason.

Decide

Decide, in its Latin root, means to "kill choice." The purpose of discussion is to eliminate some ideas from a field of possibilities and have the stronger ideas win. Groups must learn to separate people from ideas in order for this to work effectively. If ideas are "owned" by people, they are hard to kill. Ideas should belong to the group, not to the individuals. In this way they can be shaped, modified, and discarded to serve the group's greater purpose.

Consensus as the Holy Grail

Consensus is one form of decision making but not the only form. Some groups get stuck trying to use consensus processes without a consciousness of the difference between dialogue and discussion.

There are two types of consensus: (a) opening consensus, which develops through dialogue, and (b) focusing consensus, which develops through discussion.[7] Opening consensus means the consideration of perspectives and possibilities. Focusing consensus means winnowing choices by clarifying criteria and applying these criteria to the choices. Focusing consensus for complex issues depends upon effective opening consensus.

Ultimately, consensus is a value and belief system more than a decision-making process. Unless groups are willing to hang out with the process for as long as it takes, they are not usually ready for full consensus decision making.

Work at The Center for Conflict Resolution points to the following necessary conditions for effective consensus decision making:[8]

1. *Unity of purpose.* There should be basic core agreement on what the group is about and how it operates.

2. *Equal access to power.*   Consensus cannot work in formal hierarchies. Informal power also needs to be equally distributed.

3. *Autonomy of the group* from external hierarchical structures. It is very difficult for groups to use consensus processes if they are part of a larger organization that does not honor this way of making decisions.

4. *Time.*   Consensus takes time and patience. Participants have to believe in the usefulness of this method enough to follow it and not the clock or calendar.

5. *Attending to process.*   Group members must be willing to spend group time reflecting on process and modifying it as needed.

6. *Attending to attitudes.*   Group members must be willing to examine their own attitudes and be open to change. The key ingredients are trust and cooperation.

7. *Willingness to learn and practice skills.*   Communication, meeting participation, and facilitation skills must be continually honed and refined to make consensus processes work.

Most groups with whom we work are better served by "sufficient consensus." This generally means that at least 80% of the group is willing to commit and act. It also means that the others agree not to sabotage.

Sufficient consensus relies on both dialogue and discussion for its effectiveness. The norm of balancing advocacy and inquiry is essential. Any dissenting voices must be able to influence and persuade 80% of the group to carry the day. This also means that other group members can paraphrase and draw matters to a close when only a few voices line up on one side of an issue.

Norms and Values

Professional community is built on the bedrock of norms and values, which are both honed by dialogue and discussion. Strong schools have core values about how children learn, what they should learn, and how faculties should work together.

Norms about faculty work include philosophical norms (e.g., everyone can be involved in decision making; no one has to be involved, but once decisions are reached they are binding on everyone).[9] Carl Glickman calls these elements a charter, or guiding rules of governance. This type of norm signals what is important to the organization. Another type of norm specifies how the values of the organization can be achieved.

Our work with schools emphasizes the use of the seven norms of collaboration described in the previous chapter. When school faculties make these seven tools into norms—that is, normal operating behaviors in formal and informal interactions within the school—adult relationships improve, groups work skillfully to explore members' mental models and assumptions, and both dialogue and discussion are served.

These norms also have a tremendous payoff in the classroom for both teacher-student interactions and student-student interactions. In many cases faculties take them on with the dual agenda of enhancing both faculty and student performance.

Getting Started

The collaborative norms of the group have more influence on the possibility of success than do the knowledge and talents of the group facilitator. Thus, our staff development energies must go to groups, not to designated leaders of groups. We have found three components to be helpful in groups that achieve high levels of skills in the challenging talk required in professional communities.

1. *Overview.* Provide groups with a rationale and a map for the two ways of talking (Fig. 4-1). Within this framework we add key details about the seven norms, the four capabilities, the purposes of dialogue and discussion, and approaches to constructive conflict. This overview is intended to create dissatisfaction with the current state of team and working-group performance and to provide a glimpse of productive ways of working together.

2. *Inventory.* Inventorying members' perceptions of how the group uses the norms reveals beliefs about current operating practices. Groups can select one or two norms to develop and can establish monitoring systems to improve their use of the map and tools. Inventories can be simple rating scales, ranking personal and collective use of each norm, or more detailed questionnaires exploring subsets of each norm. See Appendixes B and C.

3. *Monitor.* Any group that is too busy to reflect on its work is too busy to improve. Every working group has many more tasks to do than time in which to do them and so is naturally reluctant to spend time monitoring and reflecting on its

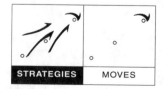

STRATEGIES   MOVES

working processes. Many groups commit themselves to a task/process ratio to overcome this tendency and budget a protected percentage of each meeting for examining how well the group is working and what it might do to improve.

Reflection can take many forms. The least effective form involves a process observer—a special role for gathering data about the frequency or distribution of behaviors that the group believes are important. Because this places the gathering of data outside the group members, they ultimately become less accurate in gathering their own data and self-assessments. The most effective form is through reflection on the four capabilities as described in chapter 3. This can occur through journal writing, round-robin reflection, and dialogue focused on personal and collective learning about the power of attention to process.

Human beings are a social species. Living and working in groups is an important part of our genetic heritage. It is ironic, then, that in many schools, professionals who are charged with preparing students to be successful collaborative citizens are themselves cut off from the rich resources offered by true collegiality. That we talk together in our schools is vitally important in these changing times. *How* we talk is just as important, for it is how we talk that influences the personal and collective satisfaction that motivates us to effectively talk together in our schools.

End Notes

[1] Amason, A. C., Thompson, K. R., Hochwarter, W. A., & Harrison, A. W. (1995, Autumn). Conflict: An important dimension in successful management teams. *Organizational Dynamics, 24* (2), 20–35.

[2] Senge, P. M., et al. (1994). *The fifth discipline fieldbook.* New York: Doubleday, p. 378.

[3] Senge, P. M. (1990). *The fifth discipline: The art and practice of the learning organization.* New York: Doubleday, p. 185.

[4] Bohm, D. (1990). *On dialogue.* Ojai, CA: David Bohm Seminars, p. 8.

[5] Isaacs, W. (1993, Autumn). Taking flight: Dialogue, collective thinking and organizational learning. *Organizational Dynamics, 22* (2), 24–39.

[6] Beyer, B. (1987). *Practical strategies for the teaching of thinking.* Boston: Allyn and Bacon.

[7] Senge, 1990, p. 248.

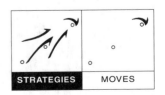

STRATEGIES   MOVES

8 Avery, M., Auvine, B., Streibel, B., & Weiss, L. (1981). *Building united judgment: A handbook for consensus decision making.* Madison, WI: The Center for Conflict Resolution.

9 Glickman, C. (1993). *Renewing America's schools: A guide for school-based action.* San Francisco: Jossey-Bass.

Chapter 5   Conducting Successful Meetings

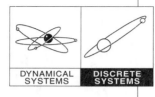

this chapter features:

Getting work done
Doing the right work
Working collaboratively
Managing systems
Developing groups
Adapting to change

MEETING success is influenced more by the collaborative norms of the group than by the knowledge and skills of a meeting facilitator. This chapter explores four structures for successful meetings. In successful meetings, a maximum amount of work is done in minimum time with a maximum amount of member satisfaction. But that is not enough. For meetings to be judged successful, sound action must result. Clear responses to four questions guide such success:

1. Who decides?
2. What topics are ours?
3. What meeting room features will support our work?
4. What are the meeting standards?

Each structure addresses one of these questions. Although all four structures are important, meeting success is guaranteed when groups become skilled at even just one of the structures.

Structure is a system organized around a set of principles. Effective structures honor the interrelationship of parts and bring them together into a workable whole. Since any group brings a variety of mental models, cognitive styles, personal histories, and individual agendas to its work, the potential for chaotic interaction always exists. Providing structures permits a full and focused expression of these differences in a manner that is useful to the work and life of the group.

However, a dilemma dogs each group. In practically every meeting, working groups have more tasks than time. While it seems logical to invest all available meeting time in work, to do so results in negligible or negative learning about *how* to work most effectively. As we have noted, any group too busy to reflect about its work is too busy to improve. Without periodic and routine self-assessment, groups are doomed to do things exactly the way they have done them in the past—or, like a rebellious child, to take giant swings on a pendulum of reaction to what has not worked in the group's recent history.

This is a common dilemma in the early stages of a group's maturational history. A group that focuses exclusively on tasks at this stage rarely produces a good product. When we train teams getting started in a working relationship, or groups with a history of dysfunction, we often advise that they devote 50% of their time to tasks and 50% to learning, monitoring, and strengthening processes. We know that this suggestion drives leaders and group members crazy, yet it is the quickest prescription for gaining group effectiveness and power. As groups develop consciousness and competence in the four meeting structures, they adjust their task/process ratio to include more time for tasks. While each situation is unique, here is a basic rule that we've found useful for mature working groups: Use about one sixth of the meeting time, in meetings of 90 minutes or less, to reflect on process. Table 5-1 is a guide to task/process ratios for mature groups.

Table 5-1. Task/Process Ratios for Mature Groups

Meeting Type	1-Hour Meeting	2-Hour Meeting	3-Hour Meeting	1-Day Meeting
Discussion	50 minutes task, 10 minutes reflection	1 hour 45 minutes task, 15 minutes reflection	2 hours 40 minutes task, 20 minutes reflection	7 hours 30 minutes task, 30 minutes reflection
Dialogue	50 minutes task, 10 minutes reflection	1 hour 30 minutes task, 30 minutes reflection	2 hours 30 minutes task, 30 minutes reflection	7 hours 15 minutes task, 45 minutes reflection

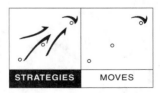

STRATEGIES   MOVES

Michael Doyle and David Straus[1] use a metaphor of gum and chewing to describe the task/process tension within a meeting. While there must always be gum (content) in meetings, there must also be chewing (process). As groups mature, they become increasingly knowledgeable about both.

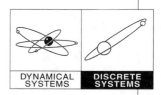

The Four Structures for Success

Every working group needs declarative knowledge of the four
success structures described in this chapter. This means that members
can describe the four structures, their parts, and the principles on
which they are based. As groups learn from their experiences,
procedural knowledge will develop, and members will become
skillful at exercising, monitoring, and self-correcting both themselves as individuals and the group. Finally, mature groups acquire a
degree of conditional knowledge, allowing them to recognize when
to "break the rules" and achieve their purpose even more effectively.
Such powerful and cumulative knowledge can be, and is, developed
with faculties, committees, task forces, cabinets, advisory boards,
and other groups. It need not be lost because of changing membership or environmental crises. We have been facilitating a statewide
group responsible for deciding how millions of dollars will be used
each year to support technology. This group meets for a full-day
meeting three times a year. Because members are appointed as
representatives from regions, membership constantly changes. Yet
after a year and a half of facilitated meetings, the consensus of the
group was that "we have become our values and operating principles." Effective groups develop a commitment to practice and
monitor their use of the four structures.

Table 5-2. Rate Your Group

Four Meeting Structures	Declarative Knowledge —can describe	Procedural Knowledge —can do	Conditional Knowledge —can break "rules" and still be effective
Decide who decides			
Define the sandbox			
Design the surround			
Develop standards			

Chapter 8 addresses broader dimensions of group development, including the development of six domains of group maturity
(working collaboratively, doing the right work, getting work done,
managing systems, developing groups, and adapting to change) and
ways to assess them.

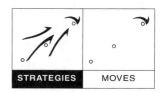

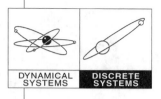

DYNAMICAL SYSTEMS   DISCRETE SYSTEMS

Decide Who Decides

This first structure addresses clarity about decision making. Often groups are not clear about who is making the final decision and what decision-making processes will be used. When this occurs, trust in processes and leadership is diminished. When members lose trust, second-guessing, resistance, or lengthy and unproductive process arguments can occur. This robs time and, more important, saps group energy, efficacy, and motivation to persevere on important agenda items.

Who decides is the question posed by this structure. Is the decision to be made by certain individuals within the group, by the group as a whole, by the person who convened the group, or even by some person or group(s) not present at this meeting?

Knowing who decides helps groups to know where to invest energy. When curriculum committees understand that a final decision will be made by the school board, they can strategically plan their time. Thus 80% of committee time might be devoted to getting as smart as possible about the recommendations they will make to the board. The other 20% might be used to study and implement ethical systems of influence.

Another benefit of knowing who decides is knowing whom to influence within the group. When the decision maker on a particular agenda item is a group member, such as an association officer or administrator, knowing this in advance allows group members to focus their attention on understanding and influencing this person. Groups are most effective and productive when they are clear about whether their role is to inform, recommend, or decide. Not all decisions should be made by consensus. Consensus matters on important items that bind commitment to collective action. For collective efficacy and protection of time and energy, a repertoire of decision-making strategies works best. The following are some possible levels of authority for decision making:[2]

- An individual or group above you
- An administrator unilaterally
- An administrator with input
- An administrator and staff by consensus
- A staff with input from administrators
- A staff by consensus
- A staff by a vote
- A subgroup of a staff with input from others

- A subgroup of a staff unilaterally
- Individual staff members, selecting from a menu of options
- Parents and community members
- Students

Ask Naive Questions

Asking a naive question is one way that group members effectively offer correction to group work. To communicate naively is to speak with innocence. It is to be artless, unaffected, and natural. Naive questions have an intonational quality of childlike inquiry in which the question being asked is truly open-ended. "Who will communicate this decision?" and "Who will be informed about this?" are examples of naive questions addressing the first structure (see sidebar for some Structure #1 questions). They serve the group in developing awareness about process, and they sometimes serve leaders because the question has been overlooked in planning.

> **"Naive" Questions for Structure #1**
>
> Who is making this decision?
>
> What are the processes for making this decision?
>
> What will be the consequence of this decision?
>
> What is our role in making this decision?
>
> How will this decision be communicated?

One of us worked with a superintendent in an eastern state who was particularly adept at maintaining clarity with groups about decisions. On one occasion, he visited each faculty to seek their information on a decision he had to make. He said to each group, "Your job is to give me the best information possible. Your job is to inform me. My job is to make a decision. When I do decide, you will hear it first from me." He then asked questions and listened. When his decision had been made, he again visited the schools. He reported to each staff, "This is the decision I made. This is my rationale. Here is how your information influenced me." He then responded to questions.

Several months later another issue emerged in which the superintendent wanted input from schools. He sent a memo describing the situation and saying that if faculty wished to inform him, please send a representative to the central office for a meeting at a designated time. Teachers said to one another, "He really means it." They had learned to trust the process. Teachers went to the meeting and informed the superintendent.

One of the best guides for clarity about decision making is a 12-step model (Table 5-3) offered by Jon Saphier and colleagues. They emphasize that the model's effectiveness comes from making it public.

We advocate sharing and teaching the process to all members in the organization through modeling and explicit discussion; this goal is critical to school improvement. All of this implies

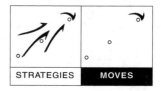

STRATEGIES   MOVES

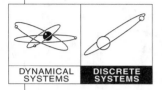

that we do not do the process "to" or "on" people, nor is it a Machiavellian model for working one's will on others. It is, rather, a set of guidelines for making good decisions that will stay made.[3]

Table 5-3. 12 Steps for Making Successful Decisions

Planning

1. Identify and explicitly state the issue, who owns it, and what the underlying goal is.
2. Find out and explain how much discretion you have to take action or not. *Must* this issue be dealt with? State how strongly you personally feel about it.
3. Every issue lands in someone's lap in the beginning. If it lands in yours, be sure to choose the proper path for who will make the preliminary and the final decisions.
4. At the beginning of the process, communicate clearly who will make the decision and identify any constraints that will affect the scope or content of the decision (e.g., staffing, budgeting, time).
5. State explicitly the values you want to maintain and why they are not negotiable, if that is the case (e.g., "Whatever proposals come forward, I want to hang on to small class size and the high quality of personal student-teacher contact we get from that").

Deciding

6. Identify and periodically check out with people what the full impact or full consequences of the decision will be and communicate them to all parties involved.
7. Involve all parties whose working conditions will be affected by the decision.
8. Make clear the timeline for deciding and implementing the decision.
9. Decide. Then make an explicit statement of the decision or recommendations, summarizing all key points.
10. Provide for exactly how and when the decision-making group will revisit the decision later to evaluate it and revise it if necessary.

Implementing

11. Close the loop. Communicate the reasons for the decision fully and clearly to all affected parties after the decision is made, including how people's input was used.
12. Plan how to monitor and support the day-to-day implementation of the decision and communicate these plans to everyone involved.

Making such a set of decision-making processes clear to everyone becomes even more important in work involving multiple stakeholders. When a group does not like a decision, it will attack the process. We watched a decision-making process in one district in which a citizen's committee studied declining enrollment patterns

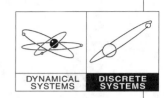

and was asked to make two recommendations to the superintendent. Should a school be closed, and if so, which one? The board was to make the ultimate decision. When the board announced that Trackview School was to be closed, the parents of that community were outraged. Rumors flew about the process, the most persistent one being that the superintendent had the name of the closing school in his bottom desk drawer before the process of community involvement had even started. Mistrust festered and interfered with the business of running a school system and educating students for a long time afterward.

Figure 5-1 summarizes the decision-making process.

Figure 5-1. Decision Making

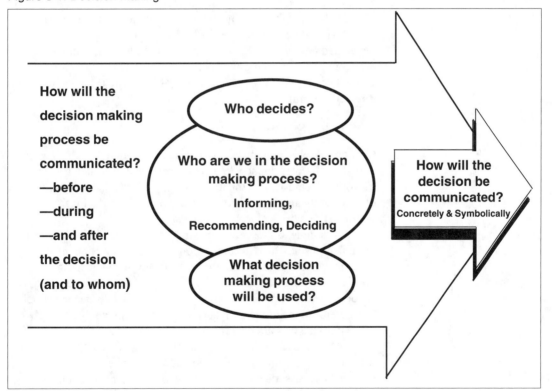

Morale problems, declining involvement, and suspicions about being manipulated are often indicators that the first structure is not being used. Most often this occurs not because meeting organizers are duplicitous but because the principles underlying this and the second structure are not being observed. The principles that underlie

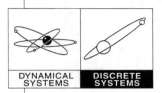

DYNAMICAL SYSTEMS   DISCRETE SYSTEMS

the first and second structures ensure that *all* members of effective groups do the following:

1. Know the game they are playing

2. Know what they can affect and what they cannot

3. Know how to influence in the areas they can affect

4. Maintain clear understandings at all times with people who are not in the meeting about the first three issues

5. Seek clarity whenever they are uncertain

These principles are grounded in values. High-performing groups continually draw on three internal resources that are valued in an adaptive organization: consciousness, craftsmanship, and efficacy. These values are founded in a belief that human energy is inexhaustible when five energy sources for high performance are accessed and developed (see chapter 8). They are also based on an assumption that the group is always the group's group, never the leader's group, and that collectively the group is in charge of itself and capable of self-directed learning.

Define the Sandbox

Groups conserve precious energy by focusing their resources where they have direct influence. When the "sandbox" in which a group is to work is clear to all members, group energy can be powerfully directed at the items it can affect. This structure works in tandem with the first structure, decide who decides.

As simple as these two concepts are, they become complex in organizations in which different groups have intersecting interests. After much deliberation, a high school faculty went on a school holiday believing that because they had voted for a change in the school schedule, it would be changed when they returned to school. They were stunned to learn that schedule adjustments could not be made until the classified staff had been consulted.

All groups have interests that intersect with other groups' decision-making authority. Considerations of collegiality, politics, and effectiveness must honor these overlapping areas of concern. Individual and collective vigilance is an essential ingredient of group success. At some time in every group's history, this structure becomes important to departments, curriculum task forces, advisory groups, grade-level teams, site councils, and faculties.

Table 5-4 is an example of how one school site council defined its sandbox. Two areas appear to be the most clear: Develop a site plan and develop budgets. The verb *develop* suggests that the council has complete authority to act in these two areas. The verbs *consult* and *review,* however, are more open to interpretation. What does it mean to consult? Will the council be informed by or seek recommendations or receive advocacies? What are the sources of criteria in reviewing student progress and other data? Finally, to whom does the council recommend?

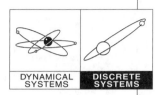

Table 5-4. Site-Council Responsibilities

- Develop site plan
- Develop budgets
- Consult with bilingual advisory committee
- Consult with Title I parents
- Review student progress
- Review other data, such as parent involvement survey
- Recommend the number of staff development days
- Review (annually) school discipline policy

"Naive" Questions for Structure #2

Should we be talking about this?

What parts of this issue live in our sandbox?

What parts of this are beyond our influence?

Who are the other stakeholders, and how are they involved?

What is the role of other groups in making decisions about this topic?

An issue common to many schools is who should be responsible for decisions about schoolwide policy and practices on student discipline. This seems like a simple sandbox question. However, even the briefest conversation will reveal that several related questions must be explored (see sidebar for some Structure #2 questions). Student discipline in what areas (gum or guns)? Within what parameters (state law or district policies)? At what level of authority (unilaterally or in consultation with the principal or parents)?

Design the Surround

David Perkins[4] defines the "surround" as the features around learners that mediate thinking and behavior. Although psychological, emotional, cognitive, and physical elements contribute to the surround, the facilitator has the greatest control over the physical arrangements in the meeting room (Table 5-5).

Schwarz[5] describes four principles for seating arrangements in meetings. To these we add a fifth and a sixth. Our list of principles for the third structure, designing the surround, is therefore as follows:

1. All participants and the facilitator should be able to see and hear each other.

Table 5-5. Designing the Surround

Physical space and room arrangement. Specific tasks require conscious room arrangement and materials provisioning. The room arrangement communicates and structures the desired interaction.

Task, norms, and standards charts. As reminders of task focus and working agreements, high-performing groups post charts stating outcomes for their tasks and charts reminding participants of collaborative norms, meeting standards, and group-member capabilities.

Charting materials. Group memory and graphic processes support learning and retention. Charting materials such as markers, tape, pads, and easels should be readily available. Wall space also should be considered. Blank walls without other artwork are best for meeting rooms. This lets each group craft the space to its own needs.

Emotional space. People come to meetings carrying unfinished business from other aspects of their day and from previous meetings. Inclusion activities support people in becoming fully present both physically and emotionally. (See Table 6-4 in chapter 6) Group-member consciousness about the emotional surround is also enhanced through processing questions that address both thoughts and feelings.

2. The seating arrangements should enable members to focus on the flip chart (or other writing devices) and the facilitator.

3. Seating arrangements should distinguish participants from nonparticipants.

4. Seating arrangements should be spacious enough to meet the needs of the group but no larger.

5. Seating arrangements should accommodate physical movement, subgrouping with different partners, and personal ownership of the entire room rather than of a single chair or table.

6. Memory displays and public recording should support the best thinking about meeting content and processes.

Participants and Facilitator Should Be Able to See and Hear Each Other

Arranging a room to accommodate this principle is rarely a problem when group size is around 20 or fewer. The semicircle, U-shape, or oval arrangements shown in Figure 5-2 will easily serve 20 to 25 participants. As group size expands up to 40 or so in a council or decision-making group, arrange a series of tables in a herringbone pattern to allow all participants to see the facilitator and the flip charts. When group size reaches 80 to 300 people, as it sometimes

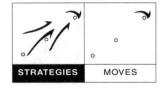

STRATEGIES   MOVES

does for community forums, facilitate from a set of risers. Position flip charts on the risers and use large markers like Sanford's Magnum® 44 Permanent Marker or Avery Dennison's Marks-A-Lot® Washable Marker. Regardless of group size, remind participants at the beginning of a meeting that any time they cannot hear one another they are to say, "Louder, please!"

Seating Arrangements Should Enable
Members to Focus on Flip Chart and Facilitator

Facilitators and recorders usually stand or sit in a location that physically distinguishes them from other group members (Figure 5-2). Like an orchestra conductor, the facilitator strategically uses space, tempo, posture, and gesture to keep the group moving together.

Figure 5-2. Room Arrangement

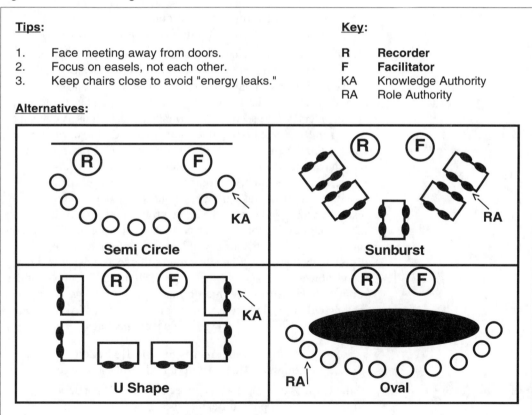

Tips:

1. Face meeting away from doors.
2. Focus on easels, not each other.
3. Keep chairs close to avoid "energy leaks."

Key:

R   Recorder
F   Facilitator
KA Knowledge Authority
RA Role Authority

Alternatives:

Semi Circle

Sunburst

U Shape

Oval

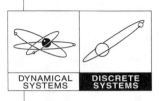

Two of the most important facilitator responsibilities are to focus the group on one topic at a time and one process at a time (see fourth structure, develop standards). Space, flip charts, other visual displays, gestures, and positioning of the facilitator's body become valuable tools for focusing the group. Additionally, all facilitator communications are enhanced when nonverbal signals are congruent with purpose and facilitation language. For example, people consciously give attention to the direction in which someone points and unconsciously attend to where the person's eyes are looking. Recorders who point to a flip chart with their eyes directed to the same spot not only focus group energies there but also insure facilitator control of focus by not looking at the group. Stand in one spot to give directions. Move to a new space to ask for clarification. This "visual paragraph" separates verbally and nonverbally the intention of the two messages. Chapter 6 describes the facilitator role in detail and describes 50 specific facilitator strategies.

Seating Arrangements Should Distinguish Participants From Nonparticipants

Many public bodies and decision-making groups work in settings in which others are present to observe, inform, or advocate. It is easier for the facilitator to monitor the moods, interactions, and energy of the members when the seating arrangements distinguish them from nonmembers. We've seen several arrangements for this. A council of 8–12 people is seated facing one another around a large conference table. Behind them are seated staff members and resource persons who may periodically be asked to "come to the table" to give a report, offer an opinion, or give information on a topic. In another arrangement, involving a group of about 40 persons of whom 15 are resource people and guests, the entire group is seated together in table groups during the dialogue portions of the meeting. The reason for this is to get a rich interplay of ideas and information from different perspectives. When the group shifts to a decision-making mode, however, the guests either leave or sit in a different part of the room. Policy boards sometimes formalize this in bylaws: "Decision making will be by 75% consensus of those present and voting. Only members shall advocate and vote in council meetings."

Seating Arrangements Should Be Spacious Enough to Meet Group Needs But No Larger

Skilled groups develop a variety of seating patterns and room arrangements to support different types of social and cognitive interactions. Planning these setups is part of the meeting design

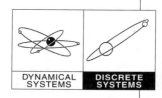

process. Groups and meeting designers who lack this awareness can get trapped by the default furniture configurations of the rooms in which they work. Moving the furniture to support productive group work is an important part of a meeting's success.

One vital consideration is to remove any empty chairs from the work area. In both dialogue and discussion settings, empty chairs bleed energy from the group and increase both the physical and psychological divide between participants. The actual physical removal of unused chairs sends a powerful message to the group about the need for connection. This is reinforced when latecomers have to move a chair to literally join the group.

Seating Arrangements Should Accommodate Physical Movement, Subgrouping, and Personal Ownership of Entire Room

When people in meetings sit where they always sit, they tend to see what they always see and say what they always say. Initially group members will sit where they are most comfortable; let them. But people unconsciously become territorial quite easily in meetings. You may have noticed that in groups that meet periodically, members will take the same space that they occupied in the last meeting. There are two generic advantages for periodically changing seating arrangements. First, it produces energy to move and sit with someone else. Group deliberations can be deadening, and thinking deadened, without physical movement. Second, subgroup conversations that are always held with the same person or small group impose limitations on thinking. Conceptual boundaries are formed by these consistent relationships, backgrounds, cognitive styles, and positions. Moving members into different conversational subgroups brings fresh thinking. Occasionally, changing seating can serve other purposes as well, such as breaking up a clique or signaling a transition from one agenda item to another.

Memory Displays and Public Recording Should Support Best Thinking of Meeting Content and Processes

Certain tasks are done more effectively with special room arrangement and materials provisioning. For example, planning, problem solving, and decision making require access to multiple kinds of data. Writing on charts and information posted on the walls become group memory devices. Many times we have witnessed a group fall silent while members scan what is on display, linking and relating information to the next task in their project.

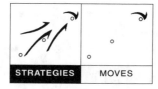

"Naive" Questions for Structure #3

Can someone record this for us?

Where are the charts from the last meeting?

What will happen with the charts from today's session?

(to another group member while pointing to the flip chart) Is that what you mean?

Perhaps more important than serving memory, what is written becomes a visual voice, always in the room, never silent, interacting with group-member thinking. Many high-performing groups post charts to clarify tasks and remind members of working agreements (see sidebar for some Structure #3 questions). Some groups keep lists of collaborative norms, meeting standards, and group-member capabilities on permanent display. Furthermore, the act of composing language for public recording interacts with thinking, forcing greater specificity, economy, and consensus. For these reasons, charting materials—markers, tape, pads, and easels—should be readily available. Blank walls without other artwork are best for meeting rooms. This lets each group craft the space to its own needs.

Benefits of public recording include the following:

- Helps the group focus on a task
- Supports visual learners
- Depersonalizes ideas and problem data
- Enhances memory of participants during and after a meeting
- Guards against data overload but holds on to all ideas and frees participants from taking notes
- Develops shared ownership
- Serves as a psychic release for participants
- Prevents repetition and wheel spinning
- Encourages participation because it respects individuals' ideas and reduces status differentials
- Enables each member to check to make sure that his or her ideas are being recorded accurately
- Increases the group's sense of accomplishment
- Makes sophisticated problem-solving methods possible by holding on to information developed in one phase for use in the next
- Makes it easy for latecomers to catch up without interrupting the meeting
- Makes accountability easier because decisions are written down in clear view of the group—who is going to do what, when

Develop Standards

Standards are agreements for ways of working together. Although each group is responsible for deciding what standards will guide its

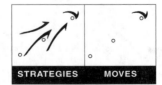

STRATEGIES   MOVES

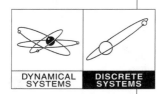

work, we advocate starting with the following simple set of standards because *whenever we have seen these standards in place, we have witnessed successful meetings:* maximum product, minimum time, and maximum member satisfaction. Additionally, when effective groups implement these standards, their levels of efficiency, efficacy, craftsmanship, and satisfaction soar. When ineffective groups adopt them, their productivity improves.

Michael Doyle and David Straus initially "discovered" these standards in the form of success principles from attending and analyzing hundreds of meetings.

> . . . we began to see that certain forces are common to all (successful) groups. A board of directors, a governmental task force, a student council, a citizen's committee, an administrative staff, a radical political group may have different values and objectives, but they all face similar problems when they hold a meeting.[6]

We have updated Doyle and Straus's principles to reflect research findings from the last few years. Our list of principles for the fourth structure is as follows:

1. Groups should address only one topic at a time.
2. Groups should use only one process at a time.
3. Meetings should be interactive and engage balanced participation.
4. Decision-making meetings should engage cognitive conflict.
5. All parties should understand and agree on meeting roles.

Address One Topic at a Time

There is a limit to what any individual can attend to in the moment. Groups are limited as well. When more than one topic is being discussed, the group lacks focus and confusion reigns. We often hear group members ask, "Which topic are we on right now?"

Multiple-topic discussions start because many issues are linked with others and/or one idea stimulates an associated idea for another person. For example, a subcommittee is meeting to recommend new textbooks for adoption. One member says, "You know, I'm really pleased that we are working on this task because the old textbooks aren't that useful. In fact, I was in the supply room the other day and I saw several books just sitting on the shelf with dust gathering. I think some teachers are not using them at all." To this, another group

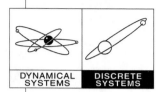

DYNAMICAL SYSTEMS   DISCRETE SYSTEMS

member responds, "Supply room! I thought we asked that it be cleaned up. I was in there the other day; it's still a mess!" Another group member says, "Has anyone seen my microscope? I've been looking for it. It was in the supply room the last time I was there."

For the linear-minded among us, this type of conversation drives us crazy. Here are several facilitator moves that can redirect the group to one topic.

Challenge relevancy. Offer a relevancy challenge by asking, "Please help us understand, Sam, how your comment relates to the topic that we are discussing." This request is made in an approachable voice and sometimes, to the surprise of everyone, Sam will indicate how his comment relates. At other times he will say, "You know, it doesn't fit right now. I'll save it for later," thereby monitoring his own participation.

"Cape" comments. Use the flip chart like a bullfighter's cape. Sam makes a comment (e.g., about cleaning the supply room), and the facilitator moves to the flip chart and writes "supply room" while saying to Sam, "Sam, I know there are several people interested in this. Let's put it here so we don't lose it. We'll come back to it later."

In this case, the facilitator has communicated respectfully, "Yes, it is important, but not now." Groups use a variety of strategies to accomplish this. They sometimes have a chart on the wall headed "Items to come back to," on which thoughts like this will be reported.

Use Only One Process at a Time

Group processes are vehicles for collective thinking. To brainstorm, to clarify, to analyze, and to evaluate require different mental operations. In order to use one process at a time, all group members must know what the process is, how it works, and why it is being used. Doyle and Straus observe that facilitators who "go slow in order to go fast" can save meeting time by front-loading detailed instructions before process.

PAG/PAU is one strategy for accomplishing this. It stands for Process As Given/Process As Understood. The facilitator will communicate each of these stages in three different mediums: space, voice, and language (Figure 5-3).

The facilitator stands in the first space and, with a credible voice, describes a process. For example: "We are about to brainstorm [see Brainstorming sidebar]. As you will recall, the ground rules for brainstorming are to report ideas, phrases, and thoughts. These do not need to be in complete sentences. There are no criticisms or questions during this time. If you do not agree with something or have a

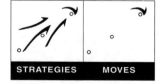

STRATEGIES   MOVES

Figure 5-3. PAG/PAU

- This space
- Credible voice
- Give directions

- This space
- Approachable voice
- Check for understanding

Brainstorming

Rules
- Allow silent think time. Don't hold back any ideas.
- The more ideas, the better.
- No discussion is allowed.
- No judgment or criticism is allowed.
- Hitchhike—build on ideas.
- Post ideas.

Sequence of events
- Review the topic, defining the subject.
- Give everyone a minute or two to think.
- Invite everyone to call out ideas.
- One team member writes down the ideas on a flip chart.

Modify this procedure to fit the group.

question about it, hold that thought for later. We will work for 4 minutes."

The facilitator then moves to a different space and, in an approachable voice, checks for understanding. "So, just to be sure I've stated this clearly, what are we going to do? What are the ground rules? George, if you have a criticism for an idea that someone has offered, what do you do with it?"

Stop and redirect.   In this example, the facilitator has taken time to make sure that group members understand a process and now has permission to use hard facilitation skills with them. For example, if Sam forgets about the ground rules in the middle of brainstorming and raises a question, the facilitator can stop Sam and redirect him. This can be done by moving toward Sam, showing him the palms of one's hand, and saying in a credible voice, "Sam, hang on to that for a minute. We'll deal with that when we are finished brainstorming."

Meetings Should Be Interactive and Engage Balanced Participation

Groups can plan, share information, problem solve, evaluate, make decisions, and define their boundaries. When you think of these purposes for working groups, it is clear that a pattern in which one person talks and the rest of the people listen is not productive. If you have 12 members in a meeting, you want 12 minds engaged. If you have 30 members, you want 30 minds engaged. Participants construct meaning and develop ownership interacting with ideas and each other.

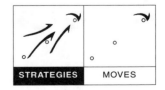

Facilitator Moves to Balance Participation

"Take a moment and jot down your ideas on this before we begin sharing."

"Turn to your neighbor and generate a few more ideas. You've got 30 seconds."

"In the context in which you are working, what is the difference between *interrogate* and *inquire?* Tell your neighbor (60 seconds)."

"In a moment, I'm going to ask you to move to a corner of the room. Stand there. When other people arrive, talk together about why you have selected that spot. Okay. Those of you who believe that option A is best, go to that corner; option B, to that corner; option C, to that corner; and option D, to that corner." (After group members have talked, ask for reports from the corners.)

STRATEGIES   MOVES

Too often we have heard the statement that the purpose of participation in meetings is for "buy-in." We encourage the disuse of this phrase because it carries with it suppositions of manipulation and inferences that the leader has something to sell and the group has an opportunity to buy it. We find, instead, that the purpose of participation is to develop ownership. When ideas are owned, when values are articulated and owned, when beliefs are admitted, when plans and programs and strategies are posed by the group, commitment is high and the likelihood of successful implementation is great. As we shall see in the next principle, ownership does not occur without disagreements.

Balanced participation does not mean that every member speaks for an equal amount of time; it means that the door is open for member participation (see sidebar). There are two forms in which group members speak: to the entire group and to a partner or a small group nearby. Facilitate participation by asking individuals to share with a partner before speaking or to get together with a group of four and identify major criteria to be brought before the group. Moves like these engage everyone richly in thinking processes. They also offer a cloak of anonymity on occasions when voices wish not to be identified.

Engage Cognitive Conflict

Meetings must be safe but not necessarily comfortable. When a group's meetings are always comfortable, the group is probably not talking about the right things. Cognitive conflict—disagreements among group members about substantive issues like goals, values, and assumptions—tend to improve team effectiveness, lead to better decisions, and increase commitment, cohesiveness, empathy, and understanding. Cognitive conflict occurs as teams examine, compare, and reconcile these differences.

The problem with encouraging cognitive conflict is that once it is aroused it may be difficult to control. If cognitive conflict slides into affective conflict, hostility, avoidance, cynicism, or apathy can result. Affective conflict focuses anger on individuals rather than ideas, and disagreement becomes personalized. It can occur when group members lack the skills to disagree gracefully. The greatest insurance against affective conflict is group-member skills and practice of the seven norms of collaboration described in chapter 3.

Amason, et al.[7] found that teams that encourage cognitive without affective conflict are characterized by focused activity, creativity, open communication, and integration (Table 5-6). They work close to the core of issues and are not distracted by trivial

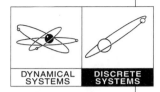

points. They encourage thinking beyond normal options, listen to the "minority voice," encourage dissenting opinions, synergize the thoughts and perspectives of different members, and approach problems from new perspectives. The researchers also found that conflict can be an asset to maintaining open communication. Members in groups with productive cognitive conflict challenge each other's assumptions. They make the fullest possible use of all their members, whereas in less effective groups there is often a dispropor-tionate contribution among members. Good teams seek out opinions of those who are less active and moderate the input of those who monopolize the conversation.

Table 5-6. Outcomes of Conflict

Cognitive Conflict	Affective Conflict
Disagreements about substantive differ-ences of opinion improve team effective-ness and produce	Disagreements over personalized, individu-ally oriented matters reduce team effective-ness and produce
• Better decisions • Increased commitment • Increased cohesiveness • Increased empathy • Increased understanding	• Destructive conflict • Poorer decisions • Decreased commitment • Decreased cohesiveness • Decreased empathy

Understand and Agree on Meeting Roles

Any team works most effectively when members know each other's responsibilities (see sidebar for some Structure #4 questions). The shortstop can anticipate the first baseman's position in relation to first base; therefore his throw is most effective. The second baseman knows that the center fielder will back him up on a long ball. Because he can count on his teammate, he stays close to second base to guard it. The same principle works for group meetings.

While there are many possible meeting roles, we would like to identify four that are most typically found in working groups. These are (a) engaged participant, (b) facilitator, (c) recorder, and (d) role or knowledge authority.

1. Engaged Participant

Because meeting success is influenced more by the collaborative norms of the group than by facilitator leadership, we call persons occupying this role "engaged participants" to illuminate the active and essential contribution they make to the group's work. Anyone, at

**"Naive" Questions
for Structure #4**

"Excuse me. Are you still in the facilitator role?"

"Would you like me to record for you while you comment?"

"Who will do what by when?"

"Who will communicate to whom?"

some time, might be an engaged participant. Standing committee members, participating guests at a special session, the recorder or facilitator *before or after* serving in those roles, and the building administrator can all at some time serve as engaged participants. What these group members know and do is critically important to group effectiveness.

In strong groups, engaged participants monitor their personal adherence to meeting standards. They notice and set aside comments they are about to make if the comment would violate the "one topic at a time" standard. They also monitor the group's adherence to standards. It is not unusual to hear an engaged participant say, "Excuse me, but I thought we were talking about 'X' and it seems as if we are now engaged in another topic" or "What process are we using now? I've lost track." (See sidebar for some Structure #3 questions.)

Engaged participants use the seven norms of collaboration described in chapter 3. They seek and provide data, clarify decision-making processes and levels of authority, and perform gatekeeping functions for others.

Gatekeeping. Susan may say to Sid, "Sid, I'm aware that you haven't talked for a little while. Is there anything that you would like to add?" Notice in this interchange that Sid is not on the spot to respond. The gate, however, has been opened. Similarly, Todd may say to Teresa, "Teresa, I know you served on a committee like this last year. Do you have anything that you'd like to say?" Kristina says to Ken, "Ken, from where I'm sitting your eyebrows look furrowed. Any comments you'd like to make?"

Set and test working agreements. Engaged participants also set and test working agreements. In this example Jose *sets* a working agreement by saying to the group, "I'm requesting that we make an agreement to start our meetings on time. I notice that some of us are here on time and others are not. Frequently, I have to wait 15 minutes before the meeting starts." Discussion ensues. The group decides to begin meetings on time. Several weeks later, June *tests* the agreement by saying, "I'd like to talk about the decision that we made several meetings ago to start meetings on time. I notice that this is not happening. What do we need to do to keep our agreement?"

Test consensus. Engaged participants informally test consensus by summary paraphrasing. Sometimes they say, "It seems that we may have agreement on this. Is that true?" or "Could we see a show of thumbs? Thumbs up if you are in agreement, thumbs down if not, thumbs sideways if you're not sure or it's not important to you."

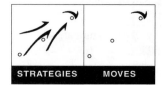

STRATEGIES   MOVES

Monitor internal processes. Engaged participants monitor their own internal processes and listen to their own listening. They become aware of when they have stopped listening to others and are following a train of thought in their own minds. They recognize their emotional responses to other speakers. When irritated, they notice it, but instead of giving in to the irritation, they locate the probable reason. Then they set the feeling aside so they can stay fully engaged in the conversation. When they are listening to understand, yet find themselves offering counterarguments in their own minds, they notice this and suspend the unproductive mental activity.

Finally, engaged participants are conscious of the assumptions they bring to a conversation and notice how these influence their listening, thinking, and speaking.

2. Facilitator

Group facilitation is a process in which a person who is acceptable to all members of the group, substantively neutral, and has no decision-making authority intervenes to help a group improve the way it identifies and solves problems and makes decisions, in order to increase the group's effectiveness.[8]

While a facilitator displays no preference for any of the solutions the group considers, no facilitator is truly neutral. To be "substantively neutral," Schwarz's term, means that facilitators give no verbal or nonverbal cues of their personal reactions to the ideas being discussed. Since the facilitator's client is the group, not certain members, this display of neutrality is important.

Facilitators are responsible for process. Ultimately they are responsible for helping groups to increase their effectiveness by improving their process, knowledge, and skills in the long run. Facilitators often start by clarifying their own role with the group: "Hi. I'll be facilitating this meeting today. My job is to support you in completing your agenda and also to assist you in staying on one topic at a time and using only one process at a time. Now, I can use a facilitation style anywhere between Rambo and Mary Poppins. Given today's topic and the time you have, where on that continuum do you want me to work?" The facilitator focuses group energy, keeps the group on task, and directs the process. Chapter 6 details facilitation functions and strategies.

3. Recorder

As groups tire, auditory acuity is the first modality to fade. Because many meetings are either long, and members begin to tire, or at the

STRATEGIES   MOVES

end of the school day, and members are already tired, public recording is critically important for the group's short-term memory. The later in the day or the more fatigued the participants, the more public recording is necessary. At the best of times, humans can manage seven items of information (plus or minus two) in their working memories.[9] Public recording keeps key data in front of a group.

Recorders, like facilitators, occupy a position of studied neutrality. Their function is to support the group by maintaining a clear visual representation of important ideas and data and to support the facilitator in managing processes as effectively and efficiently as possible. The recorder and facilitator also serve as behind-the-scenes custodians, arranging displays, clearing out unnecessary data, and arranging the room for special activities.

A great deal of knowledge is emerging about the techniques and tools of public recording. It is sufficient here to call attention to several basics of public recording:

- Print rather than write.

- Use sentence case.

- Use color—alternate green, blue, and brown for text; reserve red for headlines and black for boxes, arrows, or other organizers.

- Use only water-color pens.

- Write large enough for all members to read.

- Keep all charts visible at all times.

- Border charts for formal appearance.

- Use pictographs.

- Keep eyes on chart when recording.

- Have facilitator tell group to direct corrections.

- Have facilitator ask group what not to record.

- Point and/or stand by items as they are being discussed.

- Remain still and nondistracting.

- Move body to support facilitator's use of space.

4. Role or Knowledge Authority

We worked with principals in a state that was an early adopter of site-based decision making. Tragically, most of these principals felt neutered; they believed that their ideas or expertise did not count and that their job was to function as a noninterfering member of faculty or site-council groups. What a sad loss to the teachers and students at those schools, and what an artificial, uncomfortable position for principals.

Our guess is that this occurred from a misinterpretation of shared decision making and from the lack of a common name for a leader who is not managing a meeting of one's own staff. Leadership roles in meetings are called by many names: chairperson, convener, facilitator, leader, consultant, specialist, manager, and others. Because we see a critical leadership role in meetings that does *not* include running the meeting, we have been searching for a term that might be neutral, or at least unlike the other names we have for meeting leadership.

By what name can we designate such a leader in a meeting? The most descriptive term we've found so far is *role authority* or *knowledge authority.* The role authority might be the principal in a staff meeting, the vice principal if the principal is not there, the superintendent in a district office meeting, or the assistant superintendent if the superintendent is not there. The knowledge authority might be the social sciences consultant at a task force dealing with social science, the science consultant in a committee addressing a science curriculum, or an external consultant charged with making recommendations to the group on improving organizational effectiveness.

When the role or knowledge authority is in a meeting without a facilitator, this leader typically manages the group processes. He or she sets the agenda, decides when to move to the next topic, recognizes those who want to speak, writes meeting notes to assist remembering, and summarizes actions to be taken. In managing all these procedural tasks, the role or knowledge authority limits, or at least diffuses, the attention given to meeting content and also limits group access to the special information resources that go with this person's particular role or knowledge expertise.

Without a facilitator, the value of this leader's information is limited in two ways. First, because the leader has to balance attention between process and content, there is less time for interaction with the content. Second, and perhaps more important, it is extremely rare that a leader can maintain the neutrality required of facilitation processes and still give content information to the group. For this reason, leaders become more influential and the group proceeds on a maturational path and makes better decisions by having a person other than this leader facilitate the meeting.

When leaders such as department heads or principals use the services of a meeting facilitator, they will often set meeting schedules, coordinate topics with faculty and others, arrange to have department members rotate through the facilitator and recorder roles, and codevelop the agenda design with the next meeting facilitator. The role authority will also follow through to see that subcommittee tasks are clear, resources are available, and evaluation of processes and products is provided.

In many senses, the role or knowledge authority functions as any engaged participant in the meeting but is free from misinterpretation to inform the group about constraints, resources, and values related to their topic. Like other group members, the role or knowledge authority can advocate one's own ideas as well as inquire about the ideas of others. The primary caution is to remember that until groups have attained a high state of interdependence, actions in this role will speak louder than words.

End Notes

[1] Doyle, M., & Straus, D. (1993). *How to make meetings work: The new interaction method.* New York: Berkeley Books.

[2] Saphier, J., Bigda-Peyton, T., & Pierson, G. (1989). *How to make decisions that stay made.* Alexandria, VA: Association for Supervision and Curriculum Development.

[3] Ibid, p. 6.

[4] Perkins, D. (1992). *Smart schools.* New York: Free Press.

[5] Schwarz, R. M. (1994). *The skilled facilitator: Practical wisdom for developing effective groups.* San Francisco, CA: Jossey-Bass, p. 147.

[6] Doyle & Straus, p. 14.

[7] Amason, A. C., Thompson, K. R., Hochwarter, W. A., & Harrison, A. W. (1995, August). Conflict: An important dimension in successful management teams. *Organizational Dynamics, 24* (2), 20–35.

[8] Schwarz, p. 4.

[9] Miller, G. (1963). The magical number seven, plus or minus two: Some limits in capacity for processing information. *Psychological Review, 63,* 81–97.

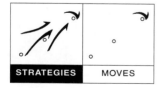

STRATEGIES   MOVES

Chapter 6   The Confident and Skilled Facilitator

WHAT IS effective facilitation? To write this chapter, we thought about skilled facilitators we know and listed what they have in common. (An example is provided in the sidebar.) We noticed the following: They are flexible. They follow principles, not rules. They improvise. They know their own cognitive and emotional styles and can work beyond them when to do so will serve the group. They are comfortable with who they are and can set aside judgments about others. They are clear about their intentions. They think about outcomes. They are reflective and learn from experience. They can direct or request, be firm or soft, be serious or light, and focus on tasks or relationships. They have abundant knowledge about processes and groups. They are effortlessly competent with many facilitation moves. They also know that they have more to learn and are continuous learners.

this chapter features:

Getting work done
Doing the right work
Working collaboratively
Managing systems
Developing groups
Adapting to change

Skilled facilitators also differ from one another. They vary in appearance, cognitive style, age, gender, culture, and ethnicity. They have different facilitation personas, unique gifts, and shortcomings, and they are at various stages on the journey from novice to expert performance.

This chapter relates facilitation to the broader aims of this book, outlines the knowledge base of successful facilitators, and identifies what facilitators pay attention to during a meeting. You will also find practical self-assessment questions and a valuable tool kit of facilitation strategies.

Why Facilitation Is Essential

Although facilitation is not more important than the hats[1] of presenting, consulting, or coaching, facilitation is the primary agent for adult

A Skilled Facilitator

Carolyn silently observes the group. As she hears a dip in the volume of the small-group conversations, she says, "Please look in this direction." She stands, silent and still until all eyes are on her. "You've just completed the first step in reaching a decision," she says. "Each group has listed criteria. Your next step is to code the ideas on your lists as either *necessary* or *nice*. As soon as you are done, have a recorder from each group list the items on your *necessary* list in front of the room." Carolyn asks, "Are there any questions about purpose or process?" She waits 5 seconds. "This step will take 5 minutes. Please begin."

As groups reengage, Carolyn scans to see that the work space is properly provisioned with chart pens, tape, and easel paper. She mentally rehearses the transition statement she will make when the lists are posted and decides how to structure the next step in the process.

group development that supports student learning—the focus of this book. Why is this so? It is clear that ". . . student learning increases substantially in schools with collaborative work cultures that foster a professional learning community among teachers and others, focus continuously on improving instructional practices in light of student performance data, and link to external standards and staff development support."[2] However, knowing this does not tell educators how to achieve collaborative work cultures that result in student learning. Nor can successful efforts be copied from one setting to another with similar results. The metaphorical wheel, and good instruction, must be reinvented at each site for each group of learners.[3] Facilitation of stakeholder thinking, problem solving, and planning is the norm in work units that make a difference in student learning. In the most effective adaptive systems, all players wear the facilitation hat because collaboration occurs in small groups and large assemblies, in coffee conversations and councils, in talks with peers and talks with parents. Facilitation provides the focusing, directing, and organizing features necessary to produce results for students from these conversations.[4]

A Brief History of Facilitation

Alaskan natives report using facilitation concepts for hundreds of years. The philosophy, mind-set, and skills of facilitation also have much in common with approaches used by the Quakers, Mahatma Ghandi, Martin Luther King, Jr., and other people in nonviolence movements over the centuries.[5] Yet formalized tools for facilitating (making easier) group work are fairly recent. When *Robert's Rules of Order* was first published in 1876, it modified American parliamentary procedures to meet the needs of "ordinary" groups. However, its complexity made it more useful in the boardroom than in the faculty room. One hundred years later Michael Doyle and David Straus made practical facilitation tools accessible with the "interaction method" of conducting, planning, problem-solving, and decision-making meetings.[6] About 20 years later, from studies at the Massachusetts Institute of Technology, dialogue emerged in management practices as another way that groups do business. With dialogue, a second type of facilitation evolved, more akin to the T-groups of the 1960s than the facilitation style used for decision-making meetings. During dialogue, in which groups talk for the purpose of developing understanding, the classical facilitation functions of maintaining one topic at a time and one process at a time are not as clearly defined as in decision-making meetings. Responsibilities for topic, process, and balanced participation become more deeply invested in the group itself. In the early stages of group development, a dialogue facilitator mediates the flow of meaning by listening for themes and paraphrasing to offer containers, make connections, and mark transitions.

The Expert Facilitator's Knowledge Base

The expert facilitator applies knowledge in the four areas displayed in Table 6-1: maps, strategies and moves, knowledge of self, and knowledge about groups. These support group work and group development.

Table 6.1 Knowledge Base for Facilitators

MAPS	SELF
Facilitators seek to understand meetings and make decisions affecting meeting dynamics with the aid of four types of mental models: 1. Universal meeting goals 2. Structures for meeting success 3. Energy management 4. Principles of effective meeting transactions, information processing, and interventions	Facilitators' most sensitive and critical asset is themselves. Self-knowledge of cognitive style, educational beliefs, emotional states, intentions, strengths, and limitations permits facilitation decisions to be based on group needs rather than personal preferences.
STRATEGIES AND MOVES Facilitators manage and direct meeting processes. They know and use a range of facilitation strategies and moves to manage group: energy, information, and action.	**GROUPS** Although all groups have common tendencies, each group has unique characteristics that facilitators must take into account: culture, developmental level, group dynamics and history, relationship with facilitator, external environment, and conflicting demands.

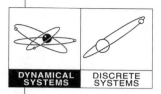

DYNAMICAL SYSTEMS | DISCRETE SYSTEMS

Mastery of any role requires mental complexity and automatic routines for fundamentals. Reflection upon facilitation practice and experience extends knowledge, efficiency and insight. Skilled facilitators can do more with less effort, are likely to be more playful in managing group energies, and compared to novices are better at distinguishing relevant from nonrelevant data in problem solving.[7]

Because there is not time in the middle of an intense meeting for a facilitator to stop and recall how to phrase a summarizing and organizing paraphrase, certain facilitation tools and maps must be overlearned to the point of automaticity. The facilitator's novice-to-expert journey is complex because the most important skills go beyond a repertoire of facilitation strategies. They are about moment-to-moment decisions regarding when to use which strategies, and, in fact, when to "break rules" of facilitation. The five metacognitive capabilities listed below support a facilitator's decisions and the capacity to learn from experience. (The first four, the reader may recall, are the group-member capabilities discussed in chapter 3.) In chapter 8 we will elaborate on how to help group members and facilitators learn these invisible resources.

The five metacognitive capabilities are as follows:

1. To know one's intentions and choose congruent behaviors.

2. To set aside unproductive patterns of listening, responding, and inquiring.

3. To know when to self-assert and when to integrate.

4. To know and support the group's purposes, topics, processes, and development.

5. To emotionally disassociate from events in order to make strategic decisions about processes.

Meetings as Dynamical Systems: Maps of the Territory

A facilitator's moment-to-moment decisions are the product of mental maps. These mental models organize and explain perception, determine what will be perceived and will not be perceived, and are the stuff with which metacognition works. The more maps a facilitator uses to understand groups at work, the more flexibility he or she brings to decisions. The greater the flexibility, the greater the influence.

Meetings are complex communication events occurring within dynamical systems. Earlier we described such systems as being subject to nonlinear logic. In these systems, tiny events cause major disturbances, everything influences everything else, you don't have to touch everyone to make a difference, and more data do not lead to better predictions. Facilitation maps are lenses for locating order within chaotic systems.

All maps are approximations of reality. They reveal as much about the cartographer's perceptions as the territory being described. Like a city map, facilitation maps are improved by showing multiple projections. Like a city map, the more detail with which they represent the territory, the more options they reveal. Unlike city maps, facilitation maps add statements of values, standards, and portrayals of idealized interactions.

To help groups be successful, facilitators manage, model, mediate, and monitor four types of maps that portray meeting territory:

1. Goals
2. Structures
3. Energy
4. Principles

Facilitators use these maps to help them manage time, task, and environment. They model facilitation principles and practices of collaboration. They mediate when they shine a compassionate ray of light on cause-and-effect relationships in group functioning and group accomplishment. They mediate when they cause the group to reflect on its work. Finally, facilitators help groups to develop the capacity to manage, mediate, and monitor each of these four types of maps on their own.

Goals

Facilitators bring three goals to their work:

1. *Task accomplishment:* The facilitator focuses the group on clear outcomes and supports the group to achieve success.

2. *Process skills development:* As the result of each meeting, improving groups have greater facility in using previously learned processes and may also learn new processes.

3. *Group development:* Working groups become more effective over time in managing themselves. They should have an increased capacity for handling their collective work, adapting to change, working through conflict, and relating to factors in their environments.

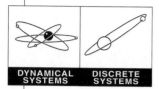

DYNAMICAL SYSTEMS | DISCRETE SYSTEMS

Facilitators working with ad hoc groups may work to achieve only the first goal and occasionally the second goal.

Structures

The four meeting success structures described in chapter 5 are invaluable maps that bring order to planning, problem-solving, and decision-making meetings.

Decide who decides. This structure provides a framework to maintain clarity about decision-making authority and processes. Who decides and how decisions will be made are the organizing questions.

Define the sandbox. This structure helps groups to be clear about which topics are within their sphere of influence and which can be acted on only by others, such as legislative bodies, other committees, or a boss.

Design the surround. This structure addresses features of the physical environment that facilitate group work.

Develop meeting standards. This structure sets standards for meetings that were discussed in chapter 5: Use only one process at a time, talk about only one topic at a time, balance member participation, engage productively in cognitive conflict, and have agreements on meeting roles.

Energy

Energy is the eternal heartbeat of a working group. To manage a group, one must first manage oneself.

Years ago, meeting master Michael Doyle taught a valuable lesson to one of the authors by example. He would frequently absent himself from dinners and social events in retreat settings where he had been hired as a facilitator. When asked about this practice, he explained that his first obligation to the group is to maintain his energy. Facilitation work demands so much in-the-moment attention that it is emotionally demanding and energy consuming. When possible, he would leave group activities to take care of himself. We deeply appreciate this strategy today, and it symbolizes for us that as facilitators we have permission to take care of ourselves in order to best serve the group.

Fifteen strategies for managing group energy are presented later in this chapter.

Principles

Principle, from the Latin *principium,* means the ultimate source or cause of something. Three categories of principles guide facilitator decisions: facilitator–group member transactions, information processing, and facilitator interventions.

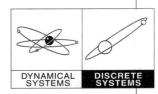

Productive transactions. The interactions shown in Table 6-2 are ideals for groups that meet regularly, are responsible for solving problems, have time to work on problems, deal with complex or nonroutine challenges, and require commitment of members to implement solutions.[8] While many of these fifteen principles are also useful to ad hoc groups, such groups rarely perform at the same high level of standards as groups that meet regularly.

Compare this to the seven norms of collaboration described in chapter 3. Groups committed to the seven norms exercise the tools necessary to achieve almost all these principles. Principles 5, 9, 10, and 15 may stand as exceptions.

Table 6-2. Principles of Effective Transactions

1. Distinguish between inferences and data.	6. Disagree openly with other members of the group.	11. Check for group-member understanding.
2. Test assumptions and inferences.	7. Jointly design ways to test disagreements and solutions.	12. Keep discussions focused.
3. State assumptions.	8. Get agreement on what words mean.	13. Discuss undiscussable items.
4. Explain reasons behind statements, questions, actions.	9. Exchange relevant information with non–group members.	14. Make decisions by consensus.
5. Focus on interests, not positions.	10. Reveal all relevant information.	15. Engage in self-critiques.

Information processing. Information processing focuses on how people acquire, transmit, store and transform information.[9] Because meetings are information intensive, skilled facilitators anticipate, monitor, and intervene to assist groups in generating, receiving, understanding, and acting on information.

Three views of mental processing converge to form a set of useful guidelines for facilitator decisions:

1. *Cognitive psychology and strategic instruction:* Learning lives at the heart of adaptive groups. From topics they address, members learn how to analyze and solve problems and how to work effectively together as a group and with the external environment. Facilitators recognize that all such learning is goal oriented, links new informa-

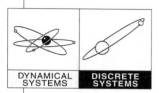

DYNAMICAL SYSTEMS | DISCRETE SYSTEMS

tion with old, and organizes information and experiences into meaningful units. Facilitators also recognize that learning occurs in phases yet is nonlinear, is influenced by a group's development, and requires the acquisition of a repertoire of cognitive and metacognitive structures.[10]

Current information-processing models describe three phases in student learning. Strategic learners use different skills and strategies at each phase. We believe that similar claims can be made for adults in meetings.

The first phase is *preparation for work*. Working groups may attend to this after a lengthy absence from the work group and/or topic or when a new challenge is introduced to the team. Some facilitation goals that will help groups prepare for work are the following: Clarify the task and success criteria; activate prior experiences and information; access topic vocabulary, categories, and structure; enrich the collective knowledge base by organizing an exchange of information; surface and clarify misconceptions; and focus mental energy on this meeting and these tasks.

The second phase is *processing and organizing information*. Some facilitation goals at this phase that will help groups are the following: Examine new information; relate prior information to current data; raise new questions; withhold judgment; integrate ideas; elaborate, test, confirm, or revise positions, predictions, and questions; and consider new information.

The third phase is the *integration and application of new information*. Some facilitation goals that will help groups are the following: Integrate and organize collective meaning; categorize; sort; summarize key ideas; conclude; decide; evaluate; plan; and commit.

2.   *Constructivist learning theory*[11]: Facilitators keep several constructivist tenets in mind as they work with groups:

*   Disequilibrium facilitates learning. Contradictions should be illuminated, explored, and discussed. Group discomfort within the context of safety is an important learning resource.

*   Reflective abstraction is essential to learning. Humans seek to organize meaning and generalize across experiences. Allowing reflection time through journal writing, dialogue groups, and/ or discussion of connections across experiences facilitates group development.

*   Dialogue engenders further thinking.

*   Learning develops cognitive structures. As groups make

meaning of their experiences, they construct progressive structural shifts in perspective. These are, in a sense, "big ideas" developed by the group that become central organizing principles generalized across experiences. This learning often requires the undoing or reorganizing of earlier conceptions.

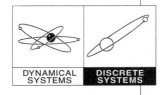

DYNAMICAL SYSTEMS   DISCRETE SYSTEMS

3. *Neurobiology:* The human brain is made up of tens of millions of relatively small neural networks. As a richly layered system of electrochemical dynamics, it both constructs itself and responds to the external environment. Our knowledge of neurobiology includes the following:

- Working memory can manage a limited number of items at one time, usually estimated at seven, plus or minus two.

- Working memory can hold more information when each item is an organized aggregate of smaller bits of information.

- Color and shape aid comprehension as well as short- and long-term memory.

- The brain attends to interruptions in patterns.

- Emotional information reaches brain systems prior to cognitive thought.

- The thicker corpus callosum of women allows them to process emotive thought and cognitive thought simultaneously. Most men cannot do this as easily.[12]

- No separation exists between body and brain. All physiological factors represent an accurate analog of internal states: breathing, gesture, posture, eye movements, language choice, tonality.

- Nonverbal communication is believed over verbal communication when discrepancies exist.

Intervention. To intervene is to interpose oneself between an experience and the person(s) having the experience. Facilitators intervene to improve either the immediate or long-term effectiveness of the group. The best interventions help a group to remain focused on substantive tasks and use a minimum amount of energy to affect a correction. Interventions can take the form of verbal transactions, facilitator use of space, or changing the room arrangement. The facilitator must decide why, when, and how to intervene. An excellent analysis of strategic considerations for interventions appears in Schwarz's book *The Skillful Facilitator.*[13] Some highlights follow.

Deciding why to intervene. Facilitators intervene to help a group be more focused and productive, learn more about pro-

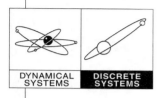

DYNAMICAL SYSTEMS   DISCRETE SYSTEMS

cesses, or develop its capacity for self-monitoring and self-correction.

Deciding when to intervene. Facilitators' interventions must balance the group's need to accomplish work with the need to learn how to function more effectively as a group. Following are some questions that facilitators consider when deciding whether or not to intervene:

1. Do I have permission?
2. Is it important enough?
3. Will it be quick or take time?
4. Can the group learn from it?
5. Are my observations accurate?
6. Am I the best person to intervene?

Deciding how to intervene. To answer yes to the first question above, you and your group must have an understanding that you will intervene to help them function more effectively and learn from their experience. If, for example, you observe side talk during a full-group discussion, you may decide that it is not important enough to address (question 2). On the other hand, you may determine that your observations are not entirely trustworthy (question 5), because despite your best intentions you find yourself annoyed by George's style, and that might be what is bringing his behavior to your attention. Besides, if this continues as a pattern, an intervention would have more influence coming from a team member (question 6).

A few minutes later you notice a pattern of "yes-but" comments from two participants. You decide that an intervention will help the two members to communicate more clearly. This is also an opportunity to support your long-term aim of developing the group's capacity to work effectively. You decide to intervene. Now the questions you must consider are the following:

- With whom will you intervene?
- What will be the focus of the intervention?
- What form will it take?

You plan to explain that "yes-and," rather than "yes-but," interactions are less confrontive and keep both persons more able to hear one another. To *whom* do you say this—the individual who initiated the "yes-but" interaction, the pair involved, or the entire group? That depends on the following consideration: Is this a pattern? Is your relationship with the individual such that you could

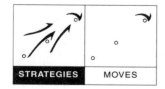

STRATEGIES   MOVES

laugh and say, "Oops, I think I heard a *but* when you were looking for an *and*." Does the group look to you for instruction on process? Often it is safest to make a general comment to the group rather than direct a public intervention to an individual.

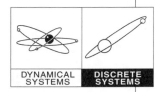

DYNAMICAL SYSTEMS | DISCRETE SYSTEMS

Second, what will be the most productive *focus* of the intervention? Will it be an action by an individual (Tom comes in late and drags a chair to the back of the room behind the group), an interaction between participants (Jim and Jane are stuck in a communication loop because they can't hear one another—some paraphrasing would clear it up), or a pattern of actions displayed by the group (a first-response tendency to argue points rather than try to understand them)?

Finally, what *form* will your intervention take: a statement of abstraction, an observation of behaviors, or an inquiry about thinking and feeling? Abstractions are the safest.

- "A common tendency is for groups to move to the first viable solution. It reduces tension but sometimes stops the group from finding some more powerful ideas."

- "You are stating assumptions more frequently. That seems to be contributing to greater understanding."

Observations of behaviors are slightly more directive. You must state them with compassion and without judgment. They can be followed with a process suggestion, question, or direction.

- "I notice that a few people have not had a chance to talk. I suggest that we see if any of them wish to add something."

- "You started talking about topic X. Now three topics are on the floor. Which one do you want to address?"

- "John, the group is still brainstorming. Please hold your question until this stage is done."

Interventions that require the greatest level of group-facilitator trust are those that illuminate thinking or feeling. This level is often the most generative of self-directed learning. "What did you notice you were feeling while that was happening? Why do you think that was so? What are you learning from this experience that can inform your work next time something like this comes up?"

Knowledge of Self

What you know about yourself allows you to rise above egocentric decisions. No person perceives or processes information the same way as another. Since much of each person's cognitive style and

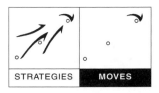

STRATEGIES | MOVES

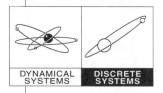

DYNAMICAL
SYSTEMS

DISCRETE
SYSTEMS

modality preferences are hardwired at birth, it is natural to not notice that your perceptions, judgments, and decisions are not "true reality" but are constructions affected by many filters. Your culture, ethnic group, unconscious assumptions, gender, and personal history all influence the meaning you make of things. The more you learn about *you,* the easier it becomes to set aside personal reactions in meetings and concentrate on group members' perceptions and needs. Although a detailed discussion of self-knowledge is outside the scope of this book, there are many excellent sources for self-study.[14] In the meantime, the inventory that follows relates aspects of self knowledge directly to your role as a facilitator.

1. Who am I? About what do I care? How much do I dare?
2. Who is my client?
3. What are my outcomes in this setting?
4. How is my expertise simultaneously an asset and a liability?
5. How can I distinguish between being right and being effective?
6. What lenses do I wear?
7. What types of capacities do I need to develop for this assignment?

Who Am I?

This is an identity question that influences your perceptions, goals, behaviors, and the responses you get from others. Each person wears, at different times, the mantle of different identities: husband or wife, child or parent, boss or employee. In each professional role you play, some metaphor of identity informs the way you play the role. While this orientation is often outside conscious awareness, it influences your work and the results you get.

The facilitator as "parent" wants the group to "grow up" strong and invested in the parent's values about being a group. This facilitator may project expectations for a dependency relationship (saving members from failure or embarrassment) and expect reciprocated love.

The facilitator as "expert" may unintentionally send messages of hierarchy to the group (the facilitator has knowledge, research, and expertise—the group must work the "right way" or develop "correct" and appropriate solutions within that framework).

The facilitator as "friend" values the relationship, companionship, and affection that friends enjoy and therefore avoids pressing the group for explanations, assumptions, or defense of positions that might endanger the friendship.

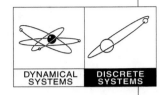

The facilitator as "boss" believes the boss will be held responsible for the group's work. This leads to direction and control. Bosses often carry an unstated emotional demand into the relationship, requesting compliance and loyalty. In turn, employees harbor an unstated emotional demand for forgiveness and protection.

The facilitator as "mediator" (from *medium,* the neutral position in the middle) communicates a relationship of equality (the group has topic expertise, the facilitator has process expertise—together we will work together as equals with different resources). This identity is closest to the role of cognitive coach[sm] and results in productivity, learning, and empowerment for both parties.

"Who am I" is also about caring. About what do you care? You are at your best as a facilitator when you care more about the group's development and task accomplishment than the decisions they make. You make the richest contribution to a group when you envision future stages of the group's maturity and make decisions that promote consciousness and growth. See chapter 7 for elaborations on these metaphors of identity.

"Who Is My Client?"

This can be a complicated question (Table 6-3). Often there is a *contact client* who initiates your services, an *intermediate client* who controls resources or sets boundaries on the task, a *primary client* with whom you will work directly, and an *ultimate client,* often the students. Clarity regarding client status should be the first order of business when agreeing to do facilitation work.

For example, after a semester in which grading policies have been studied, an assistant superintendent asks you to meet with the district's math teachers. You are to facilitate a meeting to reach a final decision about grading policies. Your parameters are the following: at least a 75% consensus, a decision in this meeting, and certain limitations on the range of options the group can consider. If the group cannot decide, the assistant superintendent will do so.

Although the assistant superintendent has provided you with goals and success criteria, you serve the math teachers in their deliberations. You serve them best by clearly representing the goals and constraints of the district as well as by helping them to think about the possible consequences of their recommendations to themselves, students, and teachers in other departments. These are stakeholders whose interests must be protected even if they are not in direct contact with the meeting processes. For teachers assigned to leadership roles that require facilitation services to their own staff, clarifying role responsibilities is even more complex. Teacher-leaders

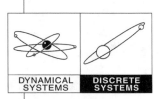

may find "The Responsibilities Dilemma of the Teacher–Facilitator Person" (Appendix D) to be a useful resource.

What Are My Outcomes?

When you are at your best, you envision goals for today's meeting as well as long-range outcomes for the group of increased interdependence, efficacy, and self-directed learning. "How much do I dare?" can remind you that whereas group interaction must always be safe, it need not be comfortable. Sometimes facilitators must resist the urge to save members or release tension in a group. Occasionally you must risk describing dynamics in the meeting room that people don't want to discuss.

Table 6-3. Who Is Your Client?

The assistant superintendent speaks for the district.	A contact client *and* intermediate client
The math teachers will receive your services.	The primary client
Several third parties will be affected by the decision: • Students • Teachers in other departments • Parents	The ultimate client
The assistant superintendent is also part of the system.	Also an ultimate client

Using My Expertise

Knowing too much about a topic is sometimes a liability; it often makes it harder to keep your opinions to yourself. To overcome this, some districts develop a cadre of trained facilitators and deploy them across departments. For example, a member of the science department might facilitate a meeting for the foreign language group.

Being Right Versus Being Effective

This poses a dilemma: A facilitator can be right but not effective. Recently, we attempted to influence leaders in a large district to clarify their outcomes in strengthening their project design before beginning facilitation services. When it became clear that we were

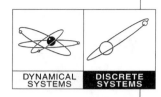

DYNAMICAL SYSTEMS   DISCRETE SYSTEMS

not skillful enough to get our points heard and acted upon, we backed off. The project floundered. Two years later, we were asked to come back to help them pick up the pieces.

What does *effective* mean? In this case, effectiveness might be a measure of the degree of authenticity and integrity we displayed during the contracting phase and while providing services. During planning we advocated clearly for what was best for the system. We knew that regardless of research in this area and what we thought was right, district decision makers must select their own course of action. We were respectful of their realities—pedagogic and political—and worked our hearts out to do the best we could for them in the situation, even though we didn't think it was promising. We maintained positive relationships with all the players. We gave up being "right" to be "effective" and were later called in to provide resources when they had come to a dead end in the course they were pursuing.

What Lenses Do I Wear?

Once while on vacation, one of the authors lost his glasses and had only prescription sunglasses to wear for almost 2 weeks. After a while he forgot that everything he saw was tempered by the color of his lenses. The more conscious you are of your personal lenses—auditory, kinesthetic, visual (detail or big picture), thinking, or feeling—the more discretion you have in making judgments. Knowing about yourself and the group is important. Cognitive styles will be varied. So will educational belief systems.[15] It is likely that some members will be oriented to goals of self-actualization, teaching philosophies that are child-centered. Some might hold a central orientation to cognitive psychology and believe that the central role of schools is to develop rational thought processes, problem solving, and decision making. Other members of your group may keep philosophical company with those committed to fostering core knowledge learning. These educators are likely to be drawn to teacher-centered instruction and the transmission of the major concepts, values, and truths of society. Still other members of your group may view education as a vehicle for social change; they would advocate that schooling should educate students to become proactive regarding the environmental problems and social injustices of the day. Others may be driven by seeking what is efficient, what is measurable, what is "scientific" in a cause-and-effect sense. Effective facilitators monitor their own lenses and observe these various filters at work in the group, allowing allocation rather than egocentric decisions.

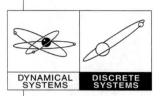

DYNAMICAL SYSTEMS | DISCRETE SYSTEMS

What Types of Capacities Do I Need?

Certain tasks will call on skills you may not have. Will fluency in team building be called for, or negotiation knowledge, conflict-resolution skills, or dealing with negative energy? Skilled facilitators anticipate what will be required. They locate and use learning resources before the event.

Knowledge of Groups[16]

Knowledge of groups involves a number of factors.

Culture

> The bottom line for leaders is that if they do not become conscious of the cultures in which they are embedded, those cultures will manage them.
>
> —Edgar Schein

Every school is unique in its culture. Culture is about "how we do things around here." One school places high value on literacy and holds annual book fairs. Another school is focused on the whole child and uses field days to promote physical fitness and math problem solving. The facilitator must assess the priorities and ways of doing things at each school in order to make sure that the sacred values of a culture are not violated.

Developmental Level

This facet of the system has to do with use of the seven norms, the five energy resources, levels of trust, and the group maturity scale in Figure 5-2. As a facilitator, decisions are driven by how the group is accessing these resources. Groups with low efficacy need greater structure than higher efficacy groups. Groups with limited flexibility require a greater number of strategies designed to understand situations from various perspectives. In groups with limited trust, activities are structured to develop trust: Facilitators overcommunicate process rationale and intent and move groups more slowly through decision-making activities.

Group Dynamics

The behavior of individuals in groups is largely determined by group-member interactions. These dynamics create tacit standards for the ways of addressing tensions. Groups and group members must balance collective interest and self-interest and resolve issues of power, dominance, and influence. A group takes on a distinct personality that supersedes the aggregate personality of its members. It becomes a social unit exerting influence on the individuals.

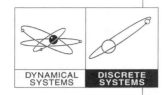

Facilitator Relationship With Group

The group exists as an entity in and of itself. Simultaneously, the group is a system that exists in relationship to the facilitator. Skilled facilitators monitor groups. Trust is essential. The facilitator works to achieve personal rapport and develop relationships of trust.

Group History

Every group has a past that shapes its future. Walk in any school and point to a chair in the lounge and ask who sits there. The information reveals something about the group. Defining events are held in group members' memories: the death of a special student, a change in principals, a year in which the student population changed dramatically.

External Environment

The external environment is the larger world in which the school lives and functions. It can be a legislative mandate such as state testing, the federal government's expectations, or the way that the media pursues an educational issue. The external environment shapes the way that members view the internal environment. This perspective is another lens by which the facilitator can understand the experiences of the group.

Conflicting Demands

Every system is influenced by demands that present mixed messages. The principal who responds to the demands of the central office may create conditions for parents to demand a charter school. Teachers driven by student learning needs may work in opposition to the demands of the state assessment system. Parents and teachers may look at a system through different eyes. Each day, there are different interpretations of the same data, and stakeholders are responding from different perspectives. A facilitator serves the system by bringing consciousness about the differing perspectives.

Two Tensions All Groups Face

Recently a school advisory committee was established at Osborne School. From the very beginning its members had to deal with two challenges. One was the committee's relationships with the broader environment: staff, parents, district office. What must it do to survive,

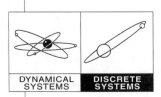

DYNAMICAL SYSTEMS | DISCRETE SYSTEMS

grow, and adapt? The second challenge was to develop effective and efficient working procedures to get work done and to learn and grow from the group's experiences. All groups face these two challenges. A group's response to these challenges form the collective assumptions and behavior patterns that become part of their culture.

The tasks listed below must be dealt with by every group to develop and maintain workable sets of relationships among its members. This is a prerequisite to coping with the external environment. The work is never done. Both challenges must be met simultaneously.

Schein regards the following as major internal issues that any group must address[17]:

1. Create a common language and conceptual categories.

2. Define group boundaries and criteria for inclusion and exclusion.

3. Distribute power and status.

4. Develop norms of intimacy, friendship, and love.

5. Define and allocate rewards and punishments.

6. Explain the unexplainable—ideology and religion.

To know groups, facilitators must know about adult developmental stages;[18] the influence of identity on beliefs, values, capabilities, and behaviors;[19] and the contributions of gender, ethnicity, and color.[20] These topics are outside the scope of this book but represent important aspects of facilitator knowledge.

Knowledge of Facilitation Strategies and Moves

Expert facilitators build a repertoire of facilitation strategies and moves. *Strategies* are patterns, processes, or structures that facilitators use to get work done. Brainstorming, for example, is a strategy. It has a structure—hot ideas only, no cold water—and is usually employed for a set amount of time or targets a certain number of ideas. Strategies often have multiple steps and require explanation and a check for understanding. They use a significant amount of meeting time. Processes performing this function are often planned before the meeting. *Moves,* on the other hand, are quick, discrete remarks or behaviors that may only take a second to perform.[21] Moves are often made to intervene, amplify, direct, or teach a group about self-management. Moves often result from facilitator decisions based on intervention principles and information processing.

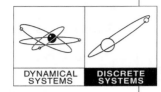

DYNAMICAL SYSTEMS   DISCRETE SYSTEMS

Many examples of facilitation strategies and moves appear throughout this book and are related to the chapter topic. For example, strategies and moves for conflict can be found in chapter 9, moves to keep meetings on track and on time are described in chapter 5. In this chapter we have organized 50 facilitation strategies and moves into three major categories: strategies for managing energy, information, and action. We hope that the examples and abstractions offered here and throughout the book will provide readers with enough information to invent new strategies.

Managing Energy

Energy is a primary resource of groups in accomplishing work. Productive energy is a by-product of productively charged human relationships. A facilitator's primary task is to amplify and direct emotional, cognitive, and physical energy to group goals. Facilitators manage energy through attention to three areas: (a) helping collections of individuals to work as a group, (b) engaging members in active participation, and (c) focusing group attention.

Becoming a group. Members in intact groups and collections of strangers need to feel included when beginning a meeting. The first three strategies in Table 6-4 are inclusion activities. The other two are activities that connect personal energy with group energy or extend consciousness of oneself as both independent and interdependent within the group. As with all facilitator strategies, you should tell participants the rationale for the activity. This creates more willing and purposeful participation.

Table 6-4. Strategies for Becoming a Group

1. Peter/Paul

Why

An inclusion activity. Use with divergent role groups like parent-teacher committees in which the aim is to encourage full participation across roles. In addition to the goals of the self-introduction inclusion activity, this allows members to develop personal knowledge of one another; useful in bridging distances across role.

How

1. Ask members to interview one another in pairs. Alert them that the purpose of the interview is for each person to introduce the partner to the group. Suggest categories, such as reason for being at this meeting, relationship to the meeting topic, feelings about being here.

2. Announce that the interview time will be either 5 or 8 minutes.

3. Model an introduction.

4. Invite participants to listen for themes during the introductions to help them understand who they are as a group.

Tip: Provide clear directions and a specific time period to motivate members to stay on task.

2. Like Me

An inclusion activity. Use with large groups and stranger groups to help members answer the question, "Who am I in relation to this group?" This inclusion activity sets norms for humor, participation, and focuses mental energy inside the room.

1. Ask members to push chairs away from tables so that it will be easy to stand if they want to do so.

2. State that the purpose of this activity is to find out who is in the room and what resources are within the group.

3. Instruct that you will be announcing some categories. Members who recognize themselves within a category should stand and look around at others who are standing. In this way they can identify persons who are like themselves in some way.

4. Announce categories. Pause until people have stood and surveyed the room. Insert humorous categories.

Tip: Be sure to include the category "other" before you are done. Otherwise some persons feel excluded.

Some category examples are: roles, levels within the system (elementary, secondary, central office), typically up before 6 a.m., length of time in the district, has more than one child in this school, had a full breakfast this morning, has worked on this topic in another setting, has a public or private passion for chocolate.

STRATEGIES   MOVES

3. Grounding[22]

An inclusion activity. Use when groups come together for important or difficult work. This final inclusion activity accomplishes several purposes: (a) sets a norm for respectful listening, (b) brings people into the present, (c) gets every person's voice into the room in a nonconfrontive way, (d) allows for people to connect with one another, (e) allows for expression of hopes and apprehensions, (f) values thinking and feeling, (g) surfaces hidden agendas.

1. Describe the purposes for the grounding.
2. Explain the procedure:
   - Members take turns talking (usually around a circle).
   - When one member talks, others are silent.
   - Full nonverbal attention is given to the speaker.
   - The first person to speak will offer a summary paraphrase of what the group has said after everyone has talked.
   - The facilitator will name the first speaker.
3. Post on a flip chart what members are to talk about:
   - My name is . . . .
   - My relationship to this topic is . . .
   - Here are my expectations . . .
   - Here is how I feel about being here . . .

Tips: For very large groups, you may wish to conduct the grounding at individual tables. When everyone is finished, have the summarizer report to the full group.

Let this activity run until everyone is finished. It is rare that groups are provided enough time to complete a task. Symbolically, this is the most important task they will undertake, as it establishes respectful listening to one another.

4. A "Pop-up" Survey

Converts fatigue or despair. Gives information to the group about how to work most effectively. Use for a transition activity after lunch, between tasks, or when a group has worked very long and hard. Pumps physical energy into the room.

1. Chart some survey questions on a flip chart.
2. Explain that "pop-up meetings" help groups to learn from their experiences. Pop-ups are time-outs from the group's task so members can lift their awareness to examine how effectively the group is working.
3. Seat members in groups of four to six. Instruct them that during the next 5 minutes they are to interview persons from other groups.
4. After surveying others, return to home groups. Share information and prepare to report a finding or conclusion.
5. Hear summary reports from groups. Ask how this information should influence the way the group works.

Tips: Some examples of survey questions are:
- What I like about our work is . . .
- What I wish we would do more of is . . .
- What I wish we would do less of is . . .
- What I'd like us to do differently is . . .
- We seem to be good at . . .
- Examples of how we are using one of our core values are . . .

Limit the number of questions to three to five.

STRATEGIES   MOVES

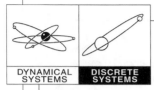

DYNAMICAL SYSTEMS — DISCRETE SYSTEMS

5. Personal Inventories

A characteristic of effective groups is an ability to see themselves not only as they are but as they might become. Inventory data allows members to see patterns of group behavior and gain insight as to why the group interacts as it does and how their own characteristics and choices contribute to group patterns. This information is fundamental to honoring and valuing diversity and making conscious choices toward more flexible responses.

1. Introduce an inventory. Describe its purpose: to learn more about self or about group to seek understanding of group dynamics.
2. Clarify that the instrument is not about what is right or wrong; rather, it seeks to reveal what is.
3. Describe processes to be used. For example:
   - Privately take inventory.
   - Facilitator will reveal a scoring key.
   - Partners will discuss how accurately they feel the instrument describes them.
   - Facilitator gathers participant data to render a simple profile of group characteristics.
   - Facilitator leads discussion of implications of this profile for group interactions.
   - Facilitator invites suggestions about choices that group members might make about their interactions based on this data.

Tips: Many inventories are available to help groups develop an understanding of themselves. We have included an inventory for the seven norms of collaboration as Appendix B. This inventory does *not* have a scoring key. One way of using this is to invite subgroups of a working unit to respond to the inventory thinking about the group as a whole. Subgroup data is reported and compared, and conflicting perceptions are explored. From this increased knowledge of group self-perceptions, one or two norms are selected to be worked on and improved. Other useful surveys inventory members' modality preferences, cognitive styles, and educational belief systems. See Appendix G for an inventory assessing group states of mind.

Engaging participation. Participation is vital to energy and meeting success. Facilitators monitor and stimulate two sources of energy: internal participation and physical participation. *Internal participation* includes thinking strategically about how to participate, keeping track of the conversation, surfacing and examining personal assumptions, and setting aside unproductive listening patterns. Internal energy is also evoked when mental tasks are changed: from auditory to visual processing, from thinking to feeling, from list making to categorizing. All of these internal activities contribute to group work. They also require activity in neural circuits that are in themselves energy producing. *Physical participation* includes movement to other places in the room, standing, sitting, walking, charting, or changing partners. The strategies in Table 6-5 are some of the ways that facilitators keep groups mentally engaged by changing cognitive activities and physically moving.

STRATEGIES — MOVES

Table 6-5. Strategies for Engaging Participation

1. Clock Partners	How
Why This adaptation of Spencer Kagan's cooperative learning work[23] is used to create both physical and mental energy. Use it as an organizing device to create movement during the meeting, change partners, and engage in new cognitive tasks. One advantage of this strategy is that a considerable amount of choice is left to the individual to select partners. Also use clock partners to break up cliques.	1. State reasons for using this strategy. 2. Distribute a representation of a clock face. Ask members to mark the numbers 12, 3, 6, and 9. 3. Explain the procedure. In a moment, each person will be on his or her feet signing up four clock partners (one for each number above). Clock partners must be from tables other than one's own, and each individual can sign up a person only once. Sit down when everyone has all four partners identified. 4. Model the process, illustrating how to write the partner's name and vice versa. 5. Specify a time within which to complete the sign-ups (1 to 2 minutes). 6. When everyone is seated again, ask for a raise of hands for those who have not found a partner at 12. Make matches. Anyone without a partner when a clock number is called, comes to the front of the room. If another person is without a partner, the two of them become a pair. If there are no other singles present, they join any pair. Repeat the process for 3, 6, and 9. Tips: Ask people to have standing conversations with a clock partner whenever there is a need for physical movement, checks for understanding, or a work task that can be started by pairs of people thinking together. Use the clock numbers to call for "pairs squared" and other variations of group size.
2. Numbered Heads[24] Use to promote full attention, interdependence, and account-ability. Use to check understanding of key concepts or publicly rehearse a summary of a meeting.	1. Group participants in teams of four or five. 2. Number off so that each person has a number. 3. Give a topic for conversation. For example, "How would you summarize the work of today's meeting?" Or "What should be the next aspect of a situation this group should address?" 4. After 4–5 minutes call for a pause in the conversations. 5. Draw a card. The person in each group with that number does a summary paraphrase of the conversation to that point. 6. Members from individual groups may report to the whole group if the goal includes checking for total group congruence or generating new ideas. STRATEGIES MOVES

3. Paired Reading

Use paired reading to modify mental activity in a group and when deep comprehension is required of some written text. Examples of uses might be a new board policy, a new legal requirement in a special program, a statement of beliefs drafted by a subcommittee, or a new policy on attendance accounting. Because paired reading requires checks for comprehension at every point along the way, it is highly engaging mentally.

1. Provide members with a brief written text, usually not more than 1½ pages.

2. Ask them to designate one of them as "A" and one of them as "B."

3. Give instructions. A is to read the first paragraph aloud. At the completion, B will provide a summary paraphrase. B will read the second paragraph aloud, and A will provide a summary paraphrase. In like manner, the pair continues until the end of the document. When they reach the end of the document, they both take pencils and mark the words, phrases, or concepts that carry the most meaning for them.

4. Check for understanding of process and signal people to start.

Tips: Because some people may be apprehensive about reading out loud, invite them to negotiate with their partner to read along silently or preread before reading aloud. Encourage them to accommodate whatever style or learning needs they have. A one-page document will typically take groups 10–15 minutes for deep processing.

4. Walk-about

Use this strategy when your goal is to stimulate energy and an interchange of ideas to activate thinking on a topic or to review and integrate a group's earlier deliberations.

1. Provide each person with an 8½ x11 sheet on which nine spaces are drawn for the recording of ideas. In the left-hand column will be three topics to support a group in recalling deliberations from earlier meetings. The three topics might be (a) recollections about group decisions, (b) recollections about what was effective about the way we worked, and (c) ideas for how to apply this information to today's meeting.

2. Members are given 4 minutes to jot down their own responses to these questions in the left-hand column.

3. Members are given 9 minutes to walk about the room and exchange information with one another. Explain that members should record the information given to them by colleagues.

4. Call members back to their original table groups and instruct them to share the information gleaned from colleagues and search for patterns or themes.

5. Invite members to name patterns and make inferences about how this information should influence thinking and actions.

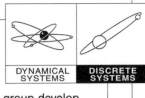

5. Multitask	1. Divide the group into ad hoc committees. Assign a different task to each. For example, in planning a conference, one group might list logistics, another list possible speakers and topics, and a third group develop marketing ideas.
Leverages group resources.	2. Clarify the task of each group. Clarify the level of decision-making authority. (Are they to inform, recommend, or decide?) Specify a time for them to report back to the full group. Instruct them to select a facilitator and a recorder.
	3. Monitor the three groups as they work. Assist in provisioning them with additional materials or information they might need.
	4. Give a 10-minute warning before the ending time.
	5. Reconvene the full group to receive reports from each subgroup.

Focusing attention. In chapter 5 we presented five principles for developing meeting standards. The first two were to stay on one topic at a time and use only one process at a time. Facilitators use language, space, flip charts, and their bodies to focus attention to these standards, to transitions, to a speaker, to information, and to many other focal points. Since each group represents a collection of minds, in even a small group it is likely that many orientations will be present: some disposed toward thinking or feeling, detail or big picture, analysis or synthesis, auditory or visual, past or future, optimism or pessimism, and many other dimensions. The facilitator's challenge is to utilize this rich diversity and simultaneously support common focus.

Strategies such as those described in Table 6-6 capture group attention and direct it to three foundations of group work: task, process, and effectiveness. Task attention requires selecting a task dimension for common work such as mission, values, goals, or strategies. Task attention also requires a common focus on forms of information; examples are directing attention to detail or big picture, examples or explanations, thinking or feeling. Task attention also requires various kinds of thinking: listing, categorizing, analyzing, theorizing, evaluating, and deciding. The attention strategies listed here capture the attention.

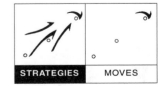

Attention to process helps a group to use only one process at a time. It also involves helping members gain sufficient process knowledge to guide their own processes. Finally, attention to group effectiveness focuses on two parts: metacognitive reflections about personal participation and working to improve the totality of group functioning.

Table 6-6. Strategies for Focusing Attention

1. Choose Voice[25]	**How**
credible voice *approachable voice* **Why** When verbal and nonverbal messages are mixed, people always pay attention to the nonverbal. Voice, its intonation, rhythms, pacing, and volume all contribute important messages about the communication. The most effective facilitators match the voice to the type of message they are sending.	Background Communication delivered in a voice with limited range in modulation, and a voice that tends to dip downward at the end of sentences, is received as credible information. Facilitators use this voice to give directions. "Please bring your attention here." "There will be four steps in this process." "You will have 5 minutes." Communication delivered in a voice with a wider range in modulation, and a voice that tends to swing up at the end of sentences, communicates approachability. Facilitators use this voice when eliciting information, reflecting, and inviting participation. "Could you say more?" "Does anyone else have ideas to add?" "Can you take another 10 minutes?"
2. Attention First To give clear directions. Ensure that each member has an opportunity to hear and understand directions. The greater the facilitator's fatigue, the greater the tendency to try to talk over group voices without getting full attention.	1. Move to the space from which you plan to speak. Stand still and erect. Place weight on both feet. 2. Using a credible voice, ask for the group's attention. Use brief phrases. They command more attention than longer sentences. "Look this direction." 3. Stand still, be quiet, and wait until the group is silent and looking at you before giving directions. 4. Give the direction with a credible voice. Use short sentences. If the directions have multiple steps, chart them. 5. Pause. Step from the spot and in an approachable voice check for understanding. "Are there any questions?" "What will you do first?" Tip: The attention first move can be made whenever a facilitator needs to focus the group; at the beginning of a meeting, at a transition between subgroup and total group conversations, or when several people are talking at once.

STRATEGIES   MOVES

3. Visual Paragraphing

Gives congruent information to portions of the brain processing spatial information and verbal information. Makes understanding easier and confusion less likely.

1. Stand in one spot. Give one message; for example, a direction in a process.

2. Pause, move without speaking a foot or so away, and give a second message; for example, ask if the directions you just gave are clear. (In this example you would want to use a credible voice to give the direction and an approachable voice to check for understanding.)

Tips: Use to separate steps in a direction to the group or in concepts. "You seem to be talking about your improved performance on the one hand [step and breathe] but on the other hand are frustrated that you are not doing better." [Now stepping away and pointing toward the two spots in the room] "Where do you want to focus?"

Also use to designate an "attention spot" in the room where you stand when you are going to call for attention. After a few times, your presence in the spot will become part of the communication that the group is to attend.

4. PAG/PAU

Saves time by ensuring that all members know the processes to be used before beginning work.

Based on a Doyle and Straus[26] principle of going slow at first in order to go fast later.

This stands for Process As Given, Process As Understood. The same process can be used in a variation called Topic As Given, Topic As Understood. (TAG/TAU)

1. In a credible voice, explain the process to be used (e.g., brainstorming).

2. Pause, silently move to a new position in the room, and with an approachable voice say you want to find out if you gave the instructions clearly. Ask for details. "What are you to do? How much time will we take?"

3. Call on individual group members. "Todd, what will you do if you have a question during brainstorming?"

4. When it seems certain that the instructions are clear, step to a new space in the room and begin facilitating the process.

Tip: This strategy, once completed, gives the facilitator permission to intervene assertively should members forget the process agreements. "Hang on to that idea, Floyd. You'll have a chance to ask that question when we are through brainstorming."

STRATEGIES   MOVES

5. Please Breathe

Members cannot attend to what is being said when they are stressed or when energy has gone inward. Shallow breathing signals that this is happening. The brain consumes about 30% of the body's oxygen yet weighs only about 3 pounds. We think best when breathing is full and deep, allowing a maximum of oxygen to the brain. As members experience stress, shock, or fear, breathing becomes shallow and members will even hold their breath, shutting off oxygen to the brain.

1. Notice when a group "stops breathing." What to look for:

   • Gaze over the heads of members, taking in a wide-angle snapshot of the whole room. When breathing has stopped, heads and shoulders will tend to be more erect. Body movements tend to be more jerky than flowing.

   • Listen for collective intakes of breath.

2. Do anything to get the group breathing again. Some ideas:

   • Get people to laugh.

   • Get people to move, stand, change seating, talk with a neighbor.

   • Say, "Start breathing again."

   • Ask, "What's going on? Why do you think you all stopped breathing?"

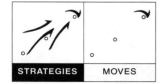

STRATEGIES MOVES

Managing Information

Information is another essential resource of working groups. Groups consume and construct information in order to plan, decide, solve problems, and take action. The facilitator's help in managing information is critical for several reasons. Information comes in a variety of packages: abstractions, examples, generalizations, details, thoughts, feelings, research, numbers, history, and dreams. There is typically too much data and too little time. Groups must select some data to study, and others to ignore, and know when to look for details and when to examine themes and patterns.

Additionally, there are limits to how much information the mind can process. To understand information, it is often necessary to engage prior data on a topic and to explore, organize, and integrate new information before it can be used for planning, problem solving, and deciding.

Some types of information are best understood in certain forms, such as graphs, tables, and charts.

Activating and engaging thinking. We believe that certain principles of information processing that are taken for granted about classroom learning are usefully applied to the business of meetings. Agreement exists among several models of thinking that an initial phase of learning is to prepare for learning.

The selection of facilitator strategies in Table 6-7 serves to activate, engage, and relate prior information to the matter at hand.

Table 6-7. Strategies for Activating and Engaging Thinking

1. Analogy

Why

Moves beyond selective thinking to generative thought. Stimulates provocative thinking before analytical thought. Opens up new pathways for exploration and fresh thinking to challenges.

How

Analogies can bring better understanding to problems and possible solution approaches. For example, for problems in maintaining enthusiasm in an overworked staff, a team might brainstorm responses to the following questions:

1. How do runners manage to have a speed-up kick left for the finish?

2. How did the stagecoaches of the American West manage to race across great distances in just a few days?

3. How do the answers to the above relate to a challenge facing the group?

The realization that stagecoaches changed horses frequently might lead to rotating and delegating school improvement tasks, or it might lead to periodic "work moratoriums" so the "horses" can rest.

2. Corners

Use to assess a group's position, identify those who agree with each other, and learn reasons for the positions.

1. Designate corners in the room for persons to stand in to represent their position on a topic.

2. Ask them to support their positions or report, with empathy, why they believe others are standing in a different corner.

3. Ask the group to summarize what they have learned about themselves.

STRATEGIES   MOVES

3. 3-2-1

Activates and brings information forward into the present.

This format can be used with a variety of stems. In one version:

1. Individuals privately record three ideas they remember from the last meeting, two questions they have about their task, and one insight relative to their work.

2. Share with a small group. Prepare to report themes to the full group.

3. Report themes to the full group.

4. Sort Cards

Activates and engages prior information on a topic. This strategy honors participant knowledge, levels the playing field of information, equalizes member status, and saves meeting time by surfacing information relevant to the topics under deliberation. Instructions to the group.

1. On your own, generate the following:
   - Knowledge or feelings you have about a topic the group is about to address
   - Standards or values that should drive a piece of work
   - Examples of strategies used in successful meetings
   Use 3 x 5 cards. Write one idea per card. Be specific so that others will know exactly what you mean.

2. In table groups, share, categorize, label categories, and make a display.

3. Discuss the work. How does this information inform you about how to proceed?

Tip: In order for each table group to gather additional ideas and have a sense of the whole group, add a museum tour.
1. Each group selects one person to stay at their display and explain items to visitors.

2. Others tour the displays and search for new ideas.

3. Members return to home base and exchange information.

5. D–YTD–? (Done–Yet to do–Questions)

Brings information forward to inform the next phase of a group's work.

1. Regarding a task the group is doing, members privately record the following:
   - D—a list of tasks done to date
   - YTD—a list of what is yet to be accomplished
   - ?—questions about getting the work done

2. In table groups, share the information. Get agreement on the next most important YTDs.

3. Report to the full group.

Generating ideas. Along with the stage in which members are preparing for learning, fresh ideas and information must be generated. "Generally, activating and engaging calls for generative and associative thinking. Activities like brainstorming, identifying, listing, and envisioning are particularly powerful."[27]

Groups generate ideas, assess them in relationship to some set of criteria, and select some to act on and some to set aside (Table 6-8). The greater the range of ideas a group has to work with, the greater the perspectives that can be brought to their work and the more expansive and ideal their choice options.

Table 6-8. Strategies for Generating Ideas

1. Existing and Desired Conditions	How
Why Builds an image of a desired state. When groups have a clear goal, work can start toward its achievement. Listing what exists reveals categories to consider in the desired state.	List existing conditions. Alongside that, chart the desired conditions. Listing desired conditions is a useful step in building a common understanding of a problem situation when group members have differing knowledge of the existing state. For example, teachers, principals, personnel managers, and clerks all have different data about problems associated with substitute teachers.
2. Brainstorming Collects ideas from all participants without criticism, judgment, or questions. Separates idea generation from analysis and decision. Protects the principle of one process at a time.	1. Name the topic, time frame, or goal (e.g., 5 minutes or until the group gets 20 ideas). 2. Remind the group that the goal in brainstorming is quantity, not quality. Encourage all ideas, even if silly. 3. Remind group of brainstorming guidelines—hot ideas only, no questions or disagreements. Tag-ons are fine. Opportunity for clarification and advocacy will follow. 4. Check for understanding of the topic and process. Allow a minute for silent reflection. 5. Begin brainstorming. Record all items on flip chart. Use more than one recorder to speed up the recording process.

STRATEGIES   MOVES

AFTER BRAINSTORMING

A group can get overwhelmed by the number of ideas generated in a brainstorming session. Here are several things a group can do after a brainstorm:

- Create categories.
- Sort data into predefined categories.
- Sort the items by *necessary* and *nice* or *what we can control* and *what we cannot.*
- Reflect on the list as a whole.
- Discuss what to do now.

Tip: *Why, how,* or *what* questions lend themselves best to brainstorming. Although any form of brainstorming is useful in generating ideas, some limitations of this approach are that it may (a) produce only superficial ideas and (b) work best when the problem is simple, specific, or limited.

One good use of brainstorming is to brainstorm a list of questions a group could be asking. Many groups tend to favor one or two question categories and create unintentional blind spots in their work. Try brainstorming for the following:

- Green questions—for possibilities of imagination
- Red questions—for descriptions of facts
- Blue questions—for judgments and opinions of value and need. "What if?" "What should?" "What is the best?"

3. Slip Method

Generates lots of ideas in a short amount of time. Equalizes group member influence and contribution, unlike brainstorming, in which the more vocal members may give a disproportionate number of ideas.

Distribute a large quantity of 3 x 5 index cards to each participant. State the problem in "how to" language. Some examples are: "How can we increase student achievement in mathematics?" "How can we raise morale?" Participants write only one idea per card. After the cards are collected, they are categorized and reported. Turn the cards the same way so they are easier to read and sort. Discard duplicate, ambiguous, and illegible items. Fifteen participants should be able to produce 150 ideas.

STRATEGIES   MOVES

4. 1-2-6

Involves each member of large groups in generation and shaping of ideas for consideration of the whole group.

Works well in group sizes from 50 to 150.

1. Each person writes an idea in response to a question (2 minutes). Questions that work well in this process sound like the following:
   - What one improvement focus should we have this year?
   - What staff development topics should we address this year?
   - What is the most important problem to solve?

2. Pairs get together, share, and agree to *one* idea (4 minutes).

3. Sixes get together and agree to *one* idea (8–12 minutes).

4. Post ideas for discussion and next steps. Each idea is written in eight to twelve words.

5. Facilitator assists the full group in clarifying and unduplicating the items.

6. Statements of advocacy are heard.

7. Each member selects a third of the items as most desirable.

8. Each item is polled. Who has this item on their list?

9. The group decides how to treat the top items.

5. Trigger Verbs

Generates ideas in classifications of thought to initiate creative ideas.

Three potent verbs:
- Magnify
- Minify
- Rearrange

Use these to focus participants on special categories of thought related to a problem. For example, to stimulate ideas regarding office space utilization, use these three verbs in questions.

1. How can we increase (magnify) our space?

2. How can we shrink (minify) our need for space?

3. How can we arrange our space more effectively?

STRATEGIES   MOVES

Other useful words are *modify, manipulate, substitute, combine, adapt*, and *reverse*.

As we have observed, information-processing studies suggest that learning occurs in three phases: preparation for learning, processing information, and integrating and applying information. Skilled facilitators are alert to a group's needs to use similar processes for planning, problem solving, or creating.

Exploring ideas. The first two information-management strategies address the first of three phases of learning, to prepare a group for learning. In the second phase of learning, information is explored and processed (Table 6-9). Thinking focuses on analysis, inference making, explaining and determining cause-and-effect relationships. Assumptions are surfaced, information is compared, and predications are attempted.

Table 6-9. Strategies for Exploring Ideas

1. Five Ws	**How**
Why	Ask *who, what, when, where,* and *why* in relation to the problem.
Specifies elements of a situation to address. Problems are often overgeneralized. Helps groups to define a problem with greater precision.	

2. Force-Field Analysis	
It is usually easier to weaken the forces restraining change than to strengthen the helping forces. This strategy is used to identify and analyze forces pressing toward a desired change and forces resisting that movement. Aids strategic thinking about where to put resources. 	1. Put up newsprint bearing the graphic below.
	2. List all forces members can think of that either support or restrain a current situation's improvement. As in brainstorming, avoid argument but, unlike brainstorming, encourage paraphrasing or questioning for clarity. Some forces may be listed on both sides of the diagram. Current situations might be figures about dropout rates, attendance, teachers involved in staff development, or student achievement.
	3. Get agreement on which forces hinder movement the most and which support improvement the most. Limit each list to about six items.
	4. Rate the forces on how feasible it will be to modify them.
	5. Select one or more to work on.

3. Futures Wheel

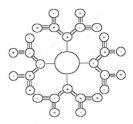

Tests possible consequences of an action. Often decisions unleash unpredictable consequences. This strategy graphically forecasts possible negative and positive effects of any decision the group might make.

1. Display the futures wheel on charts or an overhead.
2. Write the name of the event or innovation in the center of the wheel.
3. Work outward from the center to the first layer of circles. Identify two possible negative results and two possible positive ones. Have the positive and negatives be as different as possible.
4. Move to the second layer. Continue recording positive and negative effects of each item in the first layer. Continue on in this manner until at least a third or fourth layer.
5. Dialogue about the findings. How might this information influence the thinking and strategies of a planning team?

Tip: This is a forecasting, not a predictive, tool. It offers possibilities to consider, not certainties.

4. Each Teach

Checks understanding, integrates information, and identifies ideas that require clarification.

1. Partners review information, ideas, or decisions recently discussed.
2. Partner A describes a portion of information to B as if B had not been in the room.
3. Partner B describes the remaining parts of information.
4. Partners edit each other's renditions until they agree on what was said.
5. The facilitator invites requests for clarification.

5. Assumption Challenge

Surfaces assumptions on which a group's perspective, logic, and feelings are based. Since assumptions direct and distort perception, a group's clearest thinking is that in which assumptions are identified as points of view and examined.

1. Ask members to list their assumptions related to a topic. A staff development group, for example, might identify assumptions related to designing a professional development program: There is limited time for staff development, teachers have varying amounts of expertise on a topic, some teachers do not want to learn.
2. Invite the group to inquire about these assumptions. What data inform them? What inferences have been made? What might be alternative interpretations to the same data? In which aspects are the assumptions generalizable and in which aspects are they situation-specific?

Tip: Ask participants to write one assumption on a 3 x 5 card. Collect and shuffle the cards. Draw the first card and inquire about the assumption. Repeat.

Organizing and integrating ideas. During the third and final phase of a learning cycle, information developed by the group is organized, integrated, and applied (Table 6-10). Activities during this phase serve to support groups in expanding and refining their existing thinking—confirming, refining, or abandoning previously held concepts, testing new theories, and elaborating new ideas.

Table 6-10. Strategies for Organizing and Integrating Ideas

1. SPOT Analysis	
Why	**How**
Sees the forces at play affecting a group's work. Discovers how strengths, problems, opportunities and threats are interrelated. Allows a group to consider problems and opportunities in context.	1. Hang 4 x 16 poster paper on the wall and divide it into four parts. 2. Label the four sections: strengths, problems, opportunities, and threats. 3. List strengths, then list problems. 4. Rank the strengths and problems if you have time. 5. Brainstorm opportunities. Invite members to see potential opportunities within problems. 6. List threats. Discuss which ones could invalidate the work of the group. 7. Review the chart for insights and action ideas.
2. Cluster Understands relationships and interactions. Previews consequences for different courses of action.	1. Categorize elements of an issue to be addressed, such as curriculum, assessment, instruction and staff development. 2. List concerns or goals within each category. 3. Identify connections of items across categories. 4. Consider consequences of intervening at various starting places. Tip: Often best done by a subgroup.
3. Fishbone Discovers cause-and-effect reasons for existing program results. Determines focus of improvement effort. 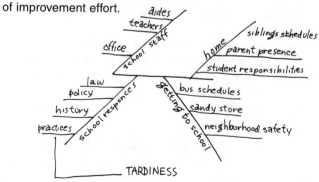	1. Prepare a fishbone chart. 2. Code sections of the chart that may be related to an existing condition of an issue. Student attitudes, school policy, neighborhood attractions, and first-period activities are examples that might be related to high levels of tardiness. 3. Brainstorm factors affecting each topic (e.g., student attitudes). Record on chart. 4. Discuss pros and cons of various combinations of solution approaches.

4. Mind Mapping[28]

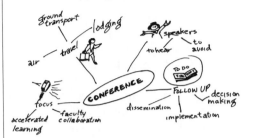

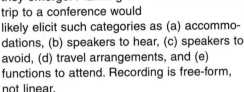

DYNAMICAL SYSTEMS | DISCRETE SYSTEMS

The recorder charts brainstormed ideas according to categories as they emerge. Planning a trip to a conference would likely elicit such categories as (a) accommodations, (b) speakers to hear, (c) speakers to avoid, (d) travel arrangements, and (e) functions to attend. Recording is free-form, not linear.

Illuminates main ideas and supporting ideas in a conversation. Aids members in sorting out hierarchies within topics and separating major themes from finer points.

Stimulates generation of random, nonsequential ideas. Displays several categories at once.

5. Is/Is Not

Determines which aspects of a situation are worthy of group energy. Pinpoints the occurrence of a problem and guides data collection or solution thinking.

This technique is drawn from a more comprehensive method developed by two former researchers at the Rand Corporation, Charles Kepner and Benjamin Tregoe. It's another way of clearly stating what you know about a problem.

In one column, write down facts you know about the problem: where it is, what its effects are, when it occurs, and so on. Then do the same for what you know is *not* part of the problem. Example: The telephone problem is "can't hear some of the incoming calls, occasionally can't get a dial tone, happens more often in early morning." The problem is *not* "callers can always hear clearly, problem does not affect other lines in the building, the intercom works well." Collectively, these statements build up to a definition of the problem without running the risk of assuming something that is not verified.

Tip: Some uses of this strategy:

- Is—Where, when, to what extent, or with whom does this situation occur?
- Is Not—Where (etc.) does this not occur?
- Therefore—What might explain the pattern of occurrence and nonoccurrence?

Managing Actions

These strategies help groups to convert ideas to actions. The word *decide* means to kill choice: Out of many options, the group selects some ideas to survive and others to be set aside. Whether decisions are made because they "feel right" or have been logically analyzed, some sort of criteria is always used to make the decision. An idea can be less costly than others, be more politically acceptable, be closest in alignment to a group's values, be judged to have greater potential, and so on.

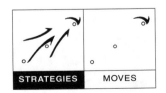

STRATEGIES | MOVES

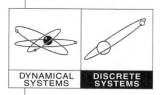

DYNAMICAL
SYSTEMS

DISCRETE
SYSTEMS

As the following strategies illustrate, there is no one correct sequence for making decisions. In one case, a group might cull a list by gut feeling before identifying conscious criteria. In another instance, a group might select criteria before advocating. In still another situation, a group might decide what it wants to abandon instead of what it wants to pursue.

Sorting and deciding.   The strategies in Table 6-11 are representative of "consensus-seeking" tools to support groups in making logically, emotionally, and politically sound selections. Each represents a different approach to categorizing and deciding.

Table 6-11. Strategies for Sorting and Deciding

1. Rule of One Third	How
Why Culls items from a proposed list for deeper consideration. This strategy is quick, does not require extensive discussion of items, and will provide an accurate reflection of a group's top and bottom items. Ranking of items below the top ones is unnecessary when the purpose is to cull a list.	1. Instruct the group that the rule of one third will be employed to identify the most desirable ideas from a list. 2. Advise the group that each person will identify a number of items most important to them. A hand tally will be made. The numbers will not determine the group's decision but will be a guide to the group to decide which items to keep for deeper consideration. 3. Instruct members to select one third plus one from a list. Do not rank them. For example, from a list of 9 items, select 4 that are most important to you. From a list of 12, select 5. 4. The facilitator asks, "Who has number 1 on your list?" Members raise hands. That number is recorded on the chart. 5. The facilitator repeats this process until all items have been accounted for. 6. The facilitator asks members to study the recorded tallies. "Which items appear to be of greatest interest to the group?" 7. The facilitator asks the group how it wishes to act on the results. For example, the group might decide to act on all the top items, give the top items to a subcommittee for study and recommendation, and pick only the top two for a pros-and-cons conversation. Tip: This method is accurate for the top and bottom third of lists, not for items in the middle.

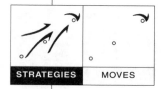

STRATEGIES   MOVES

2. Combine Opposites

Gets groups unstuck when two or more conflicting views block the group from reaching consensus. Conserves full-group time when the agenda is extensive and members are clear they *have* a position but *are* not the position.

1. Observe that the group is stuck. Suggest that one resolution that can save time is to ask persons holding divergent views to form an ad hoc subcommittee and bring a recommendation back to the full group.
2. Ask if this is agreeable.
3. Suggest times in which the subcommittee might talk (now outside the meeting room or later at a lunch break). In either case, the recommendation can be presented today. A third option is sometime after today's meeting but before the next meeting of the group.
4. Clarify the decision-making authority of the subcommittee. Will it make a decision to which the group will abide, or bring back a recommendation for group consideration?
5. Request or suggest certain members to serve on the subcommittee.

Tip: Asking the most impassioned voices to serve will make subcommittee resolutions more likely to be accepted by the full group.

3. Ranking

Gives a more accurate assessment of group preferences than the rule of one third, particularly for the middle items on a list. Time consuming but useful when groups have limited trust in the facilitator, themselves, or the process.

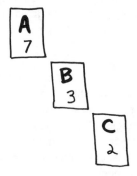

1. Explain the process.
2. If the group has identified 15 issues, each member labels (A, B, C, etc.) on 15 pieces of paper, arranges them in priority order, and rates them from 15 to 1. The papers are then stacked in 15 locations and tallied.
3. Assuming that six people are in the group, location 15 might have papers marked A, E, E, E, G, O. If location 10 reads A, A, B, B, B, O then the total of just these two stacks would be as follows:
   item A—35
   item B—30
   item E—45
   item G—15
   item O—10

STRATEGIES   MOVES

4. Subgroups tally the points each letter has earned.

Tip: This strategy becomes too cumbersome for lists of items beyond 15. Can be used with relatively large groups—50 members or so.

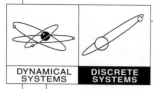

DYNAMICAL SYSTEMS   DISCRETE SYSTEMS

4. Eliminate the Negative

Saves group the time of talking about items in which no members have a strong interest. Shortens lists before advocating and selecting.

1. After a group has clarified items on a brainstormed list, ask if there are any items the group would feel OK about eliminating at this time.

2. If no one objects, remove the idea.

3. If any person objects, leave the item.

4. Move on to the next step in decision making.

5. Forced-Choice Stickers

Amplifies energy and group member interactions. Polls to sort out a group's preferences among options. Can force choice among attractive options.

1. Post the question to be resolved and chart the various options. Distribute an equal number of stickers to each member.

2. Check to see that all members understand the question.

3. Explain the process and check for understanding.

4. Instruct members to spend their stickers.

5. Members place stickers.

6. Now act from several preselected options:

   • The stickers represent a vote and are binding.

   • The group examines sticker distribution and decides which few should receive further consideration.

   • Subgroups stand by options with a large number of stickers and give reasons for their choices.

   • After advocating and inquiring about members' choices, fresh stickers are distributed and spent.

Tip: A conversation before spending influences choices. In one example, parents might talk about school goals first and then spend stickers by placing them next to goals they would like the school to emphasize.

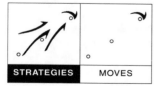

STRATEGIES   MOVES

Clarifying commitment. To decide, groups must often assess the degree of the resources available to carry out a decision. Since implementation resources are often attitudinal, facilitators use a variety of strategies (Table 6-12) to help groups assess whether they have enough commitment to proceed—or what might have to be changed in a proposal to generate more universal commitment.

Table 6-12. Strategies for Clarifying Commitment

1. Assumptions Wall

Why

Understanding group members' assumptions on a topic frees group thought from self-sealing logic and ignorance of others' thoughts and feelings. The visual template of the assumptions wall provides cognitive organizers, views beyond "selective reality," full participation, higher levels of critical thinking, and a tension that leads to energy to resolve.

How

1. Post the instructions for stage 1.
2. Advise members that this is a process in three stages. The first part is a gift of silence. During the second part the facilitator will remind members about ways of productively inquiring into another's thinking. In the third part members will seek to understand each other's assumptions.
3. Define an assumption and the influence it has on one's perceptions and thinking.
4. Seat participants in a semicircle facing a flip chart or wall. Provide each person with a sentence strip and marking pen.

PART 1

1. Silently list your assumptions about _____.
2. Record on a sentence strip the one assumption that most influences your behavior related to this topic (8 to 12 words).
3. Silently post on a team flip chart or wall.
4. Silently read and reflect.
5. Wait silently until all in your group are finished.

PART 2

1. Facilitator reminds members of, and models for them, the pause, paraphrase, and inquire pattern. Taught in chapter 3.
2. Facilitator offers categories of inquiry regarding assumptions; its importance to the author, an example, how generalizable it is, logic supporting it, its source, and its value.

PART 3

1. In round-robin fashion, one person identifies an assumption on the wall and inquires to learn more about it. Dialogue between the inquirer and the author follows.
2. When the first conversation is complete, the second person chooses an assumption about which to inquire.
3. The process continues until each person has no more need to inquire. Any person can pass at any time.

STRATEGIES | MOVES

2. Responsibility Charting Clarifies who will do what by when and produces an accountability system.	1. List all major responsibilities on the left side of a chart. List team members' names along the top. 2. Review all team responsibilities and code "R" to mean responsible for task, "A" to indicate who must authorize decisions, "S" to indicate members providing support, and "I" for those who must stay informed. Tip: Because this strategy brings focus to the roles of each person, it can become cumbersome to complete. In some settings this may be done as a subgroup task with the provision that the group approves the final responsibility chart.
3. Ask for Sabotage Ideas Surfaces hidden reservations or unconsciously held conditions under which members would not implement an activity.	1. State the agreement the group has made. 2. Say, "I know that none of you would ever sabotage this agreement, but if you were to, under what conditions would you be tempted?" 3. List the conditions under which noncompliance with the agreement might be compelling. 4. Ask members what they need to do to keep to their agreements should some of those conditions arise.
4. Reenergize Acknowledging burnout and fatigue reenergizes groups.	• Notice that the group seems tired and unfocused. • Ask each person to take some Post-it® notes and write answers to the question, "What would get me reenergized?" • Write the question on a chart as people work. • After 10–15 minutes ask everyone to post their notes. • Each person communicates his or her concern and request. • If you are conducting a regular meeting, take the communication as advice and explain how you intend to follow up. In a special meeting, ask the group if it thinks it can meet each person's request.
 **STRATEGIES** MOVES **5. Value voting** Produces public poll of positions.	Ask participants to value-vote on an item by displaying one to five fingers in response to a statement made by the facilitator. For example: "I'm satisfied with the direction the group is taking." 5 = highly satisfied, 4 = satisfied, 3 = OK, 2 = dissatisfied, 1= highly dissatisfied.

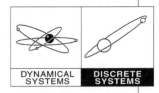

Monitoring and evaluating. Effective groups decide on, commit to, and manage activities and projects. In Table 6-13, strategies to assess the effectiveness of group action and degrees of adherence to an implementation plan are presented.

Group members may agree to proceed in a certain way, yet sometimes in the implementation phase not everyone lives by the agreement. Mutation monitoring is an important function of groups for their agreements about how to work together and the projects they have set in motion. Not all mutations are destructive. On the contrary, some are creative approaches that should be identified and shared with others.

Table 6-13. Strategies for Monitoring and Evaluating

1. Solution Analysis	How
Why Pretests and strengthens proposed solutions before implementation. Finds ways for turning a mediocre solution into a highly desirable one.	Ask: 1. What are possible disadvantages, negative consequences, or other weaknesses of each alternative? 2. What could make each alternative misunderstood, unwelcome, unsupported, or unsuccessful? 3. How likely are these to happen? How might you revise the proposed solution to avoid or minimize these factors?
2. PMI[29] Gathers information to make informed program adjustments in cases where implementation is being performed by an aggregate of individuals or teams.	1. Brainstorm a list of "pluses" about the program (what is working well, contributing to desired goals). 2. Brainstorm a list of "minuses" (what is not going smoothly, not understood, not producing intended results). 3. Brainstorm a list of "interestings" (unexpected by-products, emerging insights, some of which might be worthy of further exploration). 4. Select some of the above for analysis, problem solving, and action.

3. Activities Profile

Establishes criteria for assessing status of planned activities and judging effectiveness of program. Sets benchmarks for rethinking and correcting program design.

1. List specific activities to be conducted in order to achieve a program outcome. For example:
   • survey completion
   • parent conference attendance
   • participation in parent/student clinics

2. Determine benchmarks. For example:

Survey returns	high, 75% and above
	low, 40% and below
Parent conference	high, 95% and above
	low, 80 % and below
Clinic sign-ups	high, 18%
	low, 8%

3. Schedule data-gathering periods. Disaggregate and analyze results.

4. Recommend program refinements.

4. Curriculum or Program Audit

Reveals actual practices. Can be compared with desired practices and analyzed in relation to outcomes.

1. Construct a survey in which individuals record information about practices over a specific period of past time. For example: Examine your lesson-plan book and estimate the percentage of class time during the past 8 weeks that was devoted to the following:
   — Review of previous concepts and skills
   — Direct instruction to full group
   — Direct instruction to subgroups
   — Help to individual students
   — Full-group skills practice
   — Introduction of homework

   What percentage of content was about the following:
   — Basic operations
   — Word problems
   — Geometry
   — Algorithms

2. Gather, collate, and present data.

3. Invite inferred relationships between reported practices and student achievement.

4. Develop and test hypotheses for changes in practices that could improve student learning.

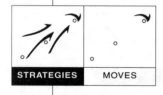

STRATEGIES MOVES

5. Sensing Interviews

Monitors and revises implementation plans in three ways. First, standardizes implementation practices when common application is important to project success. Two, discovers deviations that add unexpected power to implementation efforts. Third, discovers and corrects program weaknesses.

1. Generate descriptions of agreed-upon implementation elements. For example, in a certain literature program these might include: strategies to activate students' prior knowledge, introduction of special vocabulary, focused reading, discussion of one of preferred core curriculum concepts, and the absence of workbooks.
2. Determine what type of information you want to gather.
3. Construct sensing interview questions. For example:
   (a) What do students like about this program?
   (b) What aspects are you or students having trouble with?
   (c) What recommendations do you have?

An example of a more focused question format is the following:
   (a) On the average, what percentage of time is given each lesson to introducing special vocabulary?
   (b) How specifically are you doing that?
   (c) What are some insights and recommendations you are developing about this portion of the program?

Tip: Check for possible program mutations early, before some have a chance to become "bad habits." Mutation monitoring also sends a signal that program agreements are to be kept.

Developing Your Tool Kit

Confident and skilled facilitators develop knowledge in four areas: maps of the territory of facilitation, information about group dynamics and the specific group with which they are currently working, self-knowledge, and knowledge of facilitation strategies and moves that support groups in managing energy, information, and action. Like any complex and transactional knowledge base, it is not learned overnight, nor is it learned from a book. The preceding tool kit, tested with groups and talked about with colleagues, is a foundation for generative knowledge for each facilitator. We find that the deeper we delve into the facilitator's knowledge base of maps, strategies and moves, self, and groups, the more inventive we become, creating our own style and understandings about group facilitation.

It has been said that there are only three difficult meeting participants in the universe, but they travel around and attend every meeting. Table 6-14 lists some common problems and ideas for dealing with them. It is useful to keep in mind that behaviors that are

Table 6-14. Some Common Problems in Facilitating

PROBLEM	RESPONSE
1. Latecomer	1. Presume that there are many good reasons for being late. Start meetings on time, begin with relevant activating or sponge activities, and have members help the latecomer get oriented for arrival. If the pattern persists, invite the group to talk about their expectations for starting meetings.
2. The broken record—a person who says the same thing over and over.	2. Paraphrase and chart this person's comment. The first time that it is repeated, move to chart, underline or asterisk the original statement, and paraphrase again. The next time, move to the chart and ask what the person needs to be certain that the comment has been understood by the group.
3. Limited or apathetic group participation	3. Several moves might be tried. Have members turn to a neighbor and talk about the agenda item being discussed. Change the type of cognitive effort required to participate. For example, if the group has been dealing with theorizing, switch to brainstorming. Ask the group what is going on. Describe their behavior. Call a break to change energy and give yourself a chance to regroup.
4. Two people in a confrontive interchange	4. If the exchange is intense and disturbing the safety of the group, ask the protagonists to each select someone they trust to help them in the communication. Sit each protagonist with this person. The friend's job is to paraphrase each statement so that the partner can hear it. After a few interchanges, most people will begin to understand one another, and with this understanding, the need to confront dissolves.

STRATEGIES   MOVES

5. Yes-but	5. At an appropriate time instruct the group about the value of the language pattern, "yes-and." This will give you permission to intervene.
6. Miring in trivialities and details	6. Ask how much detail is needed to move this agenda item.
7. Domination by a highly verbal member	7. Two ideas. One that we learned from Michael Grinder is called *satisfy, satisfy, delay*. Watch the group when the highly verbal person talks. If you see distress, note it and continue to respectfully listen to the talker. The second time it happens, look again for group distress. Satisfy once more. The third time it occurs, delay listening to the talker. Several diversion moves can be made. "Can we hear first from someone who hasn't talked yet?" "George, hang on to that thought for just a moment." Or turn your back on the talker and make some appropriate comments to the group. If the high talking persists, ask this person to give the "bottom line" of the message in brief form. Occasionally when we have worked with a group for a long time, we will confidently recruit the high talker to get other persons to talk, increasing the interchange between other members.

disruptive to the group often are motivated by positive intentions—to be heard or take care of oneself in some way. Being curious about behavior rather than judgmental ("I wonder why he did that") frees us from becoming defensive or angry and allows us to access the best possible move or strategy to fit the moment.

Much of the success of any facilitation event is predetermined in the planning and contracting phases. Appendix E and Appendix F offer structures for these phases. These guidelines are useful both for facilitators and those that engage them.

One major aspect of facilitation work that we have not addressed in this chapter is meeting design. We know several groups that have cut their meeting time in half by careful attention to agenda construction. We will discuss that in the next chapter.

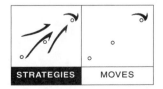

STRATEGIES   MOVES

End Notes

1 Garmston, R., & Wellman, B. (1992). *How to make presentations that teach and transform.* Alexandria, VA: Association for Supervision and Curriculum Development; and Garmston, R. (1997). *The presenter's fieldbook: A practical guide.* Norwood, MA: Christopher-Gordon.

2 Newman, F., & Wehlage, G. (1995). Successful school restructuring. Cited in Fullan, M. (1998). *Breaking the bonds of dependency: Educational leadership.* Madison, WI: Center on Organization and Restructuring of Schools, p. 8.

3 McGlaughlin, M. (1996, December). *Lessons from research.* Keynote address at National Staff Development Council Annual Conference, Chicago. Dr. McGlaughlin is Professor of Education and Public Policy at Stanford University and director of the Center for Research on the Context for Secondary School Teaching.

4 Facilitation differs from the three functions of consulting, coaching, and presenting. Elsewhere we have presented information on presenting and coaching. An excellent description of consulting skills is Block, P. (1981). *Flawless consulting: A guide to getting your expertise used.* San Francisco: Jossey-Bass. Of the four leadership hats, facilitation is most directly related to developing groups and marshalling commitment to school improvement. For the external service provider, the facilitation role is rarely the first one used with a client. "Enter as a consultant and exit as a coach," we remind ourselves in our work. Facilitation, presenting, and coaching may be done in the body of a contract, but if you are still consulting at the end of a project (getting your expertise used by others), you may not have served the client well. To exit as a coach means to leave the client independent, possessing additional tools and habits of self-improvement.

5 Kaner, S., et al. (1996). *Facilitator's guide to participatory decision making.* Gabriola Island, B.C., Canada: New Society.

6 Doyle, M., & Straus, D. (1993). *How to make meetings work: The new interaction method.* New York: Berkeley Books.

7 Sternberg, R., & Horvath, J. (1995). A prototype view of expert teaching. *Educational Researcher, 24* (6), 9–17.

8 Schwarz, R. (1994). *The skilled facilitator: Practical wisdom for developing effective groups.* San Francisco: Jossey-Bass, p. 75. Our list has been modified from Schwarz, who organizes these "ground rules" around three core values: valid information, free and informed choice, and internal commitment. He in turn has drawn from several sources in compiling his list.

[9] Marzano, R. J., Brandt, R. S., Hughes, C. S., Jones B. F., Presseisen, B. Z., Rankin, S. C., & Suhor, C. (1988). *Dimensions of thinking: A framework for curriculum and instruction.* Alexandria, VA: Association for Supervision and Curriculum Development, p. 8.

[10] Jones, B. F., Palinsar, A. S., Ogle D. S., & Carr, E. G. (Eds.). (1987). *Strategic teaching and learning: Cognitive instruction in the content areas.* Alexandria, VA: Association for Supervision and Curriculum, pp. 4–25.

[11] Constructivist learning theory is founded on the studies of Jean Piaget, Lev Vygotsky, and the later work of Jerome Bruner, Howard Gardner, and Nelson Goodman, among others.

[12] Blum, D. (1997). *Sex on the brain: The biological differences between men and women.* New York: Viking Penguin Books; and Goleman, D. (1995). *Emotional intelligence: Why it can matter more than IQ.* New York: Bantam Books.

[13] Schwarz, p. 90.

[14] Several books describe various styles of adult processing and offer ways to recognize and work effectively with them. See, for example, Costa, A., & Garmston, R. (1994). *Cognitive coaching: A foundation for renaissance schools.* Norwood, MA. Christopher-Gordon (see chapter 4, "Flexibility in Coaching," pp. 58–84); and Seagal, S., & Horne, D. (1997). *Human dynamics: A new framework for understanding people and realizing the potential in our organizations.* Cambridge, MA: Pegasus Communications.

[15] Eisner, E. W. (1994). *The educational imagination: On the design and evaluation of school programs.* New York: Macmillan College; and Eisner, E., & Vallance, E. (1974). *Conflicting conceptions of the Curriculum.* Berkeley, CA: McCutchan.

[16] Hayes, C. (1998). Private correspondence. Hayes is a former staff development director for Douglas County Schools in Colorado. The concepts in this section grew from our collaboration.

[17] Schein, E. (1992). *Organizational culture and leadership* (2nd ed.). San Francisco: Jossey-Bass.

[18] Kegan, R. (1994). *In over our heads: The mental demands of modern life.* Cambridge, MA: Harvard University Press.

[19] Dilts, R. (1994). *Effective presentation skills.* Capitola, CA: Meta.

[20] Featherstone, E. (1994). *Skin deep: Women writing on color, culture and identity.* Freedom, CA: The Crossing Press; and Garmston, R., Lipton, L., with Kaiser, K. (1998). The psychology of supervision. In G. R. Firth & E. F. Pajak (Eds.), *Handbook of research on school supervision* (pp. 242–286). New York: Simon & Schuster Macmillan.

[21] Saphier, J., & Gower, R. (1997). *The skillful teacher* (5th ed.). Carlisle, MA: Research for Better Teaching, p. 7.

[22] Chadwick, R. (1996). *Beyond conflict to consensus: An introductory learning manual.* Terra Bonne, OR: Consensus Associates. We are indebted to Bob Chadwick for this invaluable strategy.

[23] Kagan, S. (1990). *Cooperative learning: Resources for teachers.* Capastrano, CA: Resources for Teachers.

[24] Ibid.

[25] Adapted from Grinder, M. (1993). *Envoy: Your personal guide to classroom management.* Available from Michael Grinder and Associates, 16303 Northeast 259th Street, Battle Ground, WA 98604, (206) 687-3238. This is one of Michael's "seven gems" strategies for classroom management. Other strategies we've learned from Michael and have included in this table are: Attention First, Visual Paragraphing, and Please Breathe. We are grateful to him for permission to use this and other strategies from his Envoy Program.

[26] Doyle & Straus, op. cit.

[27] Lipton, & Wellman, p. 11.

[28] Margulies, N. (1991). *Mapping inner space: Learning and teaching mind mapping.* Tuscon, AZ: Sepher Press.

[29] deBono, E. (1978). *Teaching thinking.* New York: Viking Penguin.

Chapter 7 Designing Time-Efficient and Effective Meetings

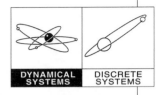

DYNAMICAL SYSTEMS | DISCRETE SYSTEMS

this chapter features:

Getting work done
Doing the right work
Working collaboratively
Managing systems
Developing groups
Adapting to change

"PREPARE more and meet less," is a motto for successful groups and effective leaders. By making a personal investment in agenda design, leaders can reduce meeting time by as much as 30%. This in turn produces dramatic increases in productivity and group-member satisfaction.

Time efficiency, enhanced morale, and better work are happening outside faculty meetings as well. Consistent with the principle that everything affects everything else in a dynamical system, department meetings are better run, ad hoc committees function more smoothly, and task forces and advisory groups feel better about their work and get more done. Being smart and proactive about meeting design pays off throughout the school.

Investing time in meeting design pays big dividends. Consider the time that you spend in meetings. At a modest 2 hours per week, you are spending more than 3,000 hours in meetings throughout the life of your career. If you translate that to a team of 12, then 1,500 24-hour days are being spent in meetings. They had better be worth it.

We define a successful meeting as a maximum amount of work being done in a minimum amount of time with a maximum amount of satisfaction. A unit with consistently good meetings has higher efficacy, better results, and less stress. A unit with consistently poor meetings spends time in meetings-after-the-meeting, has greater frustration, and expends great effort for little effect. The CEO of the Golden One Credit Union told us some time ago that the executive team spent as much time *rehearsing* for meetings as they did in the actual meetings. The result was that the company was one of the most profitable credit unions in the country, its board members felt valued and listened to, and decisions stayed made.

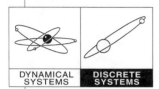

DYNAMICAL SYSTEMS | DISCRETE SYSTEMS

Designing successful meetings is simple when you attend to three organizers:

- Have clear outcomes.
- Have a task analysis–based plan to achieve the outcomes.
- Have a repertoire of agenda formats with which to work.

Have Clear Outcomes

Your first consideration is whether a meeting is necessary. Ask yourself what you want to accomplish and if meeting together is the best possible use of your group's time on this topic. Are there alternatives, such as surveys, memos, focus-group interviews, or phone conferencing, that might serve just as well?

If you decide that a meeting is appropriate, examine the potential agenda topics. Does each item on the agenda concern at least three members of the group? If not, deal with it one-to-one. Is it clear what type of action the group is to take on the item? If not, get it clarified. Can it be dealt with either initially or fully at a lower level? If so, reroute it to the appropriate group or subcommittee. Has the item for discussion been thoroughly prepared—researched, documented, and defined? If not, hold it over until preparation is complete.

Once you've decided that a meeting is the best alternative and have screened the agenda items to determine which ones must be addressed, consider who should be there. Do the agenda items pertain to the entire staff, or just some of them? If some are for all, and others pertain to just a couple of departments, schedule two adjournment times, releasing those who are not involved before starting on the final items. Are the items under consideration important or urgent enough to be on the next agenda? If not, reschedule them for a later meeting. Finally, leave room on the agenda for the unexpected or a "crisis du jour."

The type of meeting will influence the type of outcomes that can be reached. Four meeting types common to working groups are musters, assemblies, discussions, and dialogues. Chapters 4 and 5 present the purposes of dialogue (to understand) and discussion (to decide) and structures for these meeting functions. Assemblies are routine meetings of very large groups like high school faculties where, because of the large number of members, outcomes are limited to receiving and clarifying "pass down" information and sanctioning or rejecting proposals presented by a leader or subgroup.

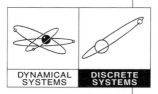

DYNAMICAL SYSTEMS | DISCRETE SYSTEMS

Musters refer to the regularly scheduled meeting of a department, an elementary faculty, or a special unit of workers such as bus drivers or principals. The function of musters is to communicate up, down, and sideways and to feel positive about the experience. They are a time for making announcements, coordinating calendars, and clarifying "pass down" information. *Never* use a muster meeting for "pass down" information in a group when a memo would do *unless* members need to ask questions, raise issues, or agree to common approaches for effective implementation. Muster meetings will often reserve a special section of time for either discussion or dialogue.

Creating clear outcomes is simple but not easy. Like a finely crafted lesson, a successful meeting will have outcomes that are behaviorally observable and that apply the same criteria as a test for individual agenda items (see sidebar for an example). Good outcomes describe a product, not a process; a destination, not a journey. "Discuss the proposal for nongraded primary" does not describe an outcome, it describes what members will do in pursuit of an outcome. "Identify pros and cons of an ungraded primary here at Anderson School," is a statement of outcome appropriate to a *discussion.* "Explore assumptions regarding ungraded primary" is a statement of outcome for a *dialogue.* In each case, a specific, observable product emerges: in the first case, a list; in the second, articulations and inquiries about assumptions.

We've had much success in designing meeting agendas within our own organizations and for groups with whom we consult by following a 5-step sequence in meeting design.[1]

1. What is the context for this meeting?
2. What are the outcomes—either cognitive, affective, or products?
3. What logistical details should be considered?
4. What is the agenda?
5. What follow-up will be required?

What Is the Context for This Meeting?

Several questions are useful to consider at this stage: Does this group have a history? Is it a newly formed working group? Is it together for more than one meeting, and if so, what is the outcome for its cumulative time together? We once facilitated a district committee that was formed to develop a set of exit outcomes for students. Table 7-1 displays the group's purpose as described at the very first meeting.

Initial Meeting Of District Steering Committee Meeting Outcomes

Steering Committee members will be able to do the following:

1. *Explain* committee purposes, final outcome, working goals, guiding principles and procedures, structures and timeline.

2. *Define* key steering committee terms.

3. *Identify* potential issues about which the steering committee should maintain sensitivity.

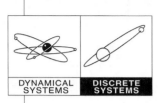

DYNAMICAL SYSTEMS   DISCRETE SYSTEMS

Other useful context questions are the following:

- What information do you want from the group leader or group members prior to planning an agenda?

- What information might you want to provide to group members prior to the meeting—for example, timelines, student data, budget figures?

- What presuppositions are contained in the stated purpose or goals of the meeting?

- Is this a single- or multiple-meeting topic?

- What level of decision-making authority will the group have?

- What other groups or processes might simultaneously be addressing or influencing this topic?

- What attitudes or feelings might group members have as they begin this meeting?

Table 7-1. District Committee Purpose

Final Outcome	Working Goals
Develop a board-adopted document that frames and commits the district to student outcomes, standards, and examples of assessment around which there is input from students and input and consensus by teachers, parents, community members, and administrators. This document will respond to the question: What do and will parents, universities, employers, and educators expect our graduates to know, do, and be like?	1. Adopt a sequence of events and processes by which stakeholders can develop consensus on exit outcomes, standards, and benchmarks for graduating district seniors necessary for successful participation in the world of the 21st century. 2. Develop exit outcomes for graduating seniors and benchmarks by _____ (date).

What Are the Meeting Outcomes?

What outcomes will be achieved by the end of the meeting, and how will you know that the meeting is a success? Outcome may be defined as cognitive, affective, or as products. Successful outcomes can be thought of as SMART outcomes (Table 7-2).

What Logistics Should Be Considered?

Our experience is that despite great attention to describing the details of room setup to another person, we must come early and check the

Table 7-2. SMART Outcomes

S	Specific: To be specific an outcome must describe the *presence* of some quality, not the absence. Not we want less of __ (e.g., tardies), but more of __ (e.g., pupils on time).
M	Measurable: What will be seen or heard as evidence of achievement? This is stated as something that participants will achieve, not that meeting leaders will provide. See the example of the district steering committee in Table 7-1.
A	Attainable: Can the outcomes be attained with the time and resources in the room? Time is most often the larger barrier to achieving success. Many groups discover that they are trying to "cover the agenda" as teachers try to "cover a curriculum," by attempting to do too much. The result is surface treatment of many items rather than deep and longer lasting attention to a few. Groups that confuse urgency with importance often fall into this trap. The resources part of the question refers to information, skills, and attitudes. Are these sufficiently in place? If not, then perhaps some different meeting outcomes are called for that will deal directly with the affective domain.
R	Relevant: How is this outcome related to the larger purposes of the meeting—the organization's vision, values, and goals?
T	Tactically sound: Is it possible that achieving the outcome, or even just working on it, could backfire in some way and endanger people? An outcome in which all members of a department express their honest feelings about the department chairperson may in fact be ecologically unsound for the individuals and the group. We have found that whenever a well-intentioned outcome carries psychological danger, we must design approaches that take that into account, or members will unconsciously and inevitably sabotage it.

room ourselves. A simple matter of furniture placement can make an enormous difference in meeting success.[2] Practical models for room design and materials are described in chapter 5. Some other logistical questions to consider are the following:

- Who should help to plan the meeting?
- Who should attend?
- What is the meeting time, date, and location?
- What materials and facility arrangements are needed?
- What communication systems will be used to support people in preparing for the meeting?
- Who is responsible for each of the above?

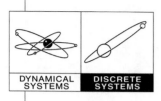

DYNAMICAL SYSTEMS   DISCRETE SYSTEMS

What Is the Agenda?

We ask ourselves the following questions with the greatest regularity when we are designing meetings. To save time in the actual agenda construction process, we use a variety of "standard formats" that will be discussed in a later section of this chapter.

- What must happen at the opening of the meeting to provide an inclusion experience, define goals and roles, and adopt an agenda?
- What terms should be defined?
- What questions, and in what sequence, must the group address to achieve its outcome?
- How much time will be assigned to meeting topics?
- What processes and language will be used to maintain group-member efficacy, flexibility, craftsmanship, consciousness, and interdependence?
- What closing activities will insure clarity on group decisions, and who is to do what by when as the next steps?

What Follow-up Will Be Required?

What will be communicated to others about this meeting, and how will it be communicated? What other follow-up will be required?

To further complicate the issue of having clear outcomes, we offer two final considerations. One is that high-functioning, intact groups should pay attention to their development as a group. Therefore, not only are outcomes thought about in terms of cognitive, affective, and product goals for this meeting, but how can the meeting be conducted in such a way that the group gets better at being a group?

Finally, regardless of your role within a meeting, or even the nature of the meeting, what specifically are your outcomes? As a group member, do you desire greater clarity about an issue, or is it your intent to influence the group on a item? If so, how will you know you've succeeded, and what might be some strategies? Mentor teachers often report to us with surprise that being clear about their outcomes has transformed one-to-one meetings with the teachers they are supporting. In our own practice we often begin a consultation conversation with the following questions: "What do *you* want as a result of this meeting? How might you know if we have achieved that? What topics should be discussed toward that goal? How much

DYNAMICAL
SYSTEMS   DISCRETE
SYSTEMS

time should we allot, and in what sequence should we discuss them?" Helping the other party to think in outcome terms, whether the meeting is a parent conference or the start of a 30-minute session with two other colleagues, helps to focus time and strategies to get results.

Have a Task Analysis–Based Plan to Achieve the Outcomes

Great meeting designers use two mental approaches to determine what must be done to accomplish outcomes during a meeting. One is that they run a mental rehearsal of the meeting from *the viewpoint of various participants* on key items on the agenda. In effect, this is what the Golden One Credit Union leaders do that contributes so highly to their success. They examine items from the perspective of individual board members and anticipate the responses. Listening in on a rehearsal for a school board meeting, we might hear something like this: "Charlie is pretty devoted to character development for students, so it's likely that he's going to ask about student choice in this proposal. How might we respond? Celita's ongoing concern is for academic rigor. What might she ask? How might the needs for both rigor and choice be accommodated in this program?"

Mental rehearsals are important to run on possible emotional states. Called "maintenance issues" in the meeting literature, these are important areas to research, because prior upsets that the group has had, which may not even be related to this meeting, can sour and derail progress. For example, we were once asked to facilitate a meeting in an organization in which participants had received a memo the preceding week that read as follows:

As you know, this is the first year of our new employee performance appraisal system. We owe it to the citizens of _____ that our work always be at the highest standards. In examining the scores this first year, we've determined that far too many "excellent" ratings were awarded. To correct this, we are initiating more intensive inservice for all supervisors.

You can imagine that this group was not very motivated to focus on the agenda that had been constructed for the meeting. They were feeling a lack of professional respect and value for their hard work and were simultaneously chiding the crazy bureaucratic logic. On such occasions, meeting leaders must discharge this energy early in the meeting. Unattended to, it remains as subterranean energy that will sabotage all valiant efforts to proceed with the tasks at hand.

There are three strategies you can add to the list on Becoming a Group (see Table 6-4 on page 106) that deal with this type of situation:

1. Use a group groan as an inclusion activity when you sense a lot of resentment in the room. Ask partners to quickly make a list of the best and worst things that could happen in the meeting. Get help to chart their ideas so as to maintain as much momentum with the group as possible. Now say you want to make an agreement with the group. Whenever anything on the negative list shows up, the group is to collectively groan. Practice it. Usually laughs will follow, and group members are reminded that they are in charge of their own experiences.

2. While reviewing the public agenda, comment that you will offer some value tips today so that group members can produce maximum value for themselves in this meeting. These tips are as follows: (a) Take care of your comfort. Coffee is here, bathrooms are there—monitor your own needs for liquid intake and outflow. Move your body if you've been sitting too long. (b) Take care of your outcomes (or learning). You each know what is important to you, related to individual agenda items, and you each know best your own cognitive style. So please be proactive, ask for clarifications, say "Louder, please" if you cannot hear someone, and influence the group on items—announcing "this is an advocacy" and telling the group why a position is important to you. (c) Misery is optional. Once again, laughter usually ensues and participants are reminded that they are adults and this is their meeting.

3. Give behavioral feedback to the group and ask what's going on.[3] Recently we facilitated a principals' meeting in which the nonverbal behavior resembled that at a funeral. "What's going on?" we asked. "This is our third meeting out of our buildings this week, and yesterday we had to distribute reduction-in-force notices." We changed the agenda.

All of the foregoing emphasis on affective issues is a task analysis of sorts. You are examining the emotional resources that are necessary to do the work and strategizing to activate them if they are not present. The other dimension of task analysis is to work from the end forward, asking what information is required, what must be decided, and what questions might be addressed that would help a group to get from the starting point to their outcome. Figure 7-1 sets the context of a meeting. The larger purpose is stated before an agenda is created.

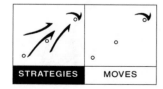

STRATEGIES | MOVES

Figure 7-1. Certificated Administrators Design Team Meeting Context

DYNAMICAL SYSTEMS

DISCRETE SYSTEMS

Date _____
7:30–11 a.m.

Sometimes agendas will describe the context for the meeting first. This two-page agenda, (shown with Figures 7-2), is an example.

The district has committed to a direction of shared decision making to support its greater mission. Today's meeting is intended to support three types of alignment:

1. An alignment of district
    • mission
    • vision
    • values
    • policy
    • practices

2. An alignment regarding the twin goals, seven norms, and five states of mind being developed at the school, team, and classroom level

3. An alignment of energies among members of the certificated administrators team

The people who are invited to attend today's meeting are being asked to serve as a design team. You represent multiple roles, perspectives, and responsibilities within the certificated administrative team. You are being asked to construct a plan to develop the capacity of the certificated administrative team to operate as a learning team.

Have a Repertoire of Agenda Formats

What follows are some agendas, each displaying different organizing principles. The most effective leaders we know have two or three types of agenda designs available and choose the best fit for each group and its issues.

The agenda of the Certificated Administrators Design Team Meeting (Fig. 7-2) is a generic form that can be used by groups to

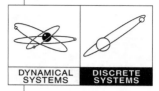

help them design their own agendas. Specific questions are posed to guide the group's deliberation. In our minds, the topics listed at 8:10, 10:00, and 10:40 a.m. are the most important for a planning group to address. If you are developing your group's capacity to design agendas, use this format and ask for written responses to these questions. The exercise reveals how difficult and how important it is to frame well-formed outcomes.

Figure 7-2. Certificated Administrators Design Team Meeting Agenda

Date _____

7:30–11 a.m.

Time	Topic	Process
7:30	Welcome Roles Context	Adopt agenda • Outcomes • Topics and times

Time	**Topic**	**Process**
8:10	What will one see and hear when the certificated administrative team is operated as a learning team?	1. Pairs generate 2. Report 3. Group adds to list
8:40	Of the above descriptors, what is essential and what is nice?	1. Group consensus
8:50	What resources (knowledge, skills, attitudes, and states of mind) are needed to attain the desired state?	1. Subgroups generate lists • Skills and knowledge • Attitudes • States of mind
9:10	Break	2. Subgroups post lists
9:20	Which of the resources are most catalytic?	1. Dialogue, advocate, inquire 2. Canvass
10:00	What are some ways that you can develop these resources using both additional vehicles and existing patterns, structures, and responsibilities?	1. List 2. Advocate and inquire
10:40	What next steps need to occur before presenting this to the full certificated administrative team?	1. List what is to be done 2. Determine who will do what by when
10:50	Summarize meeting Assess meeting	1. Summary paraphrases 2. Pluses and wishes
11:00	Adjourn	

Figure 7-3 illustrates an agenda that is designed to stimulate dialogue only, in which the purpose is to develop understanding, not make decisions.

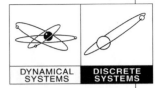

DYNAMICAL SYSTEMS — DISCRETE SYSTEMS

Figure 7-3. Desert Sands School Site-Council Agenda

Date: _____ Time: _____

Purpose:
Conduct a *dialogue* session to explore ideas related to initiating a senior citizen volunteer service program at Desert Sands School.

Assumptions:
Each of us can learn from one another on this topic. We will test this at the end of the meeting by asking for self-reports of shifts in assumptions and understandings regarding this topic.

Processes:

(15 minutes)   Develop agreement and clarity about the purpose, assumptions, and processes of this meeting.

(10 minutes)   Brainstorm questions useful to address.

(50 minutes)   Advocate and inquire on ideas stimulated by these questions.

(15 minutes)   Close
- Attempt summary paraphrase of what has been said.
- Report shifts in assumptions, understandings.
- Determine purpose of and schedule next meeting or steps.

The agenda format in Figure 7-4 is used with a standing statewide committee. Notice that the group's norms and operating principles are defined, times are estimated, and disposition of each item is named. Like a board agenda, this agenda is given to participants before the meeting, with attachments for details.

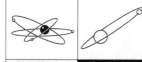

DYNAMICAL SYSTEMS | DISCRETE SYSTEMS

Figure 7-4. Coordinating Council Agenda

Date: _____
Time: 8:30 a.m. to 4 p.m.

8:30   **Organize Day**
        Welcome
        Organization of Meeting
        Introductions
        Agenda
        Inclusion Activity

Meeting Norms

Demonstrate Mutual Respect: Respect people and ideas—such respect does not represent agreement.

Employ Skillful Listening: Seek first to understand, then to be understood.

Sufficient Consensus: Each person has equal voice, the group works to understand all views, distinguish between dialogue and discussion, and 75% agreement of those present constitutes consensus.

Principles That Guide Our Work

- Make a commitment to collaboration and sharing of resources—work to coordinate the best solutions to common and differing needs across regions.
- Maintain a statewide perspective focused on student needs.
- Focus on making a difference in classrooms throughout the state.
- The Council's actions shall be built upon respect, sharing, collaboration, and communication.

Budget Information and Advocacy Phase

8:45   **Budget Process and Status—Mr. Scofield**
        Receive   Report on status of working budget
        Respond   To clarify

9:00   **Working Budget—Ms. Tappan**
        Receive   Recommended budget
        Respond   To relate budget categories to today's agenda
                   Check for understanding about processes

DYNAMICAL
SYSTEMS

DISCRETE
SYSTEMS

9:15   **Buying and Licensing Committee—Dr. Garcia**

Receive   Report on committee meeting and budget recommendations

Respond   To clarify, inquire, and advocate

Reflect   To consider recommendations for later action

10:00   **Break**

10:15   **Information Stations—Dr. Garcia, Ms. Tappan, Ms. Roberts, Mr. Moore, Dr.
Gordon, Ms. McCabe, Mr. Rodriguez**

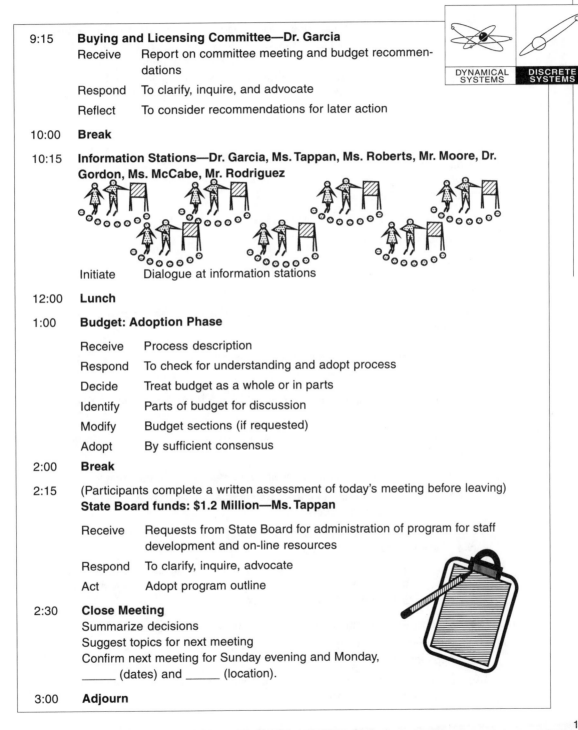

Initiate   Dialogue at information stations

12:00   **Lunch**

1:00   **Budget: Adoption Phase**

Receive   Process description

Respond   To check for understanding and adopt process

Decide   Treat budget as a whole or in parts

Identify   Parts of budget for discussion

Modify   Budget sections (if requested)

Adopt   By sufficient consensus

2:00   **Break**

2:15   (Participants complete a written assessment of today's meeting before leaving)
State Board funds: $1.2 Million—Ms. Tappan

Receive   Requests from State Board for administration of program for staff
development and on-line resources

Respond   To clarify, inquire, advocate

Act   Adopt program outline

2:30   **Close Meeting**
Summarize decisions
Suggest topics for next meeting
Confirm next meeting for Sunday evening and Monday,
_____ (dates) and _____ (location).

3:00   **Adjourn**

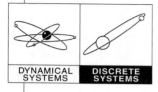

DYNAMICAL SYSTEMS   DISCRETE SYSTEMS

Much time can be saved when councils or other groups delegate tasks to subcommittees. Our experience is that 3 hours spent carefully posing the problem has saved literally hundreds of hours of committee work, eliminated false starts, and helped to keep morale and communications at healthy levels (Fig. 7-5).

Figure 7-5. Posing Problems for Group Resolution

Step 1   Leaders define the problem:

(a)   What is the problem or challenge?

(b)   Who is affected directly?

(c)   Who and what are affected indirectly?

(d)   What feelings may exist about the problem?

(e)   What time, personnel, and fiscal limitations apply to resolutions or resolving processes?

Step 2   Leaders develop resolution criteria:

(a)   What is the desired outcome?

(b)   What criteria must the outcome meet in order to reach a satisfactory resolution?

(c)   In what ways will the resolution contribute to organizational values or goals? For example:

• The management team achieving and maintaining a common focus

• Employees knowing that they are cared about and can contribute to the organization's directions

• Development of states of mind (efficacy, flexibility, craftsmanship, consciousness, and interdependence)

(d)   In what ways will the resolution procedures and processes contribute to the organization's reflection, continued learning, and systematically managed change? (See Appendix I)

Step 3   Leaders phrase the assignment for the task force or ad hoc group:

(a)   Determine the level(s) of decision-making authority the group will have. (See Appendix I)

(b)   Decide if the group is to present one resolution or three, with advantages and disadvantages for each.

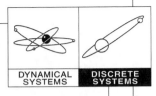

(c) Phrase the task with language such as "What might we do in order that . . ." or "In what ways might we..." This will provide the widest latitude to the task force and maximize potential for creativity.

(d) List the resolution criteria with language such as "in ways that increase group efficacy, sharpen the management team's focus, and do so within existing budget guidelines." This informs the group of organizational values and/or resolution restraints.

Step 4: Leaders present the assignment to the group and initiate processes for clarification and understanding of the task:

Example: This committee's task is to present to the superintendent of schools, by May, a *recommendation* regarding the issue stated below. The superintendent will take under advisement the committee's recommendation and will draft and recommend policy to the board of trustees, who will make a final decision at their June 8 meeting.

In what ways might we implement the county's new no-smoking ordinance in ways that do the following:

(a) Bring us into full compliance with the law

(b) Maximize individual choice

(c) Reinforce that *all* new employees know they are cared about

(d) Contribute to the states of mind of flexibility and interdependence

Time spent in agenda construction is returned a hundredfold. There is simply no other meeting device that can economize time and maximize success and satisfaction as much as a well-formed agenda. The problem, of course, is that it takes time to develop an agenda. Agenda construction, like many other tasks that educators do, is first of all a way of thinking. It is highly congruent with skills that educators have in lesson design and curriculum development. The more one practices, the easier agenda construction becomes. Here are some final planning tips.

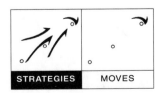

- Engage design help. In fact, part of developing your group is to increase group consciousness and skill in this area.

- Post outcomes in the meeting rooms. This forces you to construct clear language and observable goals and aids all members in knowing the reason for this meeting and how to best focus their energy. Additionally, should group members get off topic, it allows the facilitator to gesture toward the posted outcomes and ask, "Please help us to understand how your comments relate to this outcome." Sometimes they will tell us; sometimes they will monitor their own contribution, saying, "I'll save it for later."

- Determine how much content and how much process will be required to achieve outcomes related to agenda items. How much discussion, exploration, or dialogue might be needed? How much information will be required? Remember that when goals are related to attitude and behavior change, more process time is required, not less.

- Now estimate the time that each agenda item will take. Remember that if processes are involved, it takes time to explain them and check for understanding.

- Place divisive items early in an agenda to minimize the possibility of members leaving in a funk.

- Excuse the unaffected. When an item is relevant to only half the group, schedule it last and dismiss the others.

- Sometimes, when the meeting purpose is singular and brief, remove the furniture. This signals a stand-up meeting—quick, focused, and everyone out in 15 minutes.

- Finally, when you are a meeting leader, keep the first hour after the meeting to write minutes and memos and do the necessary follow-up. A leader's written follow-up to a meeting within 24 or 48 hours signals that you value people's time.

A last planning tip we offer is to consider what commitment will be made in the meeting to group development. What time, processes, and areas of group development will be addressed? At times one of the seven norms of collaboration given in chapter 3 will emerge as important to strengthen; at other times, raising conscious-ness on the five principles for developing standards for successful meetings, described in chapter 5, will be useful. This attention to group development, often overlooked, is the secret to getting better and is the focus of the next chapter.

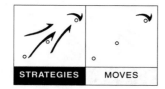

STRATEGIES | MOVES

End Notes

[1] See this volume, pp. 99–101.

[2] Perkins, D. (1992). *Smart schools.* New York: Free Press.

[3] Schmuck, R., & Runkel, P. (1985). *The handbook of organizational development in schools* (3rd ed.). Prospect Heights, IL: Waveland Press.

Chapter 8   Templates and Tools for Developing Collaborative Groups

E XPERT groups are made, not born. In adaptive schools, working groups grow, develop, learn from experience, get smarter, and become more effective at their work. In less effective schools, things stay the same, group learning is episodic and is often disjointed, and the capacity to work together and improve teaching remains relatively static.

this chapter features:

Getting work done
Doing the right work
Working collaboratively
Managing systems
Developing groups
Adapting to change

Adaptive leaders realize that developing a group is an ongoing, third agenda in their work. Stuck groups attend to the first agenda only, getting work done. Others who are beginning to move give attention to the second agenda as well, learning processes. All groups, however, work at less than full potential. The best groups regard this not as a deficiency but as a healthy dissatisfaction with their current performance. They consistently commit their resources to working together more effectively. This is the way that research teams get better at researching, basketball teams win more games, and theater casts improve from performance to performance. All groups become better at their tasks when they reflect on their work, acquire new knowledge and skills, and practice the fundamentals of their craft. Any group too busy to reflect on its work is too busy to improve.

To help groups become more effective, policy makers and leaders often focus attention and effort on *things:* money, staff, curriculum, facilities, time, and materials. Investments in energy must also occur, by increasing knowledge and skills, which are clearly significant resources. Perhaps less obvious is the importance of giving attention to other types of energy resources, those less visible and harder to quantify: staff morale, core values, and a sense of mission. Adaptive groups also work on developing five energy sources for sustained high performance: efficacy, consciousness, craftsmanship, flexibility, and interdependence. We maintain that the greatest and most long-lasting effects of developmental efforts come from enhancing these five states of mind.[1]

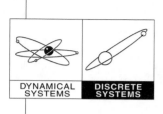

DYNAMICAL SYSTEMS | DISCRETE SYSTEMS

Premises of Group Development

Each Group Is Unique

History, cognitive styles, setting, mental models, and tasks will each contribute to developing a group personality. Each group is not only unlike other groups, it is also different from the sum of its individuals. For example, a group may be composed of efficacious individuals who nevertheless feel that they have little chance of making a difference as a group.

Some Groups Mature

Some groups will mature along a continuum from novice to expert performance. Not all groups make this journey, just as not all teachers achieve a state of expertise. David Berliner speculates that the novice stage in teaching usually lasts for the first year and that most teachers reach the third stage (competence) within 3 or 4 years. Only a modest proportion of teachers moves to the next stage of proficiency, and even fewer, says Berliner, achieve the expert stage.[2] We believe that much the same is true for group development. Sternberg and Horvath[3] note that expert teachers differ cognitively from novices in terms of knowledge, efficiency, and insight. We suspect that the parallel we have constructed in Table 8-1 approximates the truth about group development.

Attrition Need Not Block Development

The disruptive effects of attrition on group dynamics can be minimized and in many cases overcome. Groups that emphasize developing group-member capabilities and norms of collaboration informally provide induction experiences for new members (see chapter 3).

Soft Variables Affect Performance and Performance Capacity

"Soft" variables, such as the collective energies of efficacy, interdependence, consciousness, craftsmanship, and flexible perspectives, not only influence the performance of a group but also influence the group's ability to learn from its experience.[4]

Learning Organizes Itself at Hierarchical Levels

Learning occurs through different mechanisms at the levels of environment, behaviors, capabilities, beliefs, identity, and mission.

Table 8-1. Cognitive Differences Between Expert and Novice Groups

DYNAMICAL SYSTEMS   DISCRETE SYSTEMS

Knowledge

Expert groups . . .

- Have more knowledge
- Have knowledge organized more thoroughly
- Have knowledge more thoroughly integrated
- Have planning structures that are more complex and interconnected
- Have practical knowledge of the social and political context in which their work occurs

Efficiency

Expert groups . . .

- Are able to solve problems more efficiently within their domain of expertise
- Can do more in less time with less effort
- Have automated well-learned skills
- More effectively plan, monitor, and revise their approach to problems
- Use applicable cognitive processes with greater speed and accuracy
- Use think-aloud protocols that are richer and more interpretive
- More effectively use higher order executive processes to plan, monitor, and evaluate ongoing efforts at problem solving
- Spend a greater amount of time trying to understand a problem; novices invest more time actually trying out different solutions.
- Are more likely to monitor their solution attempts
- Are more playful in their approach to problems
- Are more likely to be reflective and continuously learn through experience
- Use new problems as opportunities to expand their knowledge and competence
- Reinvest cognitive resources in the progressive construction of more nearly adequate problem models

Insight

Expert groups . . .

- Are more likely to arrive at creative solutions to problems
- Reach ingenious and insightful solutions that do not occur to others
- Do better at distinguishing relevant data from nonrelevant data in problem solving
- Combine information in ways useful for problem solving
- Apply information acquired in other contexts to problems at hand

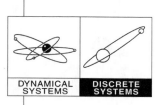

DYNAMICAL SYSTEMS | DISCRETE SYSTEMS

This learning is "nested," with interventions at some levels influencing learning at other levels. The greatest benefits of group development efforts come from strategically intervening among these nested levels of learning. We describe interventions at the various levels later in this chapter.

Maturity Manifests in Six Domains

Group maturity manifests in the ways that groups manage their day-to-day work in order to deal with their external environments. How well they perform at the following six interacting domains of being a group will determine their achievement: getting work done, doing the right work, working collaboratively, managing systems, developing groups, and adapting to change. Successful performance in each domain requires the energy sources of high performance and the application of domain-specific knowledge, skills, and structures. Each of the chapters in this book highlights the resources for developing these domains.

Six Domains of Group Development

All groups struggle for balance

All groups struggle to achieve a successful balance between managing and adapting to external relationships and maintaining harmonious and effective internal relationships.[5] In each dimension, issues of task accomplishment and process skills development compete for attention. Although it is useful for groups to realize this macro view of their work, it is difficult to assess and intervene with group development at this level. To effectively build strong groups capable of maintaining their own identity and adapting to external environments, groups must be able to function skillfully within each of six domains. Knowing the knowledge bases, skills, and structures of each domain is an essential first step. Knowing the assumptions held by the group about each domain reveals the mental models and drivers of group choices.

Getting Work Done

Leaders and groups understand the dynamic relationship between task focus and process skills development. The prevailing mental model in this domain is that the group assumes its work is manageable. Essential knowledge includes mastering of discussion and dialogue (chapter 4), conducting successful meetings (chapter 5), using facilitation skills (chapter 6), and designing efficient and effective meetings (chapter 7).

Doing the Right Work

Leaders and groups plan work to realize their vision, values, and emerging goals. The organizing presupposition of this domain in that vision, values, and goal clarity focuses group energy. Necessary knowledge includes living effectively with conflict (chapter 9), working with unmanageable problems (chapter 10), developing capacities for adaptivity (chapter 11) and creating community (chapter 12).

Working Interdependently

Leaders and groups work to create and maintain an effective environment for collaboration and interdependence. The dominant presupposition in this domain is that diversity is a necessary resource, and subcultures must connect with and value one another. The knowledge necessary to effectively work interdependently includes four group-member capabilities and seven norms of collaboration (chapter 3), mastery of discussion and dialogue (chapter 4), successful meeting management (chapter 5), facilitation skills (chapter 6), and living effectively with conflict (chapter 9).

Managing Systems

Groups develop new ways of looking at the world. An organizing presupposition here is that as systems become more complex, the ability to think systematically and know when to set aside linear logic is important. Critical knowledge includes living effectively with conflict (chapter 9), working with unmanageable problems (chapter 10), developing capacities for adaptivity (chapter 11), and creating community (chapter 12).

Developing Groups

Whatever the degree of accomplishment, groups can become better at their work. Individuals and groups need to develop resources for generating ideas and adapting to change. An important presupposition in this domain is that both individual and group orientations are necessary to produce innovations and implement them. Necessary knowledge includes information about group development (chapter 8), living effectively with conflict (chapter 9), the importance of professional community (chapter 2), and the principles of creating that community (chapter 12).

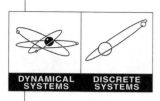

Adapting to Change

Effective groups relate to multiple communities that are external to the group. The agendas and resulting demands of these communities are often in flux and inconsistent with one another. The prevailing presupposition within this domain is that for groups to function effectively, they must constantly adapt to external environments. The more turbulent the environment, the more the energy must be focused outward. Critical knowledge includes working with conflict (chapter 9), developing capacities for adaptivity (chapter 11), and creating community (chapter 12).

Assessing the Six Domains

The six domains are inextricably intertwined; woven together they make a whole. Knowledge for one domain is also necessary in another. As in all dynamical systems, what affects one affects the others. Because of this interactive nature, an assessment instrument seeking detail about either the "things" or "energy" in each domain would contain redundancies. Mastery of discussion and dialogue, for example, are requirements in the first and third domains. To be effective at dialogue, internalization of group-member capabilities and norms of collaboration is necessary and is also a prerequisite for managing conflict in the fourth, fifth, and sixth domains. To maximize discussion effectiveness, successful meeting skills are required, which is a focus in the first and fourth domains.

In contrast to assessing "hard data," the energies in system dynamics has traditionally been harder to measure, more prone to measurement error, and therefore less relied upon as a data source for group development. "But the importance of measurement error diminishes when the investigative focus shifts from concern over the system's current state to understanding the system's behavior over time, which is often the purpose of a systems dynamics model."[6] Measurement-error importance also declines when data are used to promote conversations about how a group might strengthen itself in contrast to being used for external evaluation.

We have found the simple Likert scale displayed in Table 8-2 and the following process to be useful for group self-assessment. Organize a faculty into subgroups of three or four members each. Have them discuss each domain using the descriptions above. Have them rate their group by loose consensus on each domain, using a 1-to-5 scale.

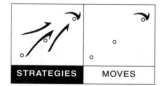

Table 8-2. Sample Likert Scale

1 Beginning	2 Emerging	3 Developing	4 Integrating	5 Innovating

Suggest that a way of calibrating their place on the scale might be to locate, in general, where the group functions along a continuum of unconscious incompetence (they don't know they don't know) to unconscious competence (performing with effortlessness). Rate the major knowledge areas in each domain.

Beginning	Unconscious incompetence
Emerging	Unconscious incompetence and conscious competence
Developing	Conscious competence
Integrating	Conscious competence and unconscious competence
Innovating	Unconscious competence

Now have subgroups report their assessments to the entire group. Search for agreements across subgroups and set those aside. Locate areas of disagreement and seek to understand the differences in perception. Come to an accommodation in ratings. From this analysis, have the group select a domain for further study and development (Table 8-3).

Table 8-3. Assessing the Six Domains of Group Development

		Low				High
1.	Getting work done	1	2	3	4	5
2.	Doing the right work	1	2	3	4	5
3.	Working interdependently	1	2	3	4	5
4.	Managing systems	1	2	3	4	5
5.	Developing your group	1	2	3	4	5
6.	Adapting to change	1	2	3	4	5

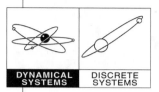

A Systems Approach for Developing Groups

Like birds lifting off from far reaches in a meadow and flocking together in flight, ideas are emerging from a variety of sources suggestive of a systems approach to developing groups. Within the literature on organizational development and school change, it is now taken for granted that teacher work and learning is largely influenced by socialization and that the culture of the workplace is significant in determining how teachers think, what they do, and how they are themselves.[7] From anthropology, cybernetics, psychology,[8] and organizational science[9] come conceptions of nested levels of learning in which learning at one level influences another. In this model, a sense of identity organizes and informs other levels of learning.

For an individual, identity is a framework for understanding oneself. This framework is formed and sustained through social interaction. Identity is what makes a person a person; it is the consistently traceable thread that is "me" over time and that distinguishes me from other people.

People construct themselves as having a set of essential characteristics, which define their self-concepts. They interpret experiences and choose behaviors intended to maintain the continuity of those self-concepts over time. Group identity too is maintained by comparisons with others. Groups seek positive differences between themselves and other groups as a way of enhancing their own self-esteem. Like individuals, they now see themselves as distinct and act as if they are unique.

Albert and Whetten[10] characterized organizational identity as a self-reflective question: Who are we as an organization? They concluded that organizational identity could be summarized in three major dimensions: (a) what is taken by the organization to be central to its work, (b) what insiders believe makes the organization distinct from other organizations, and (c) what is perceived by members to be an enduring quality of the organization.

The new sciences—quantum physics, complexity theory, and the study of fractals—portray a view of life organizing itself. Margaret Wheatley and Myron Kellner-Rogers, articulate translators of the new sciences for leadership agendas, write the following:

> Identity, then, is another essential condition for organization. It is the self of the system that compels it toward particular actions and behaviors. . . . Organizational structures emerge in response to these imperatives of identity. Identity is at the core of every organization, fueling its creation.[11]

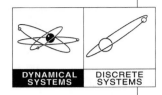

And so, in a quantum world, everything influences everything else. Individual efficacy influences group efficacy, and both influence a sense of identity for the individual practitioner and the group.

An Intervention Model

We have been working with a model of intervention conceived by anthropologist Gregory Bateson in which identity influences all lower levels of learning. Robert Dilts describes four operating principles in this model.[12] We notice their congruence with understandings of systems as dynamical entities:

1. Any system of activity is a subsystem embedded inside of another system, which is also embedded in an even larger system—and so on.
2. Learning in one subsystem produces a type of learning relative to the system in which you are operating.
3. The effect of each level of learning is to organize and control the information on the levels below it.
4. Learning something on an upper level will change things on lower levels, but learning something on a lower level may or may not inform and influence the levels above it.

The last two principles offer promise for group development. We've been testing applications with seminar groups, working teams, other individuals, and ourselves. We know others who are also applying these principles to individual and group development. The results of these efforts are promising.

Nested Levels of Learning

The brain, and any biological or social system, is organized into levels. To change behaviors, all levels must be addressed. Dilts observes the following:

> From the psychological point of view there seem to be five levels that you work with most often. (1) The basic level is *your environment, your external constraints.* (2) You operate on that environment through your *behavior.* (3) Your behavior is guided by your mental maps and strategies, which define your *capabilities.* (4) These capabilities are organized by *belief systems* . . . (5) Beliefs are organized by *identity.*[13]

Table 8-4 displays these five basic levels of organization. Each level is more abstract than the one below, but it has a greater degree of impact on the individual or group.

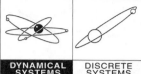

DYNAMICAL SYSTEMS | DISCRETE SYSTEMS

Table 8-4. Nested Levels of Learning

Identity

An individual or group's sense of itself. These factors organize beliefs and values. This level answers the question "Who am I?" or "Who are we?" In chapter 1, we proposed this as the first of three self-reflection questions that groups could use for adaptivity. (Who are we? Why are we doing this? Why are we doing this, this way?)

Belief System

An individual or group's values, beliefs, and meanings. This system gives rationale and permission to use or not use capabilities. Teachers who believe that they are more effective are likely to be more effective. When a group believes that their work is manageable, they will enlist the cognitive and emotional resources that allow them to persevere. This level answers the question "Why will we choose this course of action?"

Capabilities

Strategies, mental maps, metacognition, and the energy sources of efficacy, flexibility, craftsmanship, consciousness, and interdependence are all capabilities. The four group-member capabilities described in chapter 3 are examples of organization at this level. Capabilities guide and give direction to behavior choices. They answer the question "How will we use the skills and knowledge that we have?"

Behaviors

Behaviors are what individuals or groups do. They represent the application of skills and knowledge to actions and reactions. Behaviors can be singular, as in a paraphrase, or in complexes, such as listening, which includes attending, paraphrasing, making meaning, and many other singular skills. This level answers the question "What specific behaviors will I or we engage?"

Environment

Physical surroundings influence group and individual behavior. Room temperature, lighting, and access to tools and materials enhance or drain energy and focus. Attending to this level is always necessary but is not in itself sufficient for group success.

Without attention to these multiple levels of learning, professional development efforts ineffectively operate as activity-level thinking. We've observed staffs who dutifully perform collaborative activities—peer coaching, curriculum designing, serving on site-based councils—that is, going through the motions. Yet without engagement and learning at levels above these behaviors, they are only mimicking steps in a dance. No true collaboration results—that is, the cocreation of ideas or practices by people possessing different resources but working together as equals. This may, in part, explain Richard Elmore's[14] assertion that, in restructuring schools, a direct relationship cannot be found between student learning and activities like site councils, decentralized budgets, and peer coaching.

The Indelible Importance of Identity

Identity influences incorporation of information at the deepest levels, responsibility for what one has learned, and commitment to putting it into action. Group development approaches that affect identity include the construction of metaphors that can lead to expanded senses of identity, processing questions designed to stimulate reflection at this level ("How does this activity compare with your image as an educator?"), and meeting practices that shift the spotlight from members as information receivers to members as constructors.

Who are you in this interaction? Whom do you need to be? Faculty members report that these questions help them to increase consciousness and choice in professional interactions. Offer groups the metaphors of identity information in Table 8-5. Discuss how they know when they are responding to others from any of these metaphors. Explore the systems of interactions that metaphorical identities initiate. (If I respond to you as parent, you are likely to respond to me as child.) Interestingly, we find the friend metaphor is a common barrier to collegiality in many school cultures. Colleagues must be willing to experience some discomfort in solving problems together, whereas friends have a primary commitment to protect the pleasure of the relationship. While there is a time and place for each of these identities, the identity of mediator (a person without judgment in the middle) is the voice behind most successful school improvement efforts.

Identity is a major factor in personal change. A district office administrator in an eastern state talked to us recently about her superintendent's behavior in council meetings. On the one hand, the council values his leadership and contributions to the district. Yet the council remains frustrated because he takes calls during administrative council meetings and leaves the room to take care of business when a subordinate is talking. On several occasions he has been gracefully told by the council that they feel a lack of respect in this behavior. They have asked him to stop, yet the behavior persists. In exploring what seemed to motivate these patterns, a description of the superintendent's sense of identity emerged: He is a pragmatist. He takes care of things on the spot. He prides himself on providing

Table 8-5. Metaphors of Identity

IDENTITY	ORIENTATION	PRESUPPOSITIONS
Parent	Protector: I want you to grow up strong, heathy, and invested in my values.	1. Dependency 2. I am wiser and more experienced. 3. Reciprocated affection
Expert	Instructor: I will determine the correct and appropriate performance.	1. There is one right way. 2. Authority is related to knowledge and skill.
Friend	Advisor/Colleague: I want us to be companions; we will provide comfort and affection for each other.	1. There is a relationship. 2. The relationship has value. 3. The relationship must be protected.
Sibling	Brother/sister: I want you to be your best; I will support you; I might occasionally feel competitive.	1. Deep connection 2. I have permission to push you. 3. We have similar goals; we can work through adversity.
Boss	Authority; I expect compliance; I am responsible for success or failure.	1. I am responsible for you. 2. Power is hierarchical. 3. I am required to direct and control.
Mediator	Co-learner: We have an interdependent relationship in which you support my learning, and I yours.	1. Individuals have capacities to self-mediate and self-modify. 2. Resources are internal. 3. There is no one right way.

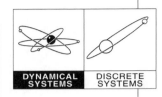

DYNAMICAL SYSTEMS   DISCRETE SYSTEMS

"We don't see things as they are, we see them as we are."
—Anais Nin

The ways in which we view the world and our role in it derives from the metaphor of identity that we hold for ourselves in specific roles. Our beliefs, values, and behaviors are congruent with our sense of identity. Each of us, at different times, constructs meaning and makes choices based on this specific orientation. Most often, our sense of identity is held at an unconscious level. However, the messages we send to others, both verbal and nonverbal, emanate from our own metaphor of identity. These messages signal our intentions and our beliefs about our professional role.

Through the language of mediation, metaphors of identity that are deeply held can be raised to a conscious level. As our metaphorical identities are articulated and examined, our capacity to explore and expand our beliefs, values, and behavioral repertoire is enhanced.

solutions to problems without delay. All these orientations are valuable resources, but their shadowy effect is the disempowerment of the administrative council. These behaviors are unlikely to change without a corresponding shift in identity by the superintendent.

Identity is the way that insiders see the organization. This is in contrast to image, the way that insiders believe that outsiders see the organization.[15] Beliefs, values, mental models, and assumptions are derived from experience interpreted through the lens of identity. They are held in deep structure and must be given form in language to be mediated.[16] Most people avoid questioning their own mental models unless they have evolved to a third stage of adult development that Robert Kegan and Lisa Lahey[17] call postinstitutional— work in a setting in which reflective dialogue is practiced and mediation of thinking is valued.

For groups, the problems of challenging their own mental models, beliefs, and values are compounded by the pattern of shared assumptions that a group develops over time. Groups will tend to cling to existing models unless a crisis intervenes. One crisis example is a dramatic change in student population, rendering old assumptions and ways of working ineffective. For groups to shift, new assumptions must be shared. This means that they must be articulated and understood, but not necessarily agreed with. Additionally, it is not enough to understand new mental models. They must be acted upon and put into practice.

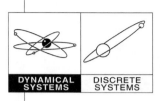

DYNAMICAL SYSTEMS | DISCRETE SYSTEMS

Changing Beliefs and Challenging Mental Models

Conduct the assumptions wall exercise described in chapter 6. In this activity, group members nonjudgmentally illuminate and examine their assumptions for sources, rationale, values, and consequences. This develops greater understanding of the presenting issue and of one another. A second way to challenge beliefs is to administer a principles assessment to help members see the degree of congruence between practices and espoused principles. Follow the assessment with individual and group analysis. This allows people to share their shock in learning that they are not living up to principles they claim to be theirs.[18] A third way to challenge mental models is to hold a values challenge seminar. Best done in a retreat setting, this is a conversation in which the group's core values are identified and then tested against a variety of increasingly complex scenarios.

Groups can challenge their own mental models by attending to different levels of data. The following strategies are common to systems thinkers who can move back and forth across multiple perspectives: (a) seeing discrete events, (b) recognizing patterns of behavior or trends over time, and (c) seeing the big picture of underlying structures.[19]

Most groups need to start at the level of discrete events.

Most groups need to start at the level of discrete events. Any of the facilitation strategies in chapter 6 will help groups to focus on the concrete. Any conversation about "facts" will also carry emotions, values, and assumptions. Use facilitation questions to get these on the table. "What are your concerns?" or "What are you noticing about your reaction to this?" or any of the *who, what, when, where, why* forms of questions can surface this class of information. Principles of dialogue encourage shared understanding of data offered by group members.

The human mind excels at pattern detection, yet this mental tendency can lead to generalizations, distortions, and misinterpretations because patterns on the surface do not always have the same structures underneath. Several facilitation tools can direct attention to this deeper level of thinking.

An Issues Agenda

This is a visual map to help a group discover emerging assumptions that are useful to challenge. It reveals issues important to the group's work and the perceptions of those issues, separates the important from the less important, and displays relationships. To make an issues agenda, distribute 3 x 5 Post-it® notes to a small group. Ask

STRATEGIES | MOVES

them to write their response to questions such as the following. Use only four to five words on each note.

- What are the most important issues from your point of view?
- What ideas do you have?
- What do you think might be holding us back?

Place the notes sequentially on the wall. Have people explain their reasoning. As this occurs, have the group begin to cluster the notes in groups. Now draw a circle around the clusters and give each a name. The clusters most important to the group will be identified and will provide conscious direction to the group's work.

Causal-Loop Diagram

This map displays multiple cause-and-effect loops. Start the process with Post-it® notes. Record the "effects" they are working to improve and the possible causal factors for the existing condition. Using the example of fourth-grade math performance declining on standardized tests, a group might chart some data as follows.

Members get out of their chairs and look at relationships between the items. In conversation they rearrange them. Clustering follows. Cause-and-effect loops are identified and drawn in with a chart pen. Causal-loop diagrams can reveal the nonlinear nature of cause-and-effect. Many of them are not visible without some sort of graphic display. Without such a strategy, a group doing event-level thinking might approach the issue of declining math performance by adding more minutes to the curriculum, bearing down harder on math facts, and slowing down instruction for students in lower tracks to ensure that they learn the basics. Such responses have tragic consequences for students and ultimately for public confidence in schools. Yet research in high schools reveals that the majority of teachers use such traditional mechanisms to respond to changing student populations and changing curricula.[20]

See the Big Picture

Step back from the patterns that emerge from agenda issues diagrams and causal-loop thinking and search for the structures that lie beneath the patterns. Three approaches are useful: (a) search for the variables, (b) ask transition questions, and (c) go to the source.

A variable is something that can increase or decrease. Kreutzer gives this example:

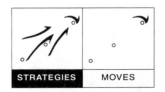

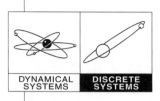

DYNAMICAL SYSTEMS | DISCRETE SYSTEMS

So if you were concerned about the economy, you might say, "We could have a depression!" A depression, however, is not a variable. Once you define a variable as eight consecutive quarters of declining GNP, you've found your variable.[21]

We note that *depression* was used in this example as a nominalization. This is one of the 10 energy traps related to conflict described in chapter 9. To nominalize, one uses language to describe dynamic processes as static things. In this regard, a group that was working to increase morale or efficacy without identifying the variables would not be successful.

Sometimes key variables can be located by examining the most important clusters on an issues diagram and asking transition questions to shift focus to an examination of the system.

- What do you really want?
- What would you see and hear if you got it?
- Who are the other key players?
- What might they want?
- How would they know if they got it?
- What would it mean to you if they got it?
- What are your key choices?
- What are the key uncertainties?

Once you understand a system, go to the source of people's behaviors within the system for the most elegant set of interventions. An elegant intervention uses minimum energy, stimulates maximum results, addresses both short- and long-range outcomes, works at the level of deep structure, and is congruent with espoused principles and values. Examining the nested levels of learning in Table 8-4, capabilities provide the most direct organizing influence on behaviors. A special class of capabilities are the five energy sources for high performance: efficacy, flexibility, craftsmanship, consciousness, and interdependence. We shall describe these in more detail.

Applying the Principles of Nested Learning

How might a group apply principles of nested learning to its development? Let's say you have selected the "Getting Work Done" domain. Behaviors and skills required for this include being an informed participant in dialogue and discussion. Skills in the seven norms are necessary. Additional behaviors will include being an

STRATEGIES | MOVES

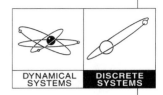

engaged participant in meetings and making good use of meetings. You choose one of these areas on which to concentrate. How will you proceed?

Begin concretely. You can generate information by administering the norms of collaboration survey. As the group reports its data, you help it to seek an understanding of conflicting perceptions. You invite a search for patterns. Either verbally or graphically you ask the group to relate the patterns in norm usage to satisfaction in meetings, quality of thinking, or impact on school programs. The group selects some norms to work on, identifies simple monitoring devices to keep itself conscious of usage and progress, and practices round-robin reflection or other metacognitve processing devices to strengthen the capabilities for the behaviors selected for improvement.

Later you might ask processing questions at the level of identity and beliefs. This coordinates learning at the levels of behavior and capabilities to more potent organizers. "How does our use of the norms relate to who we are as a collaborative group?" The group's identity in regard to being a collaborative unit is sharpened or shaken as members articulate their perception of ways they interact. Or, "Does our use of the norms reveal any differences between our espoused and behaved beliefs about working with common purpose?"

Strategic Processing Questions

Just as teachers work with taxonomies of both the cognitive and affective domains, group developers can also apply a taxonomy of intervention, seeking to direct training energies to the levels that will produce the most growth. One approach is to consistently provide processing questions that focus members' conscious attention on multiple levels in the nested learning map.

The processing questions in Table 8-6 are examples of questions designed to engage learning at different levels of organization. In this sample, the presumed skill to be learned is paraphrasing.

Five Special Capabilities: Where to Intervene

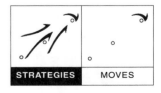

Garmston and Lipton pose two questions related to mediating teachers' growth. First, are some filters of perception more important, or do they have different implications for cognitive coaching? Second, to what degree might some of the filters be developmental and therefore subject to mediation? They postulate that certain perceptual filters represent differences in preferences about the way

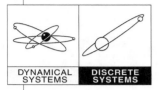

DYNAMICAL SYSTEMS | DISCRETE SYSTEMS

one knows (learning modalities, cognitive style), not about one's competence or capabilities in knowing. "They are differences in epistemological style, not epistemological capacity. They remain relatively unchanged. Capabilities do not."[22]

Table 8-6. Processing Questions at Various Levels of Learning

The Skill (Behavior) Being Taught	Sample Debriefing Questions
Paraphrase	What strategies did you employ to set aside your own autobiographical listening? (capability)
Paraphrase	How did you know your responses were useful? (capability)
Paraphrase	Why did you choose to paraphrase? (beliefs)
Paraphrase	What is it about the paraphrasing that you just did that is important to you? (values)
Paraphrase	How does paraphrasing fit with your image of yourself as a professional educator? (identity)

Our premise is that the five states of mind described in the cognitive coaching literature influence the capacity for knowing and are modifiable by mediated experience. These states of mind are related to stages of cognitive, moral, and ego development.[23] Educators can therefore maintain a developmental view in working with individuals and groups.

The following discussion centers on what we regard as developmental aspects of the states of mind. These are the energy sources of efficacy, flexibility, craftsmanship, consciousness, and interdependence. A group inventory has been developed by our colleagues Carolee Hayes and Jane Ellison of Kaleidoscope Associates (Appendix G).

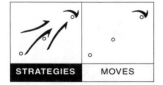

STRATEGIES | MOVES

Efficacy

Efficacy means knowing that one has the capacity to make a difference and being willing and able to do so. The RAND change-agent study found a staff's collective efficacy to be the most consistent variable related to school success.[24] Efficacy is particularly catalytic because it is a determining factor in the resolution of complex

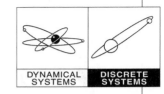

problems. If individuals or groups feel little efficacy, then blame, withdrawal, and rigidity are likely to follow. But teachers with robust efficacy are likely to expend more energy in their work, persevere longer, set more challenging goals, and continue in the face of failure. Efficacious groups regard events as opportunities for learning, are motivated by and committed to achieving shared goals, learn from experiences, focus resources where they will make the greatest difference, know what they know and do not know, and develop strategies to learn what is needed.

One study that examined the relationship between efficacy and curriculum implementation showed that two states of mind, teachers' efficacy and interdependence, significantly predicted the implementation of the new curriculum guides.[25] Neither efficacy nor teacher interactions alone produced a significant difference in use of the curriculum, but together they brought about change. Fullan regards teacher efficacy as a vital factor for successful implementation of change.[26] Rosenholtz also found that teachers' efficacy influenced students' basic skills and mastery.[27] The more certain that teachers feel about their technical knowledge, the greater the students' progress in reading. The more uncertainty that is suffered by the teachers, the less the students learn.

Flexibility

As groups develop cognitively, they value and more consistently view situations from multiple perspectives. Piaget called this overcoming egocentrism. Flexibility allows one to see others not as representatives of a role or in regard to the degree of agreement with one's own views, but from a broader perspective in which self and others are both players in a larger drama in which they are simultaneously the central cast and only playing walk-on parts.

The peak performers that Garfield studied[28] displayed an ability for flexible attention that he called micro and macro attention. Micro attention involves logical analytical computation and seeing cause and effect in methodical steps. It is important in problem analysis or curriculum planning. It encompasses attention to detail, precision, and orderly progressions. Macro attention is useful for discerning themes and patterns from assortments of information. It is intuitive, holistic, and conceptual. Macro thinking is good for bridging gaps, and it enables one to perceive a pattern even when some of the pieces are missing.

Groups who develop this energy source honor and value diversity within and outside the group, attend to both rational and

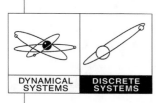

intuitive ways of thinking, can collectively shift perspective, and utilize a wide array of thinking and process skills. Such groups can also navigate the internal tensions related to confusion and ambiguity and get unstuck by generating multiple actions for moving ahead.

Flexibility is prerequisite to demonstrating respect for diverse perspectives. Flexible teachers are empathic. Flexible groups listen with their ears, eyes, heart, and mind. They are cognitively empathic with students, which enables them to predict misunderstandings and anticipate the most useful learning experiences. Flexibility, like efficacy, is related to risk taking. David Perkins[29] describes creative persons as living on the edge, always pushing the frontier, generating new knowledge, experimenting with new ways, and constantly growing into new abilities.

Craftsmanship

Studies from the League of Professional Schools[30] found that in schools where teachers are the most successful, they have the highest dissatisfaction with the results of their work. Success, for craftsmanlike groups, produces self-imposed higher standards in an ongoing cycle of improvement. In a study using cognitive coaching with university professors, Garmston and Hyerle[31] found that as craftsmanship increased, professors grew in their ability to be critically self-reflective and effective in producing self-analysis and evaluation.

To appreciate this energy source, consider the mindset of expert performers: musicians, artists, teachers, craftspersons, and athletes. They take pride in their work and consistently strive to improve current performance. Craftsmanship—the drive for elaboration, clarity, refinement, and precision—is the energy source from which persons ceaselessly learn and deepen their knowledge, skills, and effectiveness. Groups accessing this resource invest energy in honing and inventing better ways to do their work, honor in themselves and others the arduous journey from novice to expert, manage time effectively, and continually improve inter- and intra-group communications. They create, hold, calibrate, and refine performance and product standards for their work.

Consciousness

To be conscious is to be aware of one's thoughts, feelings, behaviors, intentions, and their effects. Csikszentmihayli notes the emergence of consciousness as "one of the most momentous events that

To be conscious is to be aware of one's thoughts, feelings, intentions, and their effects.

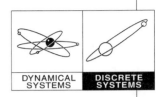

happened on our planet. . . . For the first time, it was possible for people to emancipate themselves from the rule of genes and culture. . . . [and] the illusions of the ego."[32]

Consciousness is another high-performance energy source with particular catalytic properties. It is prerequisite to self-control and self-direction. "Although every human brain is able to generate self-reflective consciousness, not everyone seems to use it equally."[33] Consciousness means that we are aware that certain events are occurring, and we are able to direct their course. While everything that we feel, smell, hear, think, see, or remember is potentially a candidate for entering consciousness, the nervous system has definite limits on how much information it can process at any given time. Groups using this energy source maintain awareness of their values, norms, and identity; monitor congruence of espoused beliefs and behaved beliefs; and stand outside themselves to reflect on its processes and products. Such groups are also aware of their criteria for decision making and of how their own assumptions and knowledge might interfere with their learning.

Interdependence

Interdependence is a recognition of the interconnections among individuals, schools, communities, cultures, and all aspects of the planet. Interdependence includes a sense of kinship that comes from a unity of being, a sense of sharing a common habitat (class, school, neighborhood) and a mutual bonding to common goals, shared values, and shared conceptions of being. Sergiovanni[34] tells us that the German sociologist Ferdinand Tonnies called this way of being *gemeinschaft. Gemeinschaft* is a community of mental life. In some respects, Sergiovanni says, these values are still central to indigenous people in Canada and the United States. *Gemeinschaft* contrasts with *gesellschaft,* in which community values have been replaced by contractual ones. This is the case in most modern organizations. Interdependent people's sense of self is enlarged from a conception of *me* to a sense of *us.* They understand that individuality is not lost as they connect with the group, only egocentricity.

Interdependent groups value and trust the process of dialogue, have awareness of their multiple relationships and identities with other groups, and regard disagreement as a source of learning and transformation. They regard knowledge as fluid, provisional, and subject to new interpretation with additional experience. Perhaps most importantly, interdependent groups see the group not just as it is, but also for its potential.

Group Development: Ways to Intervene

Group developers use at least five intervention strategies to support growth and learning: structuring, teaching, mediating, modeling, and monitoring.

Structuring

To structure is to manage the physical environment, the agenda, the tasks, and the grouping of participants in ways designed to promote certain levels of learning. This intervention acts on the level of environment in the nested levels of learning model. Stategically modifying the environment can increase the likelihood of learning at the levels of behavior, capabilities, beliefs, and identity. Some examples are as follows:

- Arrange the room so that the visual focus of members is on a chart, not each other, during problem-solving conversations. This helps put problems "out there" and not in each other. (flexibility and interdependence)

- Use the seasonal partner strategy described in chapter 6 to break up cliques. (flexibility and interdependence)

- Use role diversity as a criteria for forming subgroups. On a school site council, for example, locate a parent within each small cluster of teachers to list experiences regarding a topic. One typical by-product is respect for each other's experiences and universal perceptions about being a valued member of the group and being able to contribute. (flexibility, interdependence, and efficacy)

- Organize the agenda so that subgroups work on specific tasks during the meeting. (craftsmanship, efficacy)

Teaching

This intervention is best suited to the levels of behaviors and capabilities in the nested levels of learning. Exposition and story, as forms of teaching, can influence learning at the levels of beliefs and identity when combined with mediated experiences. Ultimately, this form of intervention includes all the repertoire of good instruction: explaining, giving examples, scaffolding, practicing, reading, and so on.

One device we have found particularly useful in regard to the norms of collaboration is to provide scaffolds. Rapid and lasting

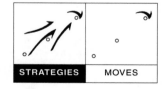

STRATEGIES   MOVES

improvements in paraphrasing occur, for example, when we display the following chart (Table 8-7) on a meeting room wall:

Table 8-7. Three Types of Paraphrasing

Acknowledge/Clarify: a brief statement in the listener's own words	**Summarize/Organize:** a statement that offers themes or containers	**Shift Conceptual Focus:** a statement that focuses on a higher logical level
• You're concerned about . . . • You would like to see . . . • You're feeling bad about . . .	• You seem to have two goals here: one is about _____ and other is about _____ • We seem to be struggling with three themes: where to _____, how to _____, and who should _____.	• So a _____ here is _____. – value – belief – goal – assumption – concept – intention

Mediating

Mediating makes its greatest contributions to learning at the levels of capabilities, beliefs, and identity. Mediating is a form of coaching in which the intention is to support a group in achieving the goals that are important to it while also extending its capacity for goal attainment and self-directed learning. Ultimately, this "hat" represents one of the four roles played at some time by all participants in an adaptive school. To mediate is to shine a judgment-free flashlight, illuminating internal or external data, the examination of which may lead to self-directed learning. The verbal tools of mediation include most, but not all, of the norms of collaboration: pausing, paraphrasing, probing, paying attention to self and others, presuming positive intentions, and inquiring. Mediation most often occurs in relation to reflecting about prior experiences, planning, or problem solving. Costa and Garmston[35] offer detailed maps for how to coach in these three dimensions.

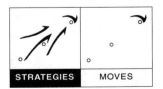

STRATEGIES   MOVES

Modeling

Leaders and group members model when they display exemplars of specific skills (like advocating) or complexes of skills (like balancing advocacy and inquiry) in work settings with colleagues. Two refinements add to the potency of modeling as a learning device. One is to talk out loud about one's rationale and metacognition related to the particular behavior being modeled. Second is to practice "public modeling," in which you announce to a group that in today's meeting you are going to work on improving your use of pausing. Reveal your reasons and ask that group members be prepared to share their perceptions on the effectiveness of your application of the behavior.

Monitoring

Monitoring involves collecting data on a dynamic of interest to the group and reflecting on ways that the data informs the group of its working patterns and ways that it might improve its effectiveness. A critical mental set is that groups are gathering and examining data to improve, not prove or judge, a level of performance. Groups gather information about how they are using the norms of collaboration, the degree of congruence with meeting standards, an assessment of operating energy sources, the inclusion of members, the valuing of diverse perspectives, and other information that they value. We are learning that the use of a process observer, a member who gathers data about participant behaviors, while the group is working, may generate more negative effects than positive. A pattern of externally provided data will often lead a group toward greater dependence on outside assessment, reduce the capacity for accurate self-assessment, and diminish its capacity for self-directed learning. Work with both students and adults has confirmed this.[36]

A strategy that employs both the interventions of self-monitoring and self-mediation involves asking two questions of group members for their private reflection: "What are some of the decisions you made about when and how to participate [in the preceding conversation]?" What are some of the influences of your decisions on you and others? After silent reflection, members might journal a response, share and interact with a neighbor, or practice a full round-robin reflection:

1. Person A speaks.

2. The group pauses.

3. Any person paraphrases and inquires.

4. Person A elaborates.

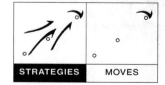

STRATEGIES   MOVES

5.   The group pauses.

6.   Repeat process with persons B, C, and so on.

Expert groups are more likely to be reflective than are novice groups. The more reflection, the greater the learning from experience. Nonreflection dooms a group to repeat the same behaviors over and over, whether they are producing desired results or not.

Every working group also has far more task than time. This contributes to a natural reluctance to take any of its precious time for monitoring and reflecting on its working processes. Some groups resolve this tension by committing themselves to a task/process ratio. They budget a certain percentage of each meeting to their own learning, exploring how well the group is working and what it might do to improve.

Perhaps no topic is as important as dealing with conflict, the focus of the next chapter. Surprisingly, the skills developed in the norms of paraphrasing and balancing inquiry and advocacy are the most important verbal tools for addressing conflict.

End Notes

[1] Costa, A., & Garmston, R. (1995, Spring). The five human passions: The origins of effective thinking. *Cogitare, 9* (2), 1–5.

[2] Berliner, D. (1988, February). *The development of expertise in pedagogy.* Paper presented at the meeting of the American Association of Colleges for Teacher Education, New Orleans, LA.

[3] Sternberg, R., & Horvath, J. (1995, August–September). A prototype view of expert teaching. *Educational Researcher,* 9–17. (Sternberg and Hovath report that novice teachers differ cognitively from expert teachers. We believe many of the same cognitive differences exist for groups. Table 8-1 on page 157 displays these differences as if they were true for groups.)

[4] Hennessy, G. (1998). Modeling "soft" variables. *The Systems Thinker, 8* (7), 6–7.

[5] Schein, E. (1992). *Organizational culture and leadership* (2nd ed.). San Francisco: Jossey-Bass.

[6] Hennessy, op. cit.

[7] Rosenholtz, S. (1991). *Teachers' workplace: The social organization of schools.* New York: Teachers College Press; Frymier, J. (1987, September). Bureaucracy and the neutering of teachers. *Phi Delta Kappan, 69* (1), 9–14; Firestone, W. (1996). Images of teaching and proposals for reform: A comparison of ideas from cognitive and organizational research. *Educational Administration*

Quarterly, 32 (2), 209–235; Newmann, F., & Wehlage, G. (1995). *Successful school restructuring.* Madison, WI: Center on Organization and Restructuring of Schools; and Louis, K., Toole, J., & Hargreaves, A. (in press). Rethinking school improvement. In J. Murphy & K. S. Louis (Eds.), *Handbook of Educational Administration.* San Francisco: Jossey-Bass.

[8] Anthropologist Gregory Bateson is generally credited with originating the idea of organizational levels of learning within organizations. Milton Erickson, M.D., developed impressive applications in clinical practice.

[9] Gioia, D. (1998). From individual to organizational identity. In D. A. Whetten & P. C. Godfrey (Eds.), *Identity in Organizations: Building theory through conversations.* Thousand Oaks, CA: Sage.

[10] Albert, S., & Whetten, D.A. (1985). Organizational identity. In L. L. Cummings & B. M. Staw (Eds.), *Research in organizational behavior* (Vol. 7, pp. 263–295). Greenwich, CT: JAI.

[11] Wheatley, M., & Kellnor-Rogers, M. (1996). *A simpler way.* San Francisco: Berrett-Koehler, pp. 85–86.

[12] Dilts, R. (1990). *Changing belief systems with NLP.* Cupertino, CA: Meta; and Dilts, R. (1994). *Effective presentation skills.* Capitola, CA: Meta.

[13] Dilts, (1990), p. 1.

[14] Elmore, R. (1995, December). Structural reform and educational practice. *Educational Research, 24* (9), 23–26.

[15] Gioia, op. cit.

[16] Garmston, R., & Lipton, L. (1998). Behaviorism to constructivism. In G. Firth & E. Pajak (Eds.), *The psychology of supervision and handbook of research on school supervision* (pp. 242–286). New York: Macmillan.

[17] Kegan, R. & Lahey, L. (1984). Adult leadership and adult development: A constructivist view. In B. Kellerman (Ed.). *Handbook on socialization theory and research* (pp. 199–229). Chicago: Rand McNally.

[18] Weinraub, R. (1995). Transforming mental models through formal and informal learning. In S. Chawla & J. Renesch (Eds.), *Learning organizations: Developing cultures for tomorrow's workplace* (pp. 417–430). Portland, OR: Productivity Press.

[19] Kreutzer, D. (1995). FASTBreak: A facilitation approach to systems thinking breakthroughs. In S. Chawla, & J. Renesch, (Eds.), *Developing cultures for tomorrow's workplace* (pp. 228–241). Portland, OR. Productivity Press.

[20] McLaughlin, M. W., & Talbert, J. E. (1993). *Contexts that matter for teaching and learning: Strategic opportunities for meeting the*

nation's education goals. Stanford, CA: Stanford University Center for Research on the Context of Secondary School Teaching.

[21] Kreutzer, D., p. 237.

[22] Garmston, & Lipton, op. cit.

[23] Kegan, R. (1994). *In over our heads: The mental demands of modern life.* Cambridge, MA: Harvard University Press.

[24] McLaughlin, M. (1990, December). The RAND Change Agent Study revisited: Macro perspectives and micro realities. *Educational Research,* 11–16.

[25] Poole, M. G., & Okeafor, K. R. (1989, Winter). The effects of teacher efficacy and interactions among educators on curriculum implementation. *Journal of Curriculum and Supervision, 4* (2), 146–161.

[26] Fullan, M., with Stiegelbauer, S. (1991). *The new meaning of educational change.* New York: Teachers College Press.

[27] Rosenholtz, S. (1989). *Teacher's workplace: The social organization of schools.* New York: Longman.

[28] Garfield, C. (1986). *Peak performers: The new heroes of American business.* New York: William Morrow.

[29] Perkins, D. (1992). *Smart schools.* New York: Free Press.

[30] Glickman, C. D. (1991). Pretending not to know what we know. *Educational Leadership, 48* (8), 4–10.

[31] Garmston, R., & Hyerle, D. (1988, August). Professors' peer coaching program: Report on a 1987–88 pilot project to develop and test a staff development model for improving instruction at California State University, Sacramento.

[32] Csikszentmihayli, M. (1993). *Flow: The psychology of optimal experience.* New York: Harper & Row, pp. 76–77.

[33] Ibid, p. 23.

[34] Sergiovanni, T. (1994). *Building community in schools.* San Francisco: Jossey-Bass.

[35] Costa, A., & Garmston, R. (1994). *Cognitive coaching: A foundation for renaissance schools.* Norwood, MA: Christopher-Gordon.

[36] Sanford, C. (1995, September/October). Myths of organizational effectiveness. *At Work.* Battle Ground, WA: Springhill, pp. 10–12.

Chapter 9   Using Conflict as a Resource

S UCCESSFUL groups know how to fight gracefully. They embrace the positive dimensions of conflict and actively minimize the negative aspects.

While conflict is an important resource for forging better practices, many groups and individuals try to avoid it. Our purpose in this chapter is to support adult groups in getting smarter about conflict, to reduce the pain of inadequate conflict mechanisms, and to increase the benefits of healthy disagreement in serving students.

this chapter features:

Getting work done
Doing the right work
Working collaboratively
Managing systems
Developing groups
Adapting to change

What We Bring to This Topic

Writing this chapter has forced us to examine our own attitudes, beliefs, and patterns of coping with conflict. We've discovered that we can't separate the professional Bob and Bruce from the personal Bob and Bruce. Our personal histories with conflict forge what and whom we bring to any work setting.

Like you, we first learned about conflict from our families. Other teachers came from the streets, playgrounds, and popular culture. Our early "studies" of conflict brought us to the formulas and advice common in the popular press. We read about win-win problem solving, six steps to problem resolution, how to get to *yes* past

no, and how to deal with difficult people. In the end we had a list of tools and some theories drawn from social psychology. But most of the ideas seemed generated from a mechanistic view of human interaction and founded on the assumptions of classical physics. Dictionaries, too, reflected this Newtonian cause-and-effect image of conflict—to strike together; to fight, battle, contend; to clash; to be antagonistic, incompatible, or contradictory.

Then, unexpectedly, we put aside much of what we knew from these sources as we learned about the martial art of Akido, explored systems thinking in relationship to conflict, and studied conflict anew from the

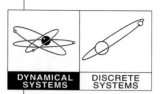

perspectives of social psychology and neurophysiology. This chapter is about what we are now learning and attempting to unlearn. It presents ways to improve the conflict quotient (CQ) of working groups everywhere.

How to Use This Chapter

We will define conflict, argue that community is not possible without conflict, describe the workings of conflict in nonlinear systems such as schools, name assumptions, identify and illustrate how to escape energy traps, and describe ideas and tools to help groups, and you, be more conflict wise.

You need two types of information to be at your most effective in situations with conflict: (a) an understanding of conflict, its dynamics, its dangers, and its opportunities, and (b) knowledge of a variety of conflict tools and ways to use them skillfully.

The sequence in which you will want this information depends on your learning style (abstract or concrete), urgency (are you thinking about conflict or in the middle of it), and personal history. If you have an urgency about learning new tools, move ahead to the section on the four disciplines (Akido, Systems Thinking, Social Psychology, and Neurophysiology) and their related tools. Come back later to more tools in the section on energy traps. If you aren't hurting at the moment, begin with the definition of conflict and read on.

What Is Conflict?

Definitions vary, illuminating different and useful understandings. Each provides a frame for living effectively with conflict.

1. Conflict is just energy in the system, nothing more, nothing less. People bring meaning to conflict. The ways they do so is influenced by personal history, cultural norms, family patterns, and the practices of the group within which they work.[1]

2. Conflict is a situation in which interdependent people express differences in satisfying their individual needs and interests and experience interference from each other in satisfying their goals. These differences can be open or hidden.

3. Like the Chinese symbol for crisis, which combines the symbols for danger and opportunity, conflict draws attention to both dimensions. Dangers emerge with violations of personal needs. Opportunities emerge when issues and possible solutions remain the focus of disagreement.

4. Conflict stems from a perceived competition for limited resources: air, water, land, food, time, wealth, power.

5. Individuals construct their own meaning of conflict; therefore, multiple meanings exist within a conflicting group.

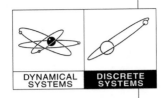

DYNAMICAL SYSTEMS   DISCRETE SYSTEMS

Truths about conflict lie somewhere in the vortex of these statements. Getting smart about conflict and having it work for you requires an understanding of conflict from all these perspectives as well as an understanding of yourself and of schools as systems. It also requires being clear about personal goals and values.

One useful distinction to make at this point is the difference between affective and cognitive conflict. Amason and his colleagues developed these frameworks from their work with teams.[2] *Affective conflict* is another name for interpersonal conflict. These are disagreements at various levels of person-to-person or group-to-group antagonism. Such interactions sap energy, sidetrack tasks, and block much group work. They can be on the surface or hidden in the substrata of group processes and instructions. *Cognitive conflict* is conflict over ideas and approaches. These "healthy fights" are one of the hallmarks of high-performing groups. In these groups, ideas and issues are separated from people. Ideas belong to the group and can be held up to the light of critical examination and analysis.

Groups need positive cognitive conflict in order to do good work. The absence of any type of conflict often leads to apathy, with decisions defaulting to the leader or the loudest voices. One major goal of group development, then, is to amplify cognitive conflict and minimize affective conflict.

Conflict Is the Other Face of Community

Authentic community, a goal of adaptive schools, contrasts dramatically with counterfeit community.[3] Counterfeit communities are communities in name only. In such groups getting along with one another is the primary goal. Faculties in which the term *team* is used as a manipulative strategy to get "buy-in" or more work from teachers are "look-good" pretenders of the real thing. Authentic communities are organized around common values and purposes. Each person is linked to the others by something more significant than oneself. Tensions between independence and interdependence are ever constant. Many authentic school communities exist, committed to shared purposes and working together as a "total village to raise a child." Conflict in these settings is a normal and necessary phenomenon of interfering energies.

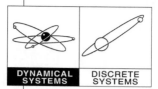

Conflict can exist without community, but community cannot exist without conflict. Adaptive schools are communities and require conflict to sort out the best practices for student learning.

Why Schools Struggle With Conflict

The nature of schools challenges the effectiveness of the traditional knowledge base about conflict. Adaptive leaders know that schools are living paradoxes, operating simultaneously as "thing" models and "energy" models. In the spirit of thingness they are organized as machines; a collection of smaller units making a part-to-whole universe: objectives-to-lessons to units-to-curriculum, a "racecourse" of relatively standardized ground that students cover in their journey toward the finish line.[4] In this model, principles of cause-and-effect prevail, values are formalized into contracts, event-level thinking is the norm, and tacit rules govern daily behavior. Transactions tend toward formality and politeness.[5] A teacher told us recently that each year students were coming to her without requisite skills, but she would be embarrassed to bring the problem up in conversation with colleagues for fear of offending.

But schools are also quantum systems—"bundles of energy in motion," more like communities than businesses. In these systems, "strange attractors"[6]—core values, vision, mission—draw people together in common purpose like magical magnets. Staffs desperately work to provide children with more than artificial belonging. In these systems the principles, passions, and conflicting energies of living systems apply.

Our central premise is that schools are enterprises of both "things" and "energy," yet "thing" mental models dominate most approaches to conflict. When educators can see schools as dynamical systems of energy and information, they are liberated to more effective ways of working with conflict. To understand how behavior operates in these systems, we have identified 10 energy traps and drawn from four disciplines: Akido, systems thinking, social psychology, and neurophysiology. Taken together, they suggest practical responses to conflict from the dual perspectives of schools as conveyor belts and quantum universes.

10 Energy Traps

Certain ways of perceiving conflict limit possibilities and constrain energy in increasingly destructive loops. Energy traps establish counterproductive, recursive patterns throughout systems. Micro-

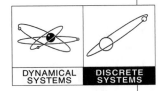

phone feedback is an example; the closer the speaker, the louder the squeal and the more grating on the nerves. One person being grumpy can set up an energy trap if other people respond to the grumpiness. To get attention, a teacher talks above the volume of a class, so the volume increases.

Recognizing traps in order to release energy is a first step in problem resolution. When energy traps are detected, conflict can be recontextualized and freed from existing solution restraints by opening space. Ten common traps, which can be reframed to provide additional solution options, are as follows:

1. Operating metaphors like the "war on drugs"

2. Time orientations that confuse past, present, and future

3. Time horizons that are too short or too long

4. Nominalizations: naming processes as things

5. The illusion of human separateness

6. Focusing on production to the detriment of production capacity

7. Fixing what shows, not what is broken

8. Accepting the myth that problems require solutions

9. Personalizing conflict

10. Being at the effect of emotion rather than having emotions

The Unhappy Elementary School

Recently we were asked to consult with an elementary school whose difficulties had reached such proportions that the school board had threatened to remove the principal unless she could "turn the school around" before the end of the year. We were contacted in March.

The previous principal had been at the school for 18 years and was a laissez-faire leader. The current principal had been there 18 months, bringing a strong curriculum background and a more directive leadership style to the role. We decided to do information interviews with each staff member in preparation for a full-day staff meeting.

Our private interviews revealed that teachers were not only complaining about the principal, they were complaining about each other. We learned that many individuals made disparaging remarks about fellow teachers to colleagues, certificated staff, and parents. Privately, a stream of vicious communication existed. "We're shooting at our wingman instead of working together," one teacher confided. Publicly the staff wore polite faces to one another and discharged their negative feelings on a common irritant, the principal. Some staff members had pipelines to board members and regularly reported their version of events at the school.

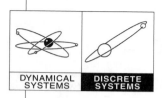

DYNAMICAL SYSTEMS   DISCRETE SYSTEMS

At the Unhappy Elementary School (see box on the preceding page), teachers were publicly griping about the principal and privately complaining about each other. The situation had reached crisis proportions, with the board poised to remove the principal. Several classical features of conflict present themselves in this example: (a) Conflict was perpetuating itself, ricocheting around in the energy traps of time orientations, nominalizations, fixing what shows, and personalizing conflict amid a labyrinth of underground communications. (b) Conflict is always contextual. In this case the school's history, a laissez-faire principal, and buildings organized into pods contributed to separate and disconnected units of teachers, each unit unique in identity, norms, and leaders. (c) The teacher leaders in this setting were bright, highly verbal, and passionately committed to action. The mix worked reasonably well with laissez-faire leadership, in which each pod was free to do its own thing, but it became an obstacle when the school was faced with a common crisis.

To release trapped energy, first you must identify the trap. Understand it as a conceptual shape that holds energy within certain configurations. Release the energy by changing the container, allowing the possibility of new resolutions into the situation. Consider a couple of issues in your work setting. Read the next section with them in mind, searching for energy traps that you might be able to identify and open.

Operating Metaphors

The human conceptual system is primarily metaphorical in nature. Concepts structure what people perceive. Language labels concepts and directs perception. A group's metaphorical language provides containers for thinking that hold unconscious assumptions, beliefs, goals, and values. The "phonics war" or the "war on poverty" are examples. Listen to groups or leaders in groups. Those thinking in war metaphors will use words like fight, position, shoot down, bomb, attack, defend. Sports metaphors drive a group into "winning" against an adversary. Others, like golf, will challenge each person against his or her individual best. But what if we never had a war on drugs, and instead had a rally for health? Changing language puts energy in new containers and opens fresh possibilities for resolution.

You can either extend concepts within a metaphor or change the metaphor. All metaphors illuminate some portions of reality and hide others. Search for unstated images within a prevailing metaphor to reframe group thinking. For example, if a committee is intent on "battling" illiteracy, focus attention on "training the soldiers" rather

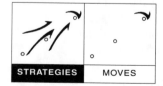

STRATEGIES   MOVES

than on the "guns." Or change the metaphor: Why not a ship instead of a war, a journey instead of an attack, a garden rather than a field of battle? What people name a thing determines their perception of it and hence their choices and behaviors.

Time Orientation (Past, Present, Future)

"We've always done it that way" identifies a speaker as focusing on the past. Energy gets stuck when groups focus exclusively on either past, present, or future or when conversations jump randomly across all three dimensions. Free energy by addressing one temporal zone at a time. In general, we find that in problem-solving conversations, energy is most freeing when it is directed toward the future. Help groups to describe the desired state. Then back up to the present or the very near future to determine what must be done to achieve the envisioned future.

In Time and Through Time[7]

One way to use time in negotiation is to pay attention to whether the opposition lives *through* time or *in* time. In-time people remember the past so vividly that it is as if the past is the present. Through-time people bury the past so that previous experiences are not terribly important to the present moment. This applies equally to last year and yesterday. The way you behaved yesterday will not affect today's negotiation, for through-time people.

Through-time people forget yesterday and start over each morning. In-time people will remember yesterday's argument as if it just happened, and their feelings about yesterday will affect today's negotiation.

Being aware of how people process time and how they relate the negotiation process to their experience of time gives you valuable insight on presenting your information and structuring your outcome.

Some groups get stuck in the past. Free them by providing a vehicle to tell their stories. Our friend and colleague, Suzanne Bailey, teaches a timeline strategy to help groups get themselves unstuck. The group designates "eras" in their history: the year the new superintendent came, the years of declining enrollment, the period of restructuring. Chart paper is hung on walls in the form of a timeline and icons used to illustrate different eras and the significant events that occurred. Groups of people complete the timeline with words, icons, and their memories delivered to one another as verbal histories. As a result, people hear about the same event from different perspectives, forming a more complex history with greater understanding of conflicting perceptions. What is expressed and understood is released.[8]

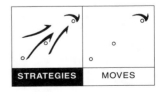

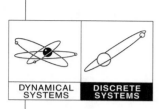

Time confusions (see box on the preceding page) will occasionally cause meeting energy to bounce off walls like a walloped ball in a racquet court. In these cases, direct the conversation to one zone at a time. "First we will talk about what has gotten us here, then we will focus on what we want."

Time Horizon

The unit of time within which parties plan to resolve a conflict limits solution options. Negotiations literature advises that everything is negotiable, including deadlines. Our friend and colleague Laura Lipton intuitively knows this and frequently moves to extend deadlines on projects. In return she gets release from deadline stress, more time for reflection, finer detail in her work, and better products.

Many time horizons are taken for granted because of past practices. Take, for example, the practice of assigning teachers to students for a single year. The moment a teacher decides to follow a class from second to third grade or from fifth to sixth grade, everything changes. Perceptions of student development burst from a 9-month window of growth to 2 years; diagnostic and relationship-building time at the beginning of the second year is practically eliminated; social norms of the class are understood and can be more effectively utilized, and parents' relationships with the teacher carry on into the second year.

Either lengthening or shortening time horizons modifies energy. A group of parents in a Colorado school wanted a principal removed. Stretching out the time period for seeking resolution to this controversy would have stirred up more problems as more people became involved and rumors multiplied. Extending time horizons can provide benefits, too. Plotting a multiyear curriculum revision allows full communication with all parties, reliable baseline data, and judiciously set expectations.

Nominalizations

Speakers nominalize when they talk about a process as a thing or an event. Teachers at the Unhappy Elementary School said the principal didn't "respect" them. *Respect* is a noun that is static, or unchanging; *respecting* is a process that is active in time with observable manifestations. Verbs are process words and imply active participation by persons or elements. As such, they imply choice and point to behaviors.

Some groups tell us that "trust" is missing in their organization. Groups cannot improve trust, they can only increase trusting behav-

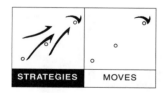

iors. We've learned to ask what people will be doing and saying when they are trusting.

"Conflict" is another nominalization. With conflict—as with love, anger, happiness, fear, or any emotion we tend to nominalize—there is a starting point, varying levels of intensity, a cooling off, and transition into another emotional state. In each case the language that labels these processes as things freezes these dynamic flowing activities into static conceptual abstractions. When groups act on the abstraction instead of the real issue, they experience failure and frustration.

Conversely, the more groups use the language of logic, emotion, and process, the greater their awareness and ability to direct and control conflicting energies.

- "We have two opposing views; let's distinguish between the data and inferences supporting each."

- "I am feeling some despair over the progress we are making."

To open traps caused by nominalizations, change conflict to conflicting, disagreement to disagreeing, relationship to relating, and responsibilities to what the person is doing (see sidebar).

Illusion of Separateness

During intense periods of shuttle diplomacy, Henry Kissinger used to say that he would remind himself of three things. First, he would remember to forget his culture; second, he would remember to forget his agenda; and third, he would remember his humanness. From such perspectives, conflict reminds people that they are irretrievably connected and that any sense of separateness is illusion.

Rusty Swigert, an astronaut in the Apollo program, tells this story about one mission. For several days they orbited the Earth until conditions were right for reentry. With relative leisure, he now had time to gaze from the spaceship to Earth below. Hurtling over the Pacific Ocean, the west coast of the United States suddenly appeared below them. He was aware of a visceral reaction, a sense of joyful belonging as he recognized his "home." Then, a little later, Cape Canaveral appeared, and he had another gut reaction of connection as he viewed the place from which the spaceship had been launched. Soon, he noticed, he began to anticipate the view of the West Coast and the launching site, and his sense of connection grew. Around and around the globe he orbited, each time anticipating the joy of recognition a little earlier, until finally he realized that he was connecting with the entire planet. It was years before Swigert could

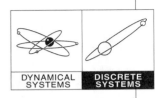

DYNAMICAL SYSTEMS | DISCRETE SYSTEMS

How to Denominalize Speech

Speaker: Our relationship with the feeder school is poor.

Respondent: How might you be relating if the situation were better?

Speaker: These students' attitudes are negative.

Respondent: What do you mean by attitude? . . . or . . .

What might they be saying and doing if they had better attitudes?

Speaker: We have a tough situation.

Respondent: How are different elements interacting to make this tough?

Ask yourself how you'd like to feel about a relationship after a conflict is over.

STRATEGIES | MOVES

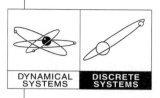

put this experience into words. When he finally did, it was in a speech in which he talked about his experience in the third person. He realized, he reported, that all the lines that separate us on Earth are artificial.

To release energy from the trap of the illusion of separateness, help groups to recognize the ways in which their members are connected. All the teachers were connected in the Unhappy Elementary School in purpose, in profession, and in humanness but were focused instead on their disconnectedness from one another and the principal.

Focus on Production to the Detriment of Production Capacity

Schools operate in demanding environments. Faculties sometimes press so hard for achievement that they forget to take care of themselves. A school in California was recently in crisis. Overnight the school population had doubled. Flooded with new students and staff, conflicting program demands and inadequate facilities, the faculty worked hard to address these issues. They ran communication-skills courses after school for two semesters in which 90% of the staff participated. The skills that were learned there helped the group to manage tough conflicts with the board, the teachers' union, themselves, and, a few years later, a districtwide strike. This staff recovered faster and better from the trauma of the strike than any other unit in the district.

Groups avoid this trap when they honor and protect time for reflection. Since adults do not learn from experience but from reflection on experience, any group too busy to reflect about its work is too busy too improve. Knowing this, some groups set task/process ratios. For every 60 minutes of meeting, for example, 10 minutes is spent on reflecting about meeting processes. Some school boards, and at least one state (Missouri), have policies establishing that a certain percentage of funding go to staff development efforts. Other schools use the first 5 minutes of faculty meetings for journal reflections.

Fix What Shows, Not What Is Broken

One common energy trap is a tendency to fix what shows rather than what is broken. Ours is a quick-fix culture. Television mysteries are solved in 30 minutes, minus time for commercials. Daily newspapers headline new solutions for schools, poverty, and crime. Legislative bodies adopt simple fixes for complex problems, and most often the

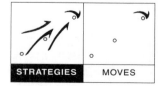

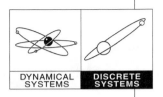

answers have nothing to do with the problem. Teacher evaluation systems are another case in point. As a profession, we've spent millions of dollars and as many hours learning and applying teacher evaluation systems, yet there is no clear evidence that such efforts improve instruction.[9]

Even as we write, politicians in California are calling for mandatory summer school.[10] About half the state's six million students would be required to attend, at a cost of $600 million. In the Compton, California, district a 1998 summer program is expected to cost $2 million just for staffing. In order to be promoted to the next grade, poorly performing students must attend summer classes and meet minimum reading standards by the end of an 8-week course. The program will only serve 1,200 of the district's 29,000 students because the district can't afford more money.

When groups fix what shows, it leads to new problems. Fixing the new conflict that shows merely leads to another. Since work is being done only at the level of appearances, the underlying tensions are left unattended and will erupt again at the next fissure.

Fixing what is broken requires a deep understanding of the interacting energies that are creating undesirable conditions. Expertise in any field is marked by a pattern of spending more time in problem understanding and less in problem solving. School staffs skilled in dialogue have the tools for this.[11]

At the Unhappy Elementary School, the board and teachers were bent on fixing what was broken: complaints about the principal. Deeper than that, however, were artificial separations of staff, communication by rumor, leadership tugs coming from multiple and uncoordinated directions, and feelings of being disempowered and disrespected. Fixing those areas could and did lead to substantive changes.

To avoid being ambushed by fixing what shows, look below the surface manifestations of a problem. Suppose fourth-grade math scores drop. On the surface it might look like number facts are the issue, calling for more drill and memorization. Underneath, however, we might find that the language of mathematics is underdeveloped and affecting performance as the math curriculum becomes more abstract.

Accepting the Myth That Problems Require Solutions

After almost a century of movie watching, most of the world uncritically assumes that problems have solutions. However, many situations exist in which no clear resolution is possible. In these cases

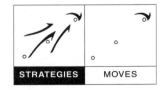

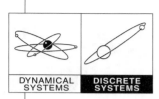

DYNAMICAL SYSTEMS   DISCRETE SYSTEMS

the wise person seeks the counsel of St. Francis's prayer, "God grant me the serenity to accept the things I cannot change, the courage to change the things I can, and the wisdom to know the difference." Turf issues in departmentalized settings are examples of problems that will never go away. They are deeply rooted manifestations of territoriality, self-interest, and survival. The most useful question to ask is how can we work together compatibly, holding service to students as our first priority while recognizing and honoring the needs of individual departments?

To avoid this pitfall, frame problems in the following manner: What do we need to do to get the best of the up side of a dimension (e.g., interdependence) and the least of the down side (e.g., autonomy)?

Personalizing the Conflict

A wise person once said that you will never grow up until you stop thinking that your parents' life was about you. To ruminate on childhood memories, pretending that we were the central characters in the play, is natural but only one version of the truth. Conflicts are hardly ever about you. They most often arise from some interference with another person's needs. To release yourself from the personalization trap, step to a mental balcony and regard the conflicting interactions as part of a system. What might possibly be going on for the other person that could open up a feeling of threat, uncertainty, or anger? Ask yourself what is the most generous interpretation of the outcome. Would it be OK with you if the person were to achieve that outcome?

Being at the Effect of Emotions Rather Than Having Emotions

Recall a recent experience of intense feeling. Were you happy, or feeling happiness? Were you angry, or feeling anger? Were you upset, or feeling upset? Language can decoy one into the energy trap of being at the cause of another person's behaviors. All emotions spring from choices. "The board makes me angry" is an inaccurate expression of reality. You get angry all by yourself. The board has better things to do than irritate you.

When you shift language from *I am* to *I am having* or *I am feeling,* you notice that you are not your feelings, you are not your thoughts, and you are not your point of view. Rather you *have* feelings, thoughts, and points of view. It is freeing to discover that whatever you are conscious of, you can direct and control. Listen for

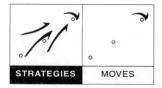

STRATEGIES   MOVES

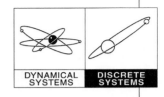

"makes me" language as a cue that either you or someone else is stuck in this energy trap. Personal power begins in your mind.

Instead of . . .	*Say . . .*
I'm disgusted	I'm feeling disgusted
He made me angry	I experienced anger when he . . .
They upset me	I felt upset when they . . .
This class makes me happy	I'm pleased with the class's behavior

How to Double Your CQ (Conflict Quotient)

We've experienced tremendous value by freeing ourselves from energy traps. Groups can easily learn to apply these ideas in their approaches to conflict, but the following information will double a group's capacity to live effectively with conflict. These are the principles and tools related to four disciplines: Akido, systems thinking, social psychology, and neurophysiology.

Principles are important because maximum success in any enterprise is guaranteed by clear outcomes and applying the principles (not rules) to achieve them. Rules are principles in chains. Rules restrict; they are useful some of the time but disastrous at other times. To start and end meetings on time is a rule. To honor a group's time and energy is a principle. Sometimes you must break the rule to maintain the principle. At a community meeting in a western state, for instance, a parent raised an important concern, about a district's effort to set student standards, 10 minutes before the announced ending time of the meeting. The superintendent wisely kept the group engaged on this topic for the next 45 minutes. By doing so, she averted 3 months of community upset and untold hours of communication and conflict-resolution efforts.

Akido

The martial art of Akido was founded by the Japanese master Morihei Ueshiba in the 1920s. To be a master, one had to accept many challenges and be consistently victorious. Yet even after reaching the pinnacle of success, Ueshiba felt unfulfilled and so retreated to the mountains to seek enlightenment. After years of search he came down from the mountains and announced to an astonished world that "the true martial art is love." "Aiki," he says, "is

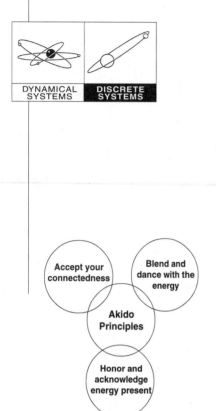

DYNAMICAL SYSTEMS — DISCRETE SYSTEMS

Accept your connectedness

Blend and dance with the energy

Akido Principles

Honor and acknowledge energy present

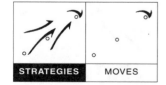

STRATEGIES — MOVES

not a technique to fight with or defeat the enemy. It is the way to reconcile the world and make human beings one family."[12] *Akido* means "the way of blending energy."

Thomas Crum, himself an Akido master, says that "the Aiki approach allows for conflicts in our lives to be resolved naturally and peacefully, with all sides being mutually supported, and it brings us closer in touch with our true self: a fully integrated mind, body and spirit."[13] Although Akido's purpose is to resolve physical conflict by rendering an attack harmless without harming the attacker, it is far more useful, Crum observes, for the practitioner. We can attest to its awesome power for both attacker and practitioner from our personal experience of using Akido principles in a group setting in which one of the authors was under vigorous and sustained verbal attack. A spirit of peacefulness prevailed for the author, and neither he nor the protagonists were harmed by the encounter.

There are three fundamental principles in Akido:

1. Honor and acknowledge the energy that is present instead of opposing it.

2. Blend and dance with the energy.

3. Accept your connectedness.

Honor and Acknowledge the Energy That Is Present

This behavior is in contrast to the natural impulse to oppose. A motorcycle rider shivers under the onslaught of frigid air penetrating to the very bone. Release is found by relaxing, allowing the cold in instead of opposing it. An attacker grabs the shoulder of an Akido master. The attack is a gift of energy. The master accepts the grab, embraces it, and places his hand on top of the attacker's, making it a part of the master. The master is then free to focus on what is more important than the hand on his shoulder—that is, the attacker. Whatever follows, he is in a position to direct the flow of energy rather than being pushed around by it.[14]

An Akido approach regards all conflict as just another form of energy. When the attacked person becomes flexible, nonrigid in response, the attacker's energy will overshoot the target. To flow with incoming energy, the first step is mental and the second is verbal. The mental state comes from being centered. Breathe. Your life does not depend on this interaction. Remind yourself that you intend the attacker no harm.

Paraphrasing heads the list of verbal tools for conflict. Remember that a paraphrase signals an attempt to understand the other person; remind yourself that you value his or her thoughts, feelings, and positions. Paraphrasing also benefits the "master" because one must concentrate on the other person to reflect his or her concerns, which effectively moves one away from ego states.

A linguistic cousin to the paraphrase is the first tool in a sequence taught by Manuel Smith in the early literature on assertiveness training.[15] He called this first tool *fogging*. It is followed by a second tool, negative inquiry.

Attacker	Respondent
I don't like your tie.	This tie disturbs you. (fog)
Yes, I think it's stupid.	You're really bothered by it. (fog)
Yes, why don't you dress better!	What might you suggest? (negative inquiry)

Smith chose to call the initial part of this interaction pattern *fogging* because however you "attack" fog, it just absorbs the energy. Fog is not damaged and does no harm to the "attacker." In fogging, the respondent is paraphrasing the attacker's perceptions, observations, and mental state, but not agreeing with them. The "What might you suggest" response begins the negative inquiry phase, still working within the thrust of the attacker's energy. This strategy is extremely effective.

In the following example, four verbal tools are used: self-disclosure, broken record, fogging, and workable compromise.

Ralph came into the school office. As head of maintenance for the district, he was responsible for seeing that OSHA safety regulations were met. A desk sat against an electrical panel on the wall.

Director of Maintenance: Bob, you have to move that desk.

Principal: I can't move the desk, Ralph. It has to stay where it is. (self-disclosure)

Director: Bob, that's against safety regs. You have to move it.

Principal: Ralph, I know it's against regulations, and I know you want me to move the desk, but I'm leaving it right there. (Broken record)

Director: Listen, Bob (heatedly), if I have a man on the roof and there is an electrical problem putting him in danger, we need easy access to this panel. You must move the desk.

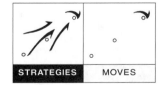

STRATEGIES   MOVES

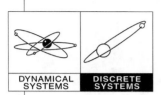

Principal: I understand, Ralph, that this is a critical situation and that you need the desk moved away from the electrical panel. But the desk stays there. (fogging and broken record)

Director: Damn it, Bob. Do I have to report you?

Principal: Listen Ralph. I've got a problem. Ever since we got more students and more staff in this office, we have not had enough room to function properly. Unless I can get more room for my staff, the desk has to stay against the wall. (self-disclosure and workable compromise)

This conversation occurred on Friday afternoon. On Monday morning, Ralph and the assistant superintendent for business were in the school office measuring space to see which walls they could remove. What made this conversation effective for Bob and, ultimately, for Ralph? We would give 10% credit to the verbal tools and 90% to Bob's mental state of centeredness, well-being, clarity about personal goals, and an intention to "love" Ralph and not hurt him.

Blend and Dance With the Energy

Crum describes an attacker who grabs you and pulls you toward him. By going with that new direction of energy, you are able to avoid a struggle and can redirect the energy to a peaceful outcome. This blending movement puts the Akido master into an optimum position to apply one of many immobilization techniques to neutralize the harmful qualities of an attack.

Using this principle in verbal conflict again begins with an inner state. Let go of any need to be right. Acknowledge the upsets felt by the other person. This receives the energy and tells the person that you value the relationship. Seek to understand: Respectfully use similar postures, gestures, and intonation to communicate respect for the other person's experience. This helps you to join in on the representation of the experience and allows you to work together.[16] The seventh collaborative norm described in chapter 3, balancing advocacy and inquiry, is a particularly effective tool for dancing with the other person's energy. So too are the principles and tools of suspension, balcony view, and dialogue described in chapter 4.

Accept Your Connectedness

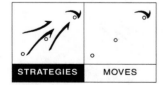

"When I accept my connectedness, I give up my attempt to manipulate and win."[17] "Connectedness is reality. Separation is an illusion."[18]

Connectedness begins by being centered. Great leaders and professionals in all fields operate from centeredness. The secret to being centered is to be in the moment, aware of oneself not as the central player in a drama but as an observing player in a dynamic interaction. Paradoxically, this state is achieved by being intensely aware of personal feelings, body sensations, and thoughts, and noticing them without attachment in the same way that one would notice other people in the room or features of the environment.

Being centered in conflict allows a sense of spaciousness and nonattachment. When one is centered, one can move beyond personal concerns into a larger perspective. Thomas Crum teaches that energy, or *ki,* is the connector to all things. Relationships are about connecting and separating. One either expands one's energy and strengthens connection to others or contracts it and increases feelings of separation. Adolescents demonstrate these principles when they become expansive, garrulous, and engaged or shift to being withdrawn, moody, and isolated.

Great athletes operate from centeredness. We recall images of Joe Montana, when he was quarterback for the San Francisco Forty Niners, calmly surveying a tumble of huge men surging across the scrimmage line to knock him down. Unflinchingly, he stayed in the moment, searching for a pass receiver in the right spot. At these times he looked as if he were above it all, a mere observer, waiting for the perfect time to pass the ball.

A fitness trainer has been patiently attempting to teach us one of the great and frustrating lessons of life related to connectedness: concentrate on the moment, not the goal. Keep attention to form, not the number of repetitions. When we follow this advice, our performance improves almost effortlessly.

Fear dissolves centeredness; it is based on being stuck in time, worrying about what might happen next because of previous experiences or apprehensions. To discharge fear, be fully aware of the moment. Notice with detail the faces and voices of others. Breathe, allowing precious oxygen to get to the brain. Notice physical sensations—chest tightness, quavering voice, trembling hands, or flushed face—both yours and theirs. Awareness alone will lesson fear and dissolve symptoms. Like Joe Montana, you will be calm in the chaotic moment, poised to make the right move.

When you breathe, exhale fully to release the energy you are holding. Move to another room if necessary. We know a department chairman who, when he realizes he is losing control of his emotions, fakes coughing spasms so he can leave the room and recenter himself.

STRATEGIES   MOVES

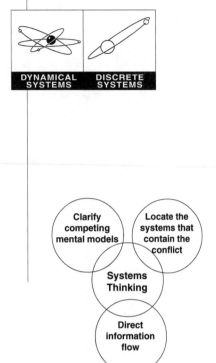

Maintaining connectedness is, in part, a matter of self-talk. We have a backpacking companion from whom we've learned the question, "What will this mean 100 years from now?" Ted raises this question for himself whenever he is on the verge of getting upset. Taken in perspective, how important is it that the other party achieves the outcome it wants? In the broad view of things, how critical is it that your preschooler has spilled watercolor paints on the living room rug? What will this really mean 10 years from now? You have a place of fulfillment that is much larger than the other party's goal, the paint on the rug, the preschooler, or this moment.

Systems Thinking

One finding from quantum physics is that everything is connected to everything else. Tiny events can cause major disturbances in complex systems. Systems thinking invites us to examine the system that may be holding conflict together and addressing that system, not its parts.

There are three basic systems thinking principles:

1. Locate the system and the feedback loops that perpetuate the conflict.

2. Direct the information flow.

3. Clarify conflicting mental models.

Locate the System and the Feedback Loops

Judy is a midlevel manager in an educational agency. She is called to a meeting at her boss's office. Three coworkers are present, and the reason for the meeting is unknown. Judy's boss, Leslie, is steamed and wants this team to help solve a problem. Leslie has learned that workers from another department are tracking the progress of legislation on childcare. Leslie considers this the domain of her department. The other department also has vested interests because the legislation could conceivably affect its operation. Leslie wants a steady and timely pipeline of information to her and has decided that Judy is the best person to take on this task. The purpose of this meeting is to figure out how to hire someone else to take Judy's present responsibilities. Judy is shocked, fearful of losing touch with the childcare program in which she has invested herself for years, and adamantly opposed to what Leslie suggests. What is her strategy?

Using Akido principles, she centers herself. From a balcony view of the meeting, she connects to Leslie's need for potency (see

sources of conflict in the section on social psychology) and regards the presenting problem as a systems issue. She dissolves her fears by concentrating on the moment. Dispassionately and skillfully, she gets all the known information on the table. When premature solutions are offered by others, she advocates for suspension of these until a more thorough understanding of the system is known. She reframes the presenting problem with a systems perspective. The critical question is not how can Leslie be kept up to date, but how can the two departments work in concert to guide proposals through the legislative process. She artfully paraphrases and inquires to guide the group in articulating the system's goals, resources, and possible responses.

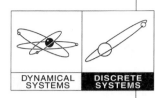

Incomplete and disconnected communication systems triggered feedback loops which set off Leslie's alarms. Without modifying the loops themselves, more problems of this nature will continue to surface. Feedback loops can be located by mapping interactions: who is involved at what points in a system, and what is the nature of their involvement? Conflicts often persist when the feedback loops do not relate to a group's mission or values. When a problem occurs, groups often examine the decisions or behaviors that are the contributing factors. Encourage them to look beneath these to locate the common values held by the group.

Direct the Information Flow

Ask what information is not in the system that, if available, would help people address the real causes of conflict. One powerful tool is the sensing interview. Arrange for 30-minute confidential interviews with the affected parties. Advise them that the source of any information will be confidential, but the content will be shared if it appears to be an observation of more than one person. Ask three questions: (a) What are you feeling good about in this situation? (b) What problems are here? (c) What recommendations do you have? Gather this data and "publish" it at a meeting of the whole group. Ask the group, did I understand this correctly? Did I make any errors in interpretation? Get the group to start talking about the data, until now publicly undiscussed, and information will flow and connect to the necessary people in the system.

This is what occurred at the Unhappy Elementary School. Complaints about the principal were serious enough to cause the board to demand that she be fired unless she could straighten up the school. In the process of interviewing staff, we discovered that teachers were complaining about each other, too. Until the data was "published" in a meeting, no one knew how prevalent the bad

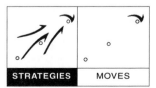

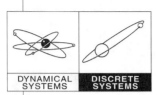

DYNAMICAL SYSTEMS | DISCRETE SYSTEMS

feelings were. As information about the system got to everyone, it changed the perception of the conflict. The teachers and the principal were able to resolve the contentions before the end of the school year.

Clarify Conflicting Mental Models

As we have previously described, at least two classes of mental models exist: "thing" models, in which success is measured by putting into place documents, policies, and procedures, and "energy models," in which attention is given to mobilizing energy toward goals. Thing models require linear thinking to understand and work with them; energy models call upon more nonlinear thought. Each class of model has its own assumptions, values, beliefs, and goals.

Recently we worked in a large school district in which the board and the central office were working heroically to develop and implement "things" to improve student achievement. Standards, benchmarks, accountability systems, mission statements, priorities, and plans were being developed centrally and encouraged locally. But teachers' responses tended toward resentment, not gratitude. They interpreted district effort as a statement about deficiency in their work. They felt blamed for low student achievement and were hearing the message that if teachers would only be organized and do these common-sense things, students would learn more.

Some of the assumptions and beliefs driving district efforts were the following: (a) To achieve something, identify a goal and its benchmarks and organize the necessary resources. (b) System success requires all teachers to work toward the same goals. (c) Clear policies, processes, and instruments are essential components. (d) Accountability is also essential. Rewards for high performance will motivate teachers, and program-review visits by peers will help staffs to devise solutions when conditions of low performance exist.

In our minds, the only assumption here that might be questioned is the fourth one. Why were there such negative reactions from the teachers? As we began our work with the teacher leaders, it seemed to us that no attention was being given to an energy model of school improvement. Different assumptions drive energy models: (a) Staff efficacy is a significant predictor of student success.[19] (b) Consciousness, flexibility, and craftsmanship are essential metacognitive skills for the improvement of any performance skill, and interdependence is necessary for group success. (c) Attitude begets the learning of knowledge and skills, not vice versa. (d) Everyone wants students to succeed and wants to be successful in helping them succeed.

What was needed in this setting was an attitude in which teachers could perceive district tools as assisting them in doing something they already wanted to do. Before the two mental models were unmasked, teachers were perceiving the tools as punishments rather than as aids.

Some specific tools for surfacing mental models are dialogue (chapter 4), the assumptions wall (chapter 6), and round-robin reflection (chapter 6).

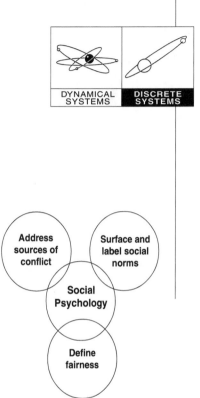

Social Psychology

Social psychologists study efforts to resolve human conflict through case histories, through mathematical models of rational thought, and by testing predictive theories about conditions and outcomes of negotiations. Advice found in the popular press usually has its origins in social psychology. In our exploration of conflict from the perspective of this field, we identify the following three principles to be of value to all educators working with any form of conflict:

1. Define fairness.

2. Surface and label the social norms for preventing conflict, regulating conflict, and finding solutions to conflict.

3. Address the sources of conflict: scarcity, power, change, diversity, civility, emotion, and values.

Define Fairness

Agreement is more likely and can be reached more quickly when a single standard of fairness is applied than when using multiple standards or no standards. It is best to negotiate the fairness criteria early in the process. Groups usually select from three definitions. Test the definitions with "what if" scenarios:

Equality.   Everybody benefits or contributes equally. Three variations of this have been observed: (a) equal outcomes, (b) equal concessions (both parties make the same degree of movement toward the middle) and (c) outside precedent (What are other districts paying teachers?).

Equity.   Benefit is proportional to work done. Merit-pay systems operate with this principle.

Needs.   Benefit should be proportional to need. Federal funding formulas for grants to schools with high populations of low-income children represent this line of thinking.

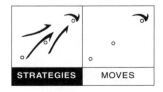

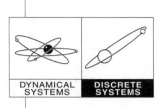

DYNAMICAL SYSTEMS | DISCRETE SYSTEMS

Surface and Label Social Norms

People will attack the process when they are not happy with a resolution. Head this off by identifying and labeling the norms that the parties will agree to use.

Norms for preventing conflict are either productive or destructive. Destructive patterns include excessive politeness, avoiding issues, using humor as a distraction, and emphasizing congeniality (making nice) over collegiality. Overregulating the processes for resolving issues with an avalanche of policies, forms, and detailed chains of command is a counterproductive approach used by some large organizations. We know a school overseas in which conflict is "managed" by banning all employee organizations. Both of these large-scale approaches drive expressions of conflict underground, affect relationships, and ultimately destroy efficacy and morale.

Productive patterns for preventing conflict include assigning resources and responsibilities on the basis of some agreed-upon definition of fairness (e.g., all teachers rotate yard-duty responsibilities except Mrs. Smith, who runs an after-school tutorial clinic). Interactive patterns for conflict prevention include the seven norms of collaboration and agreements to trace rumors to their source.

Norms for regulating conflict. To talk first with one's adversary before going to a third party is an example of regulating conflict. Groups define what constitutes fair fighting. Agreements to address issues, not personalities, or to ignore certain classes of behavior (e.g., knitting during faculty meetings) are examples of ways in which groups may define fair fighting. Agreements to discuss the undiscussable, personal feelings, values, or student achievement in the math department constitute norms for regulating conflict. Groups make regulatory agreements about language. Instead of "You are wrong," they agree to say, "I see it another way."

Norms for finding solutions. Agree first about solution criteria and solution processes (who will decide). Identify and explore the assumptions underlying the different positions. Raise questions like the following to help groups confront conflict:

- What is the worst possible outcome of addressing this?
- What is the best possible outcome of addressing this?
- What is the worst and best possible outcome of *not* addressing this?
- What outcome do you imagine that your adversary has?
- Would it be OK if your adversaries achieved their outcomes?

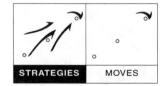

STRATEGIES | MOVES

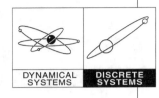

Address sources of conflict.   Scarcity, power, change, diversity, civility, emotional needs, and values can be sources of conflict. Connected to each of these are perceptions and assumptions based on personal history and mental models. Be empathic but listen below emotion. Help others to state their outcomes in several different ways. Doing so reveals the structure of mental models and opens possible avenues for satisfaction. Groups decrease the potential for conflict in these areas when they proactively educate themselves and develop norms for living with power, change, diversity, civility, and emotion.

Scarcity.   Even friends can become protagonists when fears are stimulated about scarcity. The belief that there is not enough time, money, personnel, or space stimulates survival impulses and limits creative thinking.

Power.   Develop your group's knowledge and skills in conducting successful meetings (see chapter 5). Overcommunicate the processes of decision making and influence. Clarify roles and responsibilities. Assist groups in understanding the larger contexts in which local decisions are being made.

Change.   Changing environmental conditions inevitably disturbs confidence, competence, and comfort. Change is unavoidable, however, so we must help teachers, parents, and students learn to cope with change. The most practical resource we know is the work of William Bridges.[20] In the transition process, individuals and groups go through stages. It's often helpful to identify where people are and how they're feeling. Bridges outlines a three-phase process that you can use to help groups discuss what's happening and how they feel about it. Bridges also has specific recommendations about what to do at each stage to support individuals and groups through the change process. This helps the group to "let go" of past practices and adopt new ones.

Diversity.   Humans feel a need to move toward sameness. Yet schools are increasingly multidimensional in color, culture, religion, generation, cognitive style, and community compositions. Proactively teach, touch, model, and value any one of these differences, and benefits will accrue to the rest. Start anywhere. One school's core value is to respect human dignity. Teaching is continuous at that school about what it means to be human.

Civility.   Create workplace cultures of civility. The seven norms of collaboration described in chapter 3 are an excellent foundation. Be sensitive to cultural differences. "Why does the teacher yell at me?" asks a Spanish-language student, interpreting the teacher's intonation as abuse.

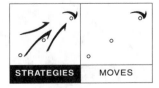

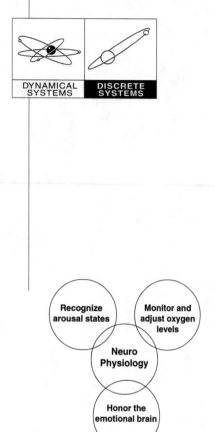

DYNAMICAL SYSTEMS · DISCRETE SYSTEMS

Recognize arousal states · Monitor and adjust oxygen levels · Neuro Physiology · Honor the emotional brain

Emotional needs. Feeling is first. When emotional needs are not addressed in problem solving, problems persist at a subterranean level, affecting everything else. People have emotional needs for influence, approval, inclusion, justice, self-esteem, autonomy, and affirmation of personal values. Listen with your heart and your eyes and with the language skills of the seven norms. Groups that practice reflective dialogue will be successful at this. Many schools that use cognitive coaching[21] in their instructional programs find an increase in teacher efficacy and satisfaction with the teaching profession.[22]

Address values, not wants. Listen to determine an adversary's hierarchy of values. Show how helping you to gain your outcome will also satisfy an important value of his or hers. Genie Laborde reports three universal classes of human values: identity, connectedness, and potency. "These needs seem to be natural processes that push for fulfillment. If you do not feel potent, you will be attracted to doing things to express your potency. If you do not know who you are, you will continue to test various traits, searching for the ones that are yours. If you do not feel connected, you will search for a partner or a cause, a religion, or a group with which to feel connected."[23]

Listen in the moment for what is most important to a person about his or her identity. Is it reputation, self-respect, success, integrity, creativity, generosity, or being "a professional"? Connectedness can be about love, honor, friendship, students' respect, religion, attractiveness, or unselfishness. Potency might be about influence, status, intelligence, choice, success, or uniqueness. At the Unhappy Elementary School, identity, connectedness, and potency were being threatened for most teachers.

Neurophysiology

"The first brain cell, or neuron, is thought to have appeared in animals about 500 million years ago. Able to form flexible connections with other cells to send and receive electrochemical messages, the neuron marked a crucial leap in evolution, second only to that of the DNA molecule that appeared some 3 billion years earlier."[24] Yet a mere moment ago in human history, modern scientists began a remarkable odyssey to understand the roles played by neurophysiology and neurochemistry in human behavior. Prior to 1969 there was no Society for Neuroscience. By 1996, the organization had 30,000 members.

While the secrets of brain geography and neurology are increasingly being revealed, practical applications of this knowledge

STRATEGIES · MOVES

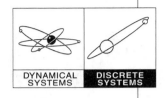

to improve behavior are still tentative. Yet enough is known already to confirm certain practices in coping with conflict and to suggest others. Our premise is that people can become more effective in conflict as they link emerging information about neurophysiology, awareness of self, and strategies for managing self and influencing others.

The following neurophysiological principles are of use in group conflict:

1. Monitor and adjust oxygen levels—one's own and others.

2. Respect arousal states.

3. Trust the emotional brain.

Monitor and Adjust Oxygen Levels

The three-and-a-half-pound mass we call the brain consumes 30% of the body's oxygen. When a person experiences stress, breathing becomes shallow, or for periods of time the breath is actually held. For the neocortex, the site of language and reasoning, to function, the brain requires a full supply of oxygen. Stress shuttles this precious resource to the limbic system to prepare the body for survival.

The study of Akido and neurophysiology intersect at this point. The word *ki,* in Japanese (*chi* in Chinese, *pneuma* in Greek and *prana* in Sanskrit), comes from the notion of breath. It is considered to be the fundamental energy that connects all things and is the source of all creative action. The Eastern martial arts share this view. By controlling the flow of *ki* in one's own body, the martial artist can achieve extraordinary powers.[25]

Educator Michael Grinder has observed in more than 5,000 classrooms. His discoveries about the nonverbal skills of classroom management and staff development[26] parallel many emerging neurophysiological findings. He has found that you can detect when breathing has stopped in a group by looking peripherally at the collection of individuals. Heads tend to jerk up as if startled, bodies are held still. A survey of torsos in the group will confirm the momentary suspension of breathing. When that happens, says Grinder, do anything to get them breathing again. Laughter, physical movement, or creating group awareness of the phenomenon are some ways to make this happen. In a one-to-one situation, moving your own body position will cause a corresponding shift in the other party and a resulting change in breathing. One cannot change physiology without an accompanying change in internal state and breathing.

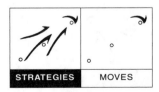

Should you notice yourself not breathing, hurry the oxygen back upstairs. Take two deep breaths—it requires two to become

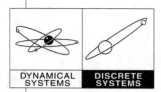

DYNAMICAL SYSTEMS / DISCRETE SYSTEMS

fully oxygenated. Center yourself. Many techniques for this exist; select one and practice it consistently until conducting the routine will effortlessly return you to a centered state.

Respect Arousal States

To respect is to notice and consider with some degree of reverence, deference, or courtesy. We choose the word *respect* quite deliberately.

The universal trigger for anger is the sense of being endangered. This can be physical danger or psychological danger; a symbolic threat to self-esteem or dignity, being treated unfairly, being insulted or demeaned, or being frustrated in achieving an important goal. These perceptions trigger a limbic surge that has a dual effect on the brain.

1. *A jump start to fight or flight.*   This stage lasts for a few minutes and is stimulated by a release of hormones called *catecholamines*. These are more commonly known as adrenaline and noradrenaline. They generate a quick rush of energy to prepare emergency conditions. The amygdala in the limbic system is the key player in this biochemical drama.

2. *A sustained arousal state.*   The second effect on the brain is another ripple driven through a branch of the nervous system, which creates a general background of action readiness. This stage can last for hours or days and helps to explain the experience of hair-trigger anger. Being repeatedly provoked, even if only by minor irritations, can take one into an arousal state. The key player is once again the amygdala.

Nonverbal language displays the presence of anger. One tool in conflict is sensory acuity of the other party's change in body state. Interestingly, the evidence is so strong that women are more adept than men in interpreting facial expression that scientists are theorizing why this might be. One line of reasoning goes to primate societies, in which dominant-submissive patterns often exist in one-to-one relationships. Female primates, often submissive, become adept at "reading" the faces of male partners. Other studies have found that men are accurate in reading unhappiness in men's faces 90% of the time but significantly less accurate in reading the same emotion in women (only 70% of the time). One theory is that in societies where males congregate and negotiate for power, the ability to discern negative emotions from another male is an important survival ability.[27]

STRATEGIES / MOVES

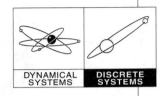

Neurologist Antonio Damasio reveals why humans behave as they do in conflict by describing what emotions are and how the whole body registers feeling (see sidebar).[28] He distinguishes *primary emotions* from *secondary emotions.*

Humans are wired at birth to respond with a primary emotion to certain features in their environment: size, types of motion, certain sounds, and certain configurations of one's own body state, such as the response to pain from a heart attack. Such features are detected and processed in the limbic system's amygdala and alter cognition in a manner that fits the state of the emotion. For this to occur, one does not need to see a specific shape, like a bear; the sensory cortexes merely need to detect and categorize key features. These primary emotions have value all by themselves because they trigger protective action—concealment from a predator, for example, or submissiveness to a large, loud adult standing too close.

For humans the next step is feeling the emotion and realizing the connection between the emotional body state and the stimulus. Some people have difficulty identifying and labeling their emotions. This is learnable except in cases of severe brain damage. The major value of this awareness is increased protection options. Once you've made the connection between stimulus X and an emotional body state, you can draw from past experiences for possible coping strategies.

The experience of secondary emotions is played out something like this. Your married daughter informs you that you are to become a grandparent. You form mental images of important aspects of this drama in your head. These stimulate modifications in different body regions. Your heart may race, your skin may flush, your lips may change size as the muscles around your mouth and eyes take on the configuration of a smile, and muscles elsewhere may relax. Or, in a different scenario, you are told that because the district is downsizing, you have lost your job or are being transferred to a position you detest. Again, representations of this event will occur in your mind, and modifications will occur in various regions of the body. Your mouth may dry up, your palms may sweat, your skin blanch, a portion of your gut contract, the muscles in your back and neck tense while your face takes on a look of sadness.

In either case, you have no choice about the electrochemical storms that surge through your body. You will experience changes in the following:

- Certain functions of viscera (heart, lungs, gut, and skin)
- Skeletal muscles attached to your bones

The essence of emotion is . . .

". . . the collection of changes in body state

that are induced in myriad organs

by nerve cell terminals,

under the control of a dedicated brain system,

which is *responding to the content of thoughts*

relative to a particular entity or event." (Emphasis ours)

—Antonio Damasio

The etymology of the word emotion *suggests a movement out, as if from the center of the body.*

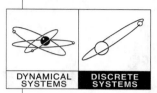

DYNAMICAL SYSTEMS | DISCRETE SYSTEMS

- Endocrine glands, such as the pituitary and adrenals
- Immune system
- Peptide modulators released from the brain into the bloodstream
- Smooth muscles in artery walls, which may contract, thinning blood vessels and causing the skin to pale, or may relax, dilating the blood vessels and causing the skin to flush

All of these responses are automatic, and many of these alterations from your normal state are observable by others. The primary emotions and secondary emotions are expressed in exactly the same neurological channels. Another way of saying this is that perception is reality. You see an angry person coming at you, and your body reacts. You *think* you see an angry person coming at you, and your body reacts the same way.

Anger, fear, happiness, love, and sadness each trigger unique bodily responses. With anger, blood flows to the hands, making it easier to grasp a weapon or strike at a foe; heart rate increases, and hormones such as adrenalin generate a pulse of energy strong enough for vigorous action. With fear, blood flows to large skeletal muscles such as the legs, making it easier to flee or fight. With happiness, increased activity in a brain center inhibits negative feelings and fosters an increase in available energy and a quieting of those feelings that generate worrisome thought. With love, tender feelings and sexual satisfaction entail parasympathetic arousal—the opposite of flight or fight; this is the relaxation response, and it facilitates calm, contentment, and cooperation. Sadness brings a drop of energy and enthusiasm for life's activities and slows the body's metabolism. This introspective withdrawal creates the opportunity to mourn a loss or a frustrated hope.

Trust the Emotional Brain

As the poet e. e. cummings wrote, feeling is first. Learning to recognize that and honor it in ourselves and others is an important resource in conflict (see box on the following page).

Neurologists have discovered several secrets of emotional functioning that help to make sense out of what appears to be illogical behavior. First is Joseph LeDoux's finding that neural pathways for feelings can bypass the neocortex. This means that there is a direct line from feeling to behavior with no intervening thought processes. Daniel Goleman, in *Emotional Intelligence*, refers to this as "hijacking the brain."[29]

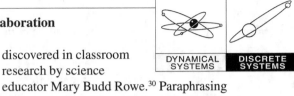

Limbic-Friendly Norms of Collaboration

Viewed from the perspective of neurophysiology, several of the norms of collaboration described in chapter 3 work directly to ease the emotional response to perceived threat. Pausing allows breathing and oxygen to the brain. Pausing also allows time for neural connections to complete their work—a longer process for kinesthetic processing than visual or auditory but, in any event, occurring between 3 and 5 seconds, the wait-time figure discovered in classroom research by science educator Mary Budd Rowe.[30] Paraphrasing affirms emotion, particularly when similar intonation is used and when feelings are named. Presuming positive intention reduces the possibility of perceived threat. Labeling intentions when inquiring or advocating signals a benign intent and reduces misunderstanding or anxiety.

A conventional view has been that the eyes and other sense organs transmit information to the thalmus and from there to the sensory processing areas of the neocortex, where signals are put together and sorted for meaning. This old theory maintains that from the neocortex, signals are sent to the limbic brain, and from there the appropriate response radiates through the rest of the brain and body. Most of the time that is so.

But LeDoux discovered a neural back alley, a shortcut that sends signals through a shorter pathway to the emotional center before the cognitive center can interpret the signals. The journey from stimulus to emotional response takes half the time of the journey to the cognitive center. So, we may spring to action before the neocortex can understand what is happening and devise a plan.

Some emotional reactions can be formed without any conscious, cognitive participation at all!

Another glimpse into emotional functioning finds that physiological processes in conflict are gender specific. Men have lower emotional flooding points than women. Once they are into negative emotions, men secrete more adrenalin into their bloodstream than women do and take longer to recover physiologically from it. Women, with higher emotional flooding points, do not mind the unpleasantness of an emotional squabble as much as men do. Additionally, perhaps because of the relatively more complete corpus callosum connection between right and left hemispheres in women, they can process emotion more quickly than men and can process emotive and cognitive thought simultaneously. This is a more difficult feat for men. In one revealing example of how these neurological differences manifest themselves, Goleman cites studies

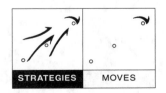

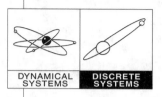

DYNAMICAL SYSTEMS | DISCRETE SYSTEMS

showing that when a husband began to stonewall in a tense conversation, his heart rate lowered by 10 beats per minute. His wife's heartbeat, however, increased to a level of stress. Both parties were engaged in a limbic dance unknown to themselves, seeking resolution in different strategies.[31]

Because neuroscience is revealing the truth beneath the claim that body states cause feelings, it validates certain tools for working with conflict. Children are often advised to feel happy and smile, to be confident and stand straight. Martial artists advise that to be calm, assume the body posture of being centered. Damasio cites research by Paul Ekman: "When he gave normal experimental subjects instructions on how to move their facial muscles, in effect 'composing' a specific emotional expression of the subjects' faces without their knowing his purpose, the result was that the subjects experienced a feeling appropriate to the expression."[32] A partially composed happy expression led to the subjects' experiencing "happiness," an angry facial expression to their experiencing "anger," and so on.

Making a fragment of the body characteristic of an emotional state is enough to produce a feeling of that emotion. The emotion produced by "faking it," though not identical, is enough to propel a person to a desired direction for coping with a situation. New evidence from electrophysiological recordings shows that make-believe smiles generate different patterns of brain waves from those generated by real smiles. This may be because a genuine smile engages the orbicularis muscle near the eyes, which is *only* under unconscious control, as well as the zygomatic muscle near the mouth, which can be controlled both consciously and unconsciously. This may also explain why people smiling for photographs often look a bit unnatural.

Finally, feelings are necessary for decisions. Contrary to the admonitions of Plato and Kant and *Star Trek's* "Mr. Spock," emotion-free forms of decision making lack efficiency. The limits of human memory make it impossible to hold all the permutations, options, and alternative decision points for even simple decisions if emotion is not present. Emotion assists decisions by producing a gut feeling associated with different scenarios you might conjure in the search for a right decision. This somatic marker will force attention either on the negative outcome of a given action or the positive outcome of another action. In effect this process reduces the number of alternatives you need to consider in any cost-benefit analysis. Somatic markers are a special instance of feelings generated from secondary emotions.

STRATEGIES | MOVES

This brief and oversimplified foray into neurophysiology suggests a variety of conflict-coping moves and tools that are in fact brain based. Some of these are the following:

- Breathe.

- Adopt body postures of calm and centerdness.

- Direct eye contact, while in rapport, can unintentionally personalize conflict and set up a limbic contest. Adopt submissive eyes when presenting information that might make the other party defensive, angry, or uncomfortable. Michael Grinder calls this three-point communication. Position yourself so that you can put printed data between you or on a chart and, keeping your eyes fixed on the data and with a gesture pointing to the data, deliver the information. With eyes and gesture still fixed on the displayed information, pause and breathe deeply, giving yourself and the other party greater access to the neocortex. Then turn, looking at the other party, and in an approachable voice state your aim in working together to either understand or resolve the problem data.

- Identify and resolve irritations as early as possible before arousal states are set.

- Notice agitated body states in the other party and do anything you can to calm them.

- Walk away when you are too tired, too hungry, or too provoked.

- Recognize and label your feelings as you are having them.

- Recognize and label the other party's feelings and legitimize them.

- Remember that all behavior has positive intention, stimulated either neurologically or physiologically in an effort to take care of oneself. Get curious, not judgmental.

- Pace and lead.

This last item is a strategic communication approach that validates the physiological states of the other party in order to move from upset to physiological readiness for reason. To pace means to meet the other person in their model of the world. A person paces to communicate, through word choices and body language, an understanding of the other person's intention, point of view, or "reality." Leading relies on a variety of language tools to expand the other party's model of the world and to evoke the internal resources necessary to achieve a desired state.

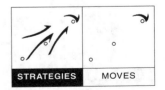

STRATEGIES   MOVES

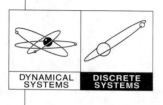

DYNAMICAL SYSTEMS — DISCRETE SYSTEMS

One paces physically by providing a mirror image of the other person's physiology—borrowing a gesture, matching posture, incorporating similar tones of voice, putting intonational stress on similar words, and communicating to the other person, through these and other out-of-awareness areas, empathy and understanding of the other person's reality. However, to meet the other person at his or her model of the world is not to live there. In the lead portion of the pace and lead, one leads by using linguistic tools to expand the other's model of the world, evoke the internal resources necessary to achieve the desired state, and expand choices available to the person.

Costa and Garmston describe the language of pacing in their work with cognitive coaching. "An effective pace includes four steps: expressing empathy, reflecting content, stating a goal, and presupposing a search for a pathway. The first two of these steps are embodied in any well-formed paraphrase. The fourth element marks the beginning of a statement that can lead the teacher to a new mental state."[33]

For example: (a) Express empathy by matching intonation and accurately describing the person's feeling: *"You're frustrated. . . ."* (b) Accurately reflect the speaker's content: "You're frustrated *because that department is blocking your attempt to change the schedule. . . ."* (c) Infer the goal the speaker is trying to achieve. Sometimes this includes a third-party goal, but always and ultimately, it will also involve a goal for the self. "You're frustrated because that department is blocking your attempt to change the schedule, and *you'd like them to be open to possibilities. . . ."* (d) Presuppose the person is seeking a pathway to attain the goal: "You're frustrated because that department is blocking your attempt to change the schedule, and you'd like them to be open to possibilities, so *you're searching for a way to make that happen."*

When you are presented with conflict, you bring your entire personal history to the stage. You also bring consciousness, the human capacity to overcome conditioning and to work effectively with physiological responses to fear, anger, disagreement, discomfort, and conflict. When you notice that your response to conflict and your strategies for dealing with it change according to whom you are in conflict with, it is a reminder that conflict begins inside of you. Help yourself and others to (a) concentrate on developing the capacity for good fighting by cultivating a group's shared emotional intelligence; (b) learn ways of calming down and calming down other parties; (c) practice empathy for yourself and others; and (d) develop the capacity for graceful fighting. "Graceful fighting" consists of the following:

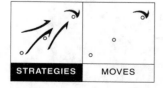

STRATEGIES — MOVES

- Search for energy traps in any problem.

- Continue to learn about conflict as viewed from Akido, systems thinking, social psychology, and neurophysiology.

- Teach the seven norms of collaboration.

- Teach groups to dialogue and discuss.

- Value human diversity. Engage groups in a self-study of what makes each person unique—cognitive style, educational belief system, culturally held assumptions, learning-style preferences—and how, collectively, each adds resources to the group.

- Listen well to yourself and to others.

In this chapter we've laid a foundation for understanding and living more effectively with conflict.[33] But what about situations in which problems are so complex that they overwhelm our normal coping capacities? Special tools for addressing unmanageable problems will be addressed in the next chapter.

End Notes

[1] Crum, T. (1987). *The magic of conflict*. New York: Touchstone Books.

[2] Amason, A. C., Thompson, K. R., Hochwarter, W. A., & Harrison, A. W. (1995, Autumn). Conflict: An important dimension in successful management teams. *Organizational Dynamics, 24* (2), 20–35.

[3] Sergiovanni, T. (1994). *Building community in schools*. San Francisco: Jossey-Bass.

[4] Zais, R. (1976). *Curriculum principles and foundations*. San Francisco: Harper & Row, p. 6.

[5] Sergiovanni, op. cit.

[6] Briggs, J. (1992). *Fractals: The patterns of chaos. Discovering a new aesthetic of art, science and nature*. New York: Touchstone, pp. 138–139. Andrei Kolmogorov, a Soviet scientist, plotted the chaos of the orbits in the asteroid belt. The mathematics in his theorem can be plotted out as a torus: a three-dimensional shape looking much like a section of a distorted bagel. This provides a visual image of the "choppy mess" when you take into account several contending planetary motions. Kolmogorov termed this torus a *vague attractor*. The term *strange attractor* was first coined as an attempt at scientific humor when scientists wanted to study similiar forces in dynamical systems like weather or mountain streams. In these systems, every movement affects every other

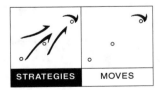

STRATEGIES   MOVES

movement, yet while weather is constantly changing, it also stays within the boundaries of what we call *climate,* just as a rushing stream stays within its banks. In such systems each iteration of feedback folds into a new region of space within the outline of its strange attractor. In similiar fashion, when a school is organized around values, the values become a strange attractor. Respect for human differences may be manifested in respect for students, which influences respect for staff, which influences respect for community members, which influences views about cooperation and conflict, and so on.

[7] Laborde, G. Z. (1984). *Influencing with integrity: Management skills for commmunication and negotiation.* Palo Alto, CA: Sytony.

[8] Bailey, S. (1996, August 8) *Sensing and managing the surround: Physical dimensions, social dimensions, symbolic and emotional dimensions.* Presented at The Adaptive School Leadership Institute, Tahoe City, CA.

[9] Iwanicki, E. (1998). Evaluation in supervision. In G. Firth & E. Pajak (Eds.), *Handbook of research on school supervisison* (pp. 138–175). New York: Macmillan. Findings on the positive relationship between teacher evaluation and teaching improvement are mixed. Iwanicki notes that "the current attention to rewards and sanctions is somewhat surprising, because there is no evidence to support the theory that accountability models aimed at sanctioning programs or personnel have had a positive effect on the quality of education" (p. 141).

During the 1970s and 1980s, many teacher evaluation programs became committed to "weeding out" less effective teachers, and *evaluation* became a four-letter word. Other programs committed themselves to improving, not proving, and often gained reputations for high-quality programs.

See also Darling-Hammond, L., & Sclan, E. (1992). Policy and supervision. In C. Glickman (Ed.), *Supervision in transition* (pp. 7–29), Alexandria, VA: Association for Supervision and Curriculum Development. Some teacher evaluation programs make teaching worse, not better. For example, in a study seeking to validate Georgia's Teacher Performance Assessment Instrument, two of the instrument's behaviors actually produced significant negative correlations with teachers' effectiveness, as measured by student achievement gain.

[10] Mecoy, L. (1998, July 27). District turns up the heat on poor students. *The Sacramento Bee,* pp. A1, A10.

[11] Garmston, R., & Wellman, B. (1998). Teacher talk that makes a difference. *Educational Leadership, 55* (7), 30–34.

[12] Cited in Crum, T. (1987). *The magic of conflict.* New York: Touchstone Books, pp. 243, 252.

[13] Ibid, p. 53.

[14] Ibid.

[15] Smith, M. (1975). *When I say no I feel guilty.* New York: Bantom Books.

[16] The importance of rapport in human interactions is treated many places. A good source is Costa A., & Garmston, R. (1985). *Cognitive coaching: A foundation for renaissance schools.* Norwood, MA: Christopher-Gordon. See especially chapter 3, pp. 34–55. Another is O'Conner, J., & Seymour, J. (1990). *Introducing neuro-linguistic programming: The new psychology of excellence,* (pp. 36–41). London: Mandala, pp. 34–55.

[17] Garmston, R., & Wellman, B. (1998, March). *Exploring vital questions about conflict, interdependence and group development.* Paper delivered at ASCD Annual Conference, San Antonio, TX.

[18] Crum, p. 109.

[19] Teacher efficacy has been identified as a variable accounting for individual differences in teaching effectiveness. Studies by Armor, Berman, & McGlouglin and Brookover, Brophy, & Evertson support this finding. See Gibson, S., & Dembo, M. (1984). Teacher efficacy: A construct validation. *Journal of Educational Pyschology, 76* (4), 569–582. More recently, in a 3-year study investigating the results of cognitive coaching on teacher efficacy (among other factors) and student success, similiar results were found. See Edwards, J., Green, K., Lyons, C., Rogers, M., & Sword, M. (1988). *The effects of cognitive coaching and non-verbal classroom management on teacher efficacy and perceptions of school culture.* Paper presented at the Annual Meeting of the American Educational Research Association, San Diego, CA.

[20] Bridges, W. (1980). *Making sense of life's changes: Transitions.* New York: Addison-Wesley; and Bridges, W. (1991). *Managing transitions: Making the most of changes.* Reading, MA: Addison-Wesley.

[21] Costa, A., & Garmston, R. (1994). *Cognitive coaching: A foundation for renaissance schools.* Norwood, MA: Christopher-Gordon.

[22] Edwards, J., Rogers, S., & Swords, M. (1998*). The pleasant view experience.* Golden, CO: Jefferson County Public Schools.

[23] Laborde, G. (1984). *Influencing with integrity: Management skills for communication and negotiation.* Palo Alto, CA: Syntony, p. 163.

[24] Kotulak, R. (1996). *Inside the brain: Revolutionary discoveries of how the mind works.* Kansas City: Andrews and McMeel, p. 14.

[25] Leonard, G. (1991). *Mastery: The keys to success and long term fulfillment.* New York: Penguin Books, pp. 161–162.

[26] Grinder, M. (1993). *EnVoy: Your personal guide to classroom management.* Battle Ground, WA: Michael Grinder & Associates.

[27] Blum, D. (1997). *Sex on the brain: The biological differences between men and women.* New York: Viking, p. 79.

[28] Damasio, A. (1994). *Descartes' Error: Emotion, reason, and the human brain.* New York: Avon Books, p. 139.

[29] Goleman, D. (1995). *Emotional intelligence: Why it can matter more than IQ.* New York: Bantam Books, p. 14.

[30] Rowe, M. B. (1983). Getting chemistry off the killer course list. *Journal of Chemical Education, 60* (1), 954–956.

[31] Goleman, p. 139.

[32] Damasio, p. 139.

[32] Costa, & Garmston, p. 145.

[33] We are greatful to Robert Chadwick of Consensus Associates in Terrebonne, Oregon for much practical information about working with conflict. His views and approaches have richly influenced our work.

Chapter 10 Working With Unmanageable Problems

IT WAS THE best of times, it was the worst of times, it was the age of wisdom, it was the age of foolishness, it was the epoch of incredulity, it was the season of light, it was the season of darkness, it was the winter of despair, we had everything before us, we had nothing before us, we were all going direct to heaven, we were all going direct the other way—in short, the period was so far like the present period, that some of its noisiest authorities insisted on its being received, for good or for evil, in the superlative degree of comparison only.

—Charles Dickens
A Tale of Two Cities

this chapter features:

Getting work done
Doing the right work
Working collaboratively
Managing systems
Developing groups
Adapting to change

In a world where change itself is changing, educators are caught between trusted assumptions about how things work and a slow, dawning awareness that current ways of thinking and long-trusted tools are no longer capable of solving the problems that beset them. The emerging organizational and professional landscape holds both "a high, hard ground of technical knowledge—conveyed as discrete practices, methods, techniques, and tips—and a low-lying swamp of messy problems, persistent dilemmas, and perennial perplexities for which no evident technical knowledge exists."[1] Our purpose in this chapter is to honor and illuminate the increasing complexities that surround practitioners and to propose lenses and approaches for recognizing, correctly identifying, and grappling with the persistent problems that beset and entangle present-day schools and schooling. Such persistent problems are wicked in their complexity. They often defy logical solutions, especially when educators attempt to apply tools best suited to tamer issues.

We were recently at a school that had become concerned about its report cards and reporting practices. The staff members who surfaced this issue were committed professionals. They convened a task force, invited parents to participate,

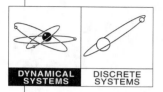

collected examples of report cards from other districts and schools, and set about in a rational and orderly process to resolve this issue. Then things got messy. Parents not on the task force grew apprehensive about the proposed move away from letter grades. If familiar points of reference were lost, how would they really know how their children were doing? Several teachers worried about the added paperwork, and others were concerned about being criticized for seemingly subjective ratings. The local press made connections to a similar controversy happening in a nearby district. The school board got involved, and soon there were advocates on all sides of the issue. The poor beleaguered teachers who had started the project were overwhelmed and depressed. All they had wanted was to improve the reporting system so that parents would have better and more timely information about their children's progress.

The problem here stemmed from using tried and trusted planning and problem-solving strategies on the wrong type of problem. By applying traditional, step-by-step, linear problem-solving approaches to problems that are, at their core, nonlinear and filled with complexities, we encounter unpredictable barriers. These lead to more tangles and frustrations that sap the creative problem-solving energies of individuals and groups. Over time, this drains the will to persist or to even attempt to resolve issues. Avoidance and apathy are then the ultimate by-products and outcomes of these attempts.

These are rapidly changing times, with increasing demands for accountability and higher-than-ever stakes both socially and politically. Educators need to increase their resourcefulness and their repertoires for dealing with complexity, problems generated by other problems, and attempted solutions to those problems.

Certain types of problems occur repeatedly. In slightly different form, in new costumes, the same types of problems appear as a changing cast of characters. Attempts to fix them often make something else in the system worse. These problems, as Ross Perot might say, are creating a giant sucking sound in our schools, vacuuming away efficacy and the will to persist and proactively address them.

Our own frustration and curiosity about these issues has driven us to explore the literature in four areas to better understand these phenomena: private sector organizational development; systems theory; the new sciences—especially the work on chaos theory, ecoliteracy, and complexity theory; and the reexamination of problem solving in organizations in the work of Rosabeth Moss Kanter, Kurt Lewin, and Gareth Morgan.[2] We are currently testing fresh ideas and tools with the groups with whom we are working.

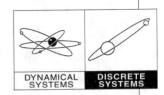

This chapter presents our learning from this work-in-progress and some emerging, cautious conclusions.

To begin our explorations, we started by taking a closer look at the terms we were using. Language holds layers of meaning, and we wanted to get below the surface and explore options and nuances.

Four Key Terms

The key terms in our journey are *solutions*, *tame problems*, *wicked problems*, and *adaptive responses*.

Solutions

Conventionally, a solution is a resolution to an undesirable situation. A solution approach is a method or process of solving a problem. A problem is a condition that is deemed undesirable. The word *problem* carries a subtext or assumption, which is that once identified, it has or requires a solution. A solution is also the answer to a question. As we will explain later in this chapter, question formation may be more important than solution seeking.

In the physical sciences, the term *solution* carries a two-part meaning. First, a solution is a spontaneously forming homogeneous mixture of two or more substances. Notice the language here—*spontaneously*—meaning in the moment without identifiable outside agents, and *homogeneous*—meaning blended together. Adding cream to a cup of coffee forms a homogeneous solution between the cream and the coffee that cannot be undone by simple means. The second part of the scientific definition of solution is that when two or more substances come together in this manner, they maintain a homogeneous constitution in all subdivision, down to the molecular level.

This last notion is important when dealing with certain types of problems in schools and districts. Many problems get "solved" at the policy level but remained entrenched at the school and classroom level or within teacher-to-student relationships or adult-to-adult relationships. It also works in the other direction, such as when teachers attempt to develop more democratic classrooms and more democratic schools. The existing power relationships in the school, district, state, or province are unlikely to shift, and the system stays stuck in hierarchical arrangements.[3]

Tame Problems

Tame problems have predictable barriers, established means, and clearly defined outcomes (Fig. 10-1). Tame problems can be com-

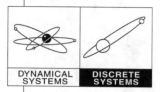

plex, but they eventually bend to conventional strategies and working methods. Known algorithms apply, and the problem can be worked "inside the box." Cause-and-effect relationships are discernible and usually close together in time. These interactions may be complex, but they do not have the dynamical, nonlinear nature of wicked problems. In tame problems, the properties of the system maintain their identity before, during, and after interactions.

Figure 10-1. Tame Problems

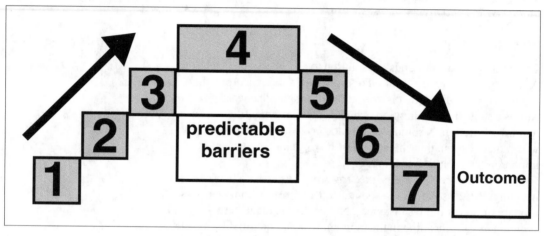

A broken automobile is a prime example of a tame problem. A skilled mechanic isolates the cause of the breakdown, removes the broken part, installs the new part, readjusts the system, and hands the owner the bill. All other properties of the automobile system are unchanged by the breakdown and retain this same integrity after the offending part is replaced.

Action research in schools is one approach to tame problems. Committed educators gather data, generate interventions, and compare results with goals. Modifications arise from emerging action-knowledge.

One school with which we worked confronted the problem of poor spelling in this way after the school secretary pointed out that students were misspelling words that were on the "official" high-frequency-usage lists. These errors appeared in daily work and in notes to the office. Teachers and other staff members collected examples of misspellings, informally interviewed younger students on their attitudes toward correct spelling, and held dialogues with the older students about this issue. One month later the staff gathered after school to pool information, draw conclusions, and appoint a

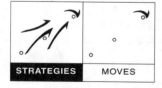

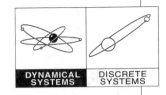

task force to develop an intervention plan. The problem as they now understood it was that students did not think that daily spelling was important. The solution centered on ways to change this attitude by sending a united message to students and parents that this mattered both in school and in life outside school.

Districts draw from their repertoire of tools for tame problems when they work to get out the "yes" vote for bond elections. This solution approach finds hard-working administrators and board members talking to their peers in other districts, interviewing political consultants, tapping the knowledge base of professional organizations, and crafting plans for positively influencing potential supporters and motivating them to vote on election day.

While this example has greater complexity than the spelling scenario, tame approaches still carry the day. The weight of collective wisdom, effort, and solid execution of details prevails in such situations as long as good choices are made regarding strategy and implementation.

Wicked Problems

Wicked problems are tenacious and nonlinear. They contain unpredictable barriers and recur, folding back on themselves. With each iteration, wicked problems increase in complexity as they cycle within and through the system (Fig. 10-2). Existing ways of thinking cannot handle wicked problems. Individuals and groups require new mental models for problem finding and problem approaches.

The distinction between tame and wicked problems was first developed by the German physicist Horst Rittel.[4] Physics seemed to Rittel to be a "normal science." This latter term was coined by the philosopher of science, Thomas Kuhn,[5] to describe the typical "tame" problems that well-applied scientific methods can solve. Many of these problems are difficult and require hard thinking and number crunching, but they eventually yield to logic and classical mathematics.

In turning his attention to the field of operations research, Rittel encountered problems in the specialized fields of architecture and city planning that seemed to defy common ways of thinking. The problems in this new field were often difficult to define, let alone solve. Solutions to parking problems generated sticking points in traffic flow, which drove more people to public transportation, which soon become overcrowded, which created the need for additional buses and trains, which further jammed traffic, and so on.

Many wicked problems cannot, in fact, really be solved. They need to be understood by individuals and organizations who learn

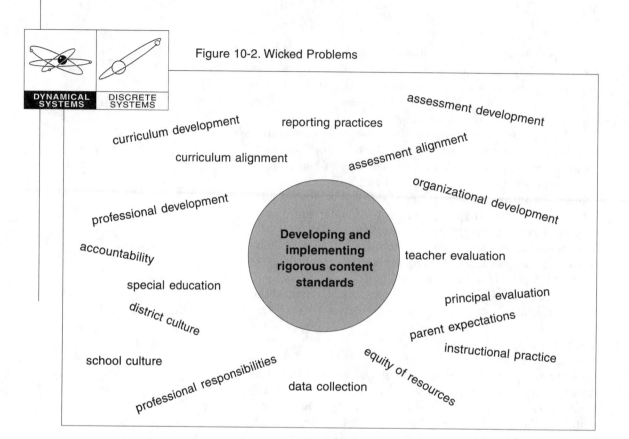

Figure 10-2. Wicked Problems

DYNAMICAL SYSTEMS

DISCRETE SYSTEMS

curriculum development

reporting practices

assessment development

curriculum alignment

assessment alignment

organizational development

professional development

Developing and implementing rigorous content standards

teacher evaluation

accountability

principal evaluation

special education

parent expectations

district culture

instructional practice

school culture

professional responsibilities

data collection

equity of resources

how to correctly identify wicked problems and live effectively with them. Such problems force groups to work outside past patterns and practices. Individual schools cannot import ready-made solutions from other sources. Chaos theory holds that each setting is subtly different and that potential solutions have a sensitive dependence on initial conditions.[6] The culture of an organization; its social, political, and technical resources; and the community it serves are just a few of the variables that set the stage differently for the same proposed solution.

Wicked problems have a fractal nature. They operate across the levels of the organization, with repeated images at each level. Fractal geometry is the basic pattern of nature.[7] A stem of broccoli follows the fractal pattern. As you cut it apart, each stalk looks like a smaller version of the larger stalk. Schools operate with many fractal patterns, both good and bad. How people talk to one another at any level is a fractal image of the whole. Respect and consideration at one level repeats throughout the system. The issues of power and control

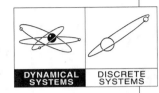

commented on by Seymour Sarason[8] are another fractal pattern. Legislatures try to control school boards, who try to control superintendents, who try to control principals, who try to control teachers, who try to control children.

Wicked problems surround schools today. Educational goal tensions tug at political and curriculum processes in many communities. How do schools both prepare students for an unknowable future and conserve the values of the majority culture? Changing demographics find many communities unprepared for issues and concerns that are supposed to be happening only in other places. The exploding special education population and the push for greater inclusion of children with disabilities finds budgets and teacher capacities strained and barely coping in many places. Proponents and opponents line up on all sides of these issues, unable to hear each other through the filters of their own beliefs. Psychologist Robert Kegan[9] calls this self-sealing logic. Beliefs and values form institutions of thought that reinforce themselves and exclude contrary data and viewpoints.

These and similar problems are not likely to go away. The level of complexity in society and in schools is likely to increase, not decrease. These changes, in turn, will spawn other changes not yet imaginable.

Table 10-1 shows the differences between tame and wicked problems.

Table 10-1. Tame vs. Wicked Problems

Tame Problems	Wicked Problems
• An algorithm exists	• Known algorithms are inadequate
• Can be worked "inside the box"	• Require new mental models
• Lend themselves to action research	• Are dynamical, producing emergent phenomena within systems and subsystems
• Direct and discernible cause-and-effect relationships are apparent	• Have a fractal nature
• Interactions may be complex but are not dynamical	• Recur, folding back on themselves and amplify with each iteration
• Properties of the system maintain their identity before, during, and after interactions	• Contain values conflicts rooted in self-sealing logic

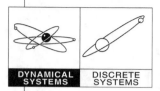

DYNAMICAL SYSTEMS   DISCRETE SYSTEMS

Developing and implementing rigorous content standards is a vivid example of a wicked problem that many schools, districts, states, and provinces are confronting these days. On the surface it looks like a logical and straightforward proposition. School districts form committees of content experts who define what students should know and be able to do at selected checkpoints. They then float these drafts for educator and citizen review and sit back waiting for constructive feedback. As most such committees have discovered, the various belief systems soon collide with battles over just what content is most important, the place of a multicultural perspective within the curriculum, and the balance of content with process skills development.

This is just the beginning. Developing content standards is not the same as assessing them. Just what is good work? What are appropriate quality and performance standards at each level? How many different assessments does a student need to complete before the system has confidence in his or her knowledge and skills? What is the place of norm-referenced testing in this new standards system? And what are the new graduation requirements?

The assessment issue is one of many related issues. No part of the system can remain untouched if this devilishly wicked problem is going to be worked through successfully. We have shared the graphic in Figure 10-2 with several groups and asked them to fill in any missing elements. Most groups double the number of items inside the circle that require addressing related to developing and implementing rigorous content standards.

We know of very few districts that have embraced the complexity of this issue. We were told in one district not to even bring up the issue of aligning the teacher contract and evaluation system with the adopted academic standards. The personnel office and school board had recently, and to their minds successfully, completed a new contract negotiation with the teachers' association. The fact that the contract was based on outdated modes of instruction and norms of professional behavior was swept aside in the relief that this task was finished. Any thoughts that the new contract would in fact stall and possibly mutate the implementation of the content standards were not to be considered at this time.

Adaptive Responses

School faculties, site councils, teams, and departments all need to expand their repertoires of adaptive responses if they are to successfully learn to address wicked problems. These responses contain both cognitive and emotional resources.

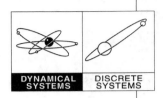

Difficulties arise from several patterns of human behaviors. At W. L. Gore & Associates, the makers of GoreTex™, teams well trained in communication and meeting skills still run into difficulty when confronting wicked problems.[10] Hardworking groups there still have the following patterns and tendencies:

1. Prematurely locking into problem definitions and particular solutions

2. Widely different recall of key issues, decisions, and proposed courses of action by group members after a meeting

3. A desire to operate as small teams, working by consensus, and not always wanting to engage a larger team with greater perspective

4. Becoming impatient and so lost in issues and tasks that group members forget to use effective meeting processes

Leaders and planners at W. L. Gore & Associates eventually realized that there was a mismatch between the types of tasks confronting teams and the resources that teams brought to bear on those tasks. In essence they were using tame processes for wicked problems.

Similar difficulties burden most schools today. The problems before them overmatch the resources within them. We offer the following adaptive responses as a beginning set of resources for groups to cultivate. These responses help groups to correctly identify problem types as tame or wicked. They also help groups frame questions within each problem type. These eight response patterns interact with one another. They are not presented in priority order. Each influences the others. The adaptive responses are as follows:

1. Locate the system.
2. Challenge assumptions.
3. Engage and value cognitive conflict.
4. Capacitate post-institutional thought.
5. Develop norms of dialogue.
6. Name the elephants.
7. Manage the surround.
8. Engage double-loop learning.

Locate the System

Margaret Wheatley reminds us that a system isn't a system unless it knows it is a system.[11] The challenge for individuals and groups is in

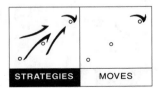

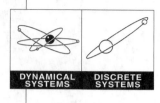

learning to look for and to see the systems and subsystems of which they are a part. Wicked problems live inside systems in which everything influences everything else. Gaps in cause-and-effect sequences hide the foundations of difficulties from those who are confronting the issues. The roots of low math performance in the eighth grade, for example, lie not in the seventh grade but lower still, somewhere in elementary school. Information gaps between schools keep such information hidden from the system, and hardworking middle-school math teachers struggle onward year by year.

Biologists Humberto Maturana and Francisco Varela remind us that natural systems cannot be directed, only disturbed.[12] No intervention can magically turn a system to a new way of being or a new way of operating. Systems choose what to notice and where to pay attention. Since tiny events create a major disturbance, the trick is to focus energy on positive tiny events that disturb the system productively. The seven norms of collaboration form one set of tiny positive events that operate with fractal qualities across the levels of the system. The next chapter presents a section on systems thinking and places to intervene in a system.

Challenge Assumptions

Assumptions define reality.

Assumptions and mental models define reality and frame problem definitions and solution approaches. Any list of brainstormed ideas and brainstormed questions contain embedded assumptions. When these assumptions go unexamined, they guide and distort thinking to fit the pattern of the mental models. Tremendous resources can then be spent solving the wrong problem.

Individuals, organizations, and cultures are guided by operating metaphors. The so called "war on drugs" is a case in point. We have been fighting this war for a generation at a cost of billions and billions of dollars. Borders are patrolled, prisons fill, people die, and vast sums of money corrupt officials here and abroad. But since we are fighting a war, all this makes sense.

What if the government ran a quest for health instead of a war on drugs? What tools and approaches would be needed? Where would money be spent? What new social and political institutions might arise to manage such a quest?

Working groups need to learn to surface and inquire into their own and others' assumptions. The assumptions wall described in Chapter 6 is one way to do this. In general, group members need to develop the skills of inquiry to get below the surface of language and concepts. The seven norms of collaboration presented in chapter 3 are vital to this process.

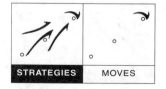

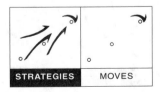

Question brainstorming is another way to surface assumptions. Given a topic, group members brainstorm all the questions they have about the topic. When a reasonable number of questions emerges, they are categorized and labeled. The group then steps back and names the assumptions that produced the questions.

Engage and Value Cognitive Conflict

Ideas are honed by dialogue and discussion. Conflict is the instrument of this honing. The previous chapter described ways to get smart about conflict and the differences between cognitive and affective conflict. We mention it here again to emphasize the point that groups without cognitive conflict get stuck in the opinions and mental models of leaders and the most vocal members. Inquiry and cognitive conflict push past this pattern and engage the group's collective mind in problem definition and solution finding.

Capacitate Post-Institutional Thought

Developmental psychologists Robert Kegan and Lisa Lahey outline three stages of adult development.[13] Not all individuals successfully move through all three stages; some maintain stability at a given stage for most of their adult life. The first stage is called the *interpersonal stage*. Relationships with people and or ideas govern this stage. Validation comes from external criteria. The values and beliefs of others are uncritically internalized. There is a dependency on others—"I am my relationships."

The second stage is labeled the *institutional stage*. Self-authorship, self-ownership, and self-initiation define this stage. Validation comes from internal criteria. Personal standards and self-evaluation shape values and beliefs, which form the institution of self. This "institution" holds assumptions about how the world works and one's place in it. People at this stage operate independently of others—"I have relationships."

The third stage is called the *post-institutional stage*. Most people who achieve this phase do not do so before the age of 40. Here identity develops through reflection and modification of the self within the systems of which the self is a part. Validation comes from openness to questions, possibilities, conflict, and reconstruction. Continual inquiry and data from outside oneself shape values and beliefs. Adults at this stage are consciously interdependent with others—"There are relationships, and I am part of them."

To capacitate post-institutional thought, groups need to be able to surface their mental models and step outside them for examination

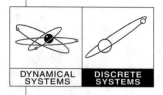

DYNAMICAL SYSTEMS | DISCRETE SYSTEMS

and reflection. Dialogue and graphic tools like mind mapping offer new insights and perspectives.

Develop Norms of Dialogue

In chapters 3 and 4, we presented seven norms of collaboration and the differences between dialogue and discussion. These skills and the practice of dialogue within groups form the basic tool kit for wicked problems. Talking together about how problems are being constructed by the group offers viewpoints not always available to individuals grappling with such problems alone.

Name the Elephants

Organizational theorist Chris Argyris claims that all organizations have defensive routines to protect them from facing hard truths.[14] To intervene in these systems, he looks for ways to "name the elephants in the living room" that no one wants to talk about. To do so he asks his clients, "What don't you talk about around here?" and "Why don't you talk about the fact that you don't talk about it?"

These two simple questions offer up the deep structure of the organization for examination and modification. The high school that sends 80% of its students on to post-secondary education learns to ask about and talk about the other 20% as more than unmotivated problems to live with until graduation day. The middle school that chews up and spits out principals every few years learns to look at itself and stop looking for saviors. And the elementary school with chronically low reading scores looks for the system that builds literacy instead of the system that drives standardized test scores.

Manage the Surround

This concept comes to us from the work of David Perkins in his book *Smart Schools,*[15] in which he defines the surround as the features around learners that by their very presence mediate thinking and behavior. Designing the surround is one of the meeting success principles we described in chapter 5. It is especially important for work on wicked problems. Graphic displays of thinking in the form of charts, graphs. focusing questions, systems maps, and the like all support shared cognition and perspective development.

The emotional space for work with wicked problems is especially important. The environment must be safe for individuals to surface deeply held beliefs and assumptions. Paraphrasing and use of the most approachable voice are essential if reluctant group members are to gather the courage to think out loud with others.

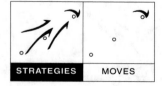

STRATEGIES | MOVES

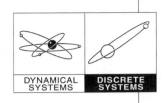

Engage Double-Loop Learning

Chris Argyris and Donald Schon developed the concept of double-loop learning (Fig. 10-3) to help individuals and organizations locate deep-seated problems.[16] With single-loop learning, problem solvers get caught in loops of action and reaction. Action does not always lead to accomplishment. In some schools, working hard and caring about kids gets lost in these unproductive rounds.

Figure 10-3. Double-Loop Learning

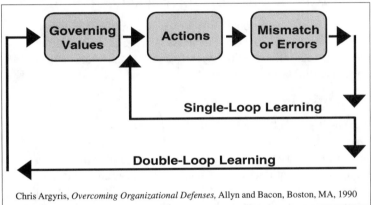

Chris Argyris, *Overcoming Organizational Defenses,* Allyn and Bacon, Boston, MA, 1990

Double-loop learning assumes that if significant mismatches occur between action and results, the problem may lie elsewhere. Usually it is found in the governing beliefs and values of the organization. The call for more alternative schools for students who are maladapted to traditional programs is one such example of the single-loop problem. Some districts now have alternative-to-the-alternative programs.

This problem definition assumes that there is a "real school" that fits the needs of most students, and that those who are outside this norm need an alternative. The governing values here do not see all students as needing options, flexibility, and close relationships with adults. Assumptions about economies of scale may require reexamination in light of higher retention rates, higher dropout rates, and alienated learners.

To engage double-loop learning, groups search for the values and beliefs beneath both their questions and their answers. Who benefits from the proposed solutions? What beliefs about learning and change seem to be at work here? Who loses what as this plan moves forward?

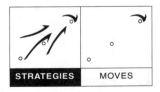

These eight adaptive responses and the strategies described in this book provide both a road map and a tool kit for persistent problems. The first step for groups is to learn to identify and correctly categorize problems as being either tame or wicked. When wicked problems are identified, groups need to emotionally prepare themselves for new ways of thinking, including inventing process tools. Posting the eight adaptive responses on the wall is one way to remind group members that this problem requires care and thoughtfulness.

Additional Tools for Wicked Problems

Here are several additional tools for wicked problems. These tools help groups to see complex and messy issues and support group members to develop flexibility, craftsmanship, and consciousness about their thinking.

Futures Wheel

The futures wheel is a graphic tool for forecasting ripple effects resulting from an innovation or a disaster. It is based on the premise that any event has both positive and negative ripple effects. The aftermath of a natural disaster is an excellent case in point. The physical destruction creates many ongoing negative effects on the environment and on peoples' lives. Often, however, building codes are reexamined and rewritten based on what scientists and engineers learn by examining the wreckage.

Well-intended innovations also have positive and negative ripple effects. The quest for higher standards in schools raises the bar once again for special-needs students. Higher graduation requirements may in fact demotivate some learners. This in turn upsets parents who have struggled to keep kids in school and off the streets, which in turn creates political upset and challenges to inflexible barriers.

On the other side of this coin comes the need for better communication between teachers and schools. Higher standards drive home gaps in assessment systems and in teachers' knowledge of assessment, which in turn promotes a desire and need for professional development activities. This leads to deep conversations about teaching and learning, which opens up teachers' sense of themselves and of their collective mission.

Leaders and facilitators need to help groups look for intended and unintended ripple effects. This tool is one way to do this. To apply it to a task, innovation, or project, share the graphic organizer in Figure 10-4.

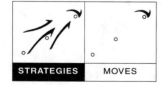

STRATEGIES MOVES

Figure 10-4. The Futures Wheel

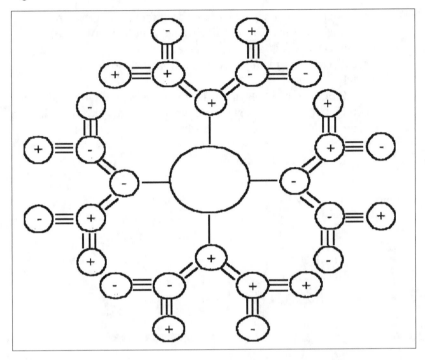

To use the futures wheel, proceed with the following steps:

1. Write the name of the event or innovation in the center circle.

2. Work outward. At the first inner layer of circles, notice that there are two negatives and two positives. For maximum thinking stretch, the negatives and positives at each layer should be as diverse as possible from one another.

3. Now proceed to the second layer. Notice that each negative and each positive leads to its own negative and positive ripple effect.

4. Move to the third layer in a similar manner. Group members are often surprised at the possible positive and negative effects at the third layer.

5. Depending on the topic, group members can now explore potential changes in policy or can brainstorm options that might thrive in the new environment.

The futures wheel is an excellent launching point for study groups and task forces.

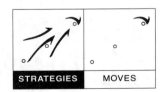

STRATEGIES   MOVES

Desired-State Map

Groups have a tendency to get stuck describing, and therefore sometimes wallow in, the existing state of a problem. War stories accumulate, energy flags, and progress toward solution stalls. In these cases, group members focus on what they don't want, not on what they do want.

Prominently displaying a desired-state map (Figure 10-5) in a meeting room creates a key element in that group's surround, shaping and modifying behavior by its presence and message. Within experienced groups, someone invariably notices the stalled conversation and references this guidepost.

Figure 10-5. Desired-State Map

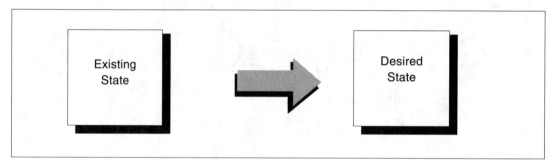

Groups skilled in applying this map learn to articulate a positive desired state rich in detail about what they would see and hear in the environment and in groups or individuals who are the locus of change. They also learn to operate within the arrow, developing resources and strategies to manifest the desired state.

For a more detailed look at this process, we offer the next planning tool.

Outcome Mapping

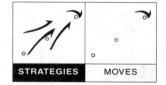

The outcome map (Figure 10-6) is a tool for planning backwards. It is developed from right to left. When completed, the plan can then be run forward to achieve the desired outcomes.

The group first identifies the problem in column 1. In column 2, group members craft an outcome statement that captures this ideal state in its positive form. Such statements describe what the group wants to have happen, not what it does *not* want to occur. (Example:

Figure 10-6 Outcome Mapping

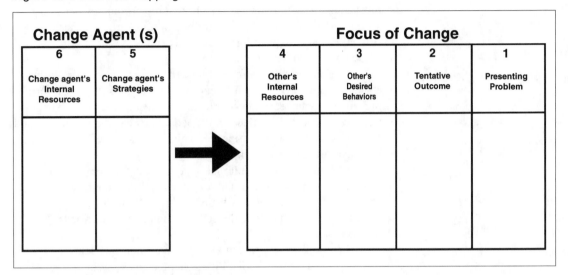

We want to see and hear low-performing students demonstrate and articulate good study skills and knowledge of their own learning styles in action. Not: We don't want to see low-performing students fall further behind in our classes.)

In column 3, identify the desired behaviors by individuals or groups that are the focus of this change. Such behaviors must be explicit and specific. This is the toughest and most difficult section of the outcome map. The norm of probing for specificity is an important listening and linguistic tool to apply to this task.

Behaviors must be "SMART." We described these in chapter 7 on page 141 (see Table 7-2) in relation to meeting design. They are so important in outcome mapping that we are restating them here:

S   Specific

M   Measurable (how many times, at what frequency, where, and when)

A   Attainable (in reach of the targeted person or group)

R   Relevant (to larger purposes, for the change agents and for the focus of change)

T   Tactically sound (fitting the ecology of the culture and of individuals, not expecting people to radically change behaviors that are deeply embedded and safe because this may be expecting too much too soon)

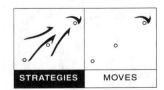

Lists of behaviors must be winnowed to those that are deemed most catalytic within the setting. Often three or four key behaviors set up positive ripple effects for individuals and groups. These behaviors can then be monitored as the prime assessment and feedback system for this change effort.

This is another example of how tiny events have major influences and how everything influences everything else. Low-performing students who learn to understand how they learn best will begin to advocate for their own learning needs. They can then plan time and strategies with greater confidence, which builds self-efficacy and produces greater success in the classroom.

Column 4, Other's Internal Resources, is the true focus of change in this process. Internal resources include knowledge, skills, attitudes, and the five energy sources described in chapter 8. These are the resources that drive the catalytic behaviors described in the previous step.

In our example, student knowledge of their own learning styles, both strengths and liabilities become an essential first resource. This is followed by skills that match and stretch these styles, such as various outlining tools, graphic organizers, and content reading skills. Key attitudes might include the connection between effort and success and the payoffs of delayed gratification.

Completion of these first four columns is a prerequisite to working on the left side of the map. For novice groups, this will take some discipline. Typical problem solving approaches promote this stage before most groups are ready for it. Without clearly defined outcomes and clear measures of success, groups get lost in activity thinking instead of outcome thinking. Each type of thinking sets up a different assessment system, both formally and informally. Activity thinking values hard work and effort. Outcome thinking values results, feedback, and "on-the-fly" modifications aimed at achieving the goal.

In column 5, planners brainstorm and select strategies to develop the internal resources of individuals and or groups that are the focus of change efforts. Again, planners select the most catalytic behaviors to apply to this setting. Doing a few things well and consistently usually outperforms a shotgun approach. Successful change agents follow through on the details, keep detailed anecdotal records, collect other data and artifacts, and assess as they go.

In order to work the plan that develops, change agents need access to their own internal resources. These are defined in column 6. Knowledge, skills, attitudes, and energy sources drive change-agent behavior.

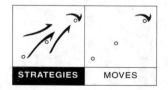

STRATEGIES   MOVES

In our example on page 235, the adult change agents themselves need knowledge of learning styles and how that knowledge is best developed in students of all performance levels. They then need self-awareness of their own teaching styles and how those styles support and limit the learners about whom they have the greatest concerns. This in turn drives the need for flexibility in planning, teaching, and assessing student learning.

Most deeply entrenched and wicked problems require resources of patience, compassion, and persistence on the part of change agents. Problems that develop over years do not usually go away with simple solutions.

Outcome mapping can also be applied by groups to themselves. In this case the right-side of the map will suffice. The group becomes its own focus of change by articulating an outcome for itself and developing vivid examples of desired behaviors to see or hear in their interactions with one another. They then move on to clarify their needed internal resources. The final part of this plan is to develop ways to support the internal resources as they do other important work.

Planning Models

Groups need to develop a variety of planning models. We propose the following as examples to draw from and to modify for a variety of problems and issues. One type, Action Planning (Fig. 10-7), works with tame problems. Keep in mind that such problems may be complex, but the parts can be isolated and addressed separately. The other type, Dynamical Action Planning (Fig. 10-8), works with wicked problems. This type of planning is much harder to capture graphically. It requires three-dimensional thinking and fluidity in action.

Action Planning

Action planning consists of the following steps:

1. **Clarify outcomes.** Outcome thinking is central to all planning processes. For the typical tame problem, this is a necessary first step.

2. **Anticipate challenges.** What barriers might be encountered along the way? What interest groups should be consulted to offer perspectives and concerns? What technical resources will be required?

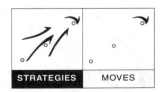

Figure 10-7. Action Planning

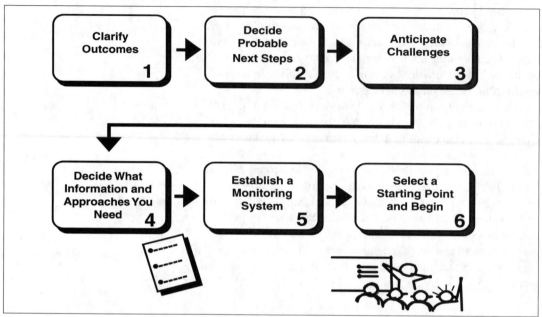

3. **Decide probable next steps.** Who will do what by when? What ripple effects might be encountered?

4. **Decide what information and approaches you need.** These include: data, ideas, decision criteria, forecasts, connections, consensus, understanding, perspective, shared goals, analysis, articulation, and ownership.

5. **Establish a monitoring system.** How will you know that you are making progress? What indicators of success or mismatch are most vital? What form will data take? Who will collect and analyze the data?

6. **Select a starting point and begin.** Based on steps 4 and 5, select an avenue of entry, marshal your resources, and begin. Monitoring data along the way allows for course corrections and changes in direction.

Dynamical Action Planning

Dynamical action planning requires that following steps:

1. **Clarify values.** Framing wicked problems within the values that hold them allows groups to clarify those values and examine what keeps the problem in place. Values also guide

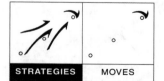

STRATEGIES | MOVES

Figure 10-8. Dynamical Action Planning

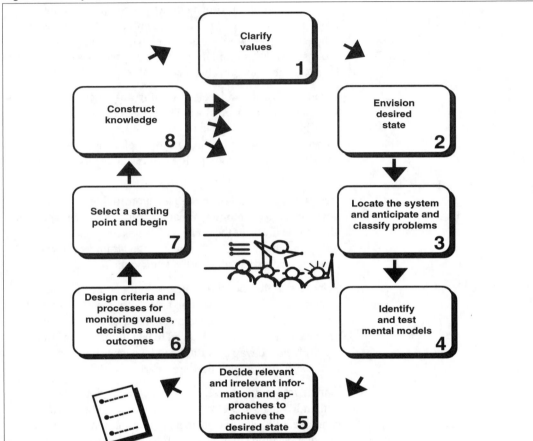

approaches to wicked problems. They become the governing system for choices, interventions, and measures of success.

2.   **Envision a desired state for individuals, for groups, and for greater systems.** Rigor and thoroughness at this stage drives all the other stages of this process.

3.   **Locate systems and anticipate and classify problems.** Within any wicked problem lie other problems. Some are themselves wicked; others are of a tamer nature. What is the greater system and subsystems that keep this problem in place? What current feedback loops reinforce the system and motivate it to continue as is?

4. **Identify and test mental models.** Mental models exist for both the change agents and others in the system that holds the problem. These mental models sometimes overlap and sometimes are at odds with one another. To test mental models, groups use the assumptions wall and assumptions challenge processes described in chapter 6.

5. **Decide relevant and irrelevant information and approaches to achieve the desired state.** The list given in stage 4 of action planning (page 238) applies here as well. Data overload sometimes burdens planning groups. Selecting the most catalytic resources from the list will release energy in the group and move it forward.

6. **Design criteria and processes for monitoring values, decisions, and outcomes.** What criteria determines success at all of these levels of the process? What is the standard for judgments about success? How will the group monitor progress and stay true to the values articulated in the first stage?

7. **Select a starting point and begin.** Entry points with wicked problems begin with a learning agenda for the planners and change agents, who soon realize that to approach wicked problems successfully they need to be willing to confront themselves, the way they think, and the ways they are shaped by the system of which they are a part.

8. **Construct knowledge.** Knowledge construction occurs for both individuals and groups. Each influences the other. Groups cannot learn if individuals do not learn. Individuals who learn together develop smart groups. To solve problems is to learn. Active learning groups know this and acknowledge the messiness of the process. The multiple arrows branching off from step 8 indicate that knowledge construction sends groups in many different direction, often simultaneously.

Figure 10-8 provides a rough guide to the process. It provides some comfort to group members who need to know where they are at a given point and where they are going next. In the midst of nonlinear problems, this too is a problem. Comfort with ambiguity is an essential personal and collective resource in a world of both tame and wicked problems.

The next chapter details the capacities for adaptivity that help organizations and individual professionals function better in a rapidly changing world.

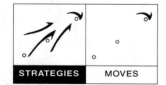

STRATEGIES   MOVES

End Notes

1 Schon, D. (1983). *The reflective practitioner*. Cited in Wilson, S. M., Peterson, P. I., Ball, D. L., & Cohen, D. K. (1996). Learning by all. *Phi Delta Kappan, 78*, 466.

2 Lewin, K. (1948). *Resolving social conflicts*. New York: Harper & Row; Kanter, R. M. (1983). *The change masters: Innovation & entrepreneurship in the American corporation*. New York: Simon and Schuster; and Morgan, G. (1997). *Images of organizations*. Thousand Oaks, CA: Sage.

3 Sarason, S. B. (1990). *The predicable failure of educational reform: Can we change course before it's too late*? San Francisco: Jossey-Bass.

4 Pacanowsky, M. (1995, Winter). Team tools for wicked problems. *Organizational Dynamics, 23* (3), 36–51.

5 Kuhn, T. (1970). *The structure of scientific revolutions*. Chicago: University of Chicago Press.

6 Glick, J. (1987). *Chaos: Making of a new science*. New York: Penguin Books.

7 Briggs, J. (1992). *Fractals: The patterns of chaos*. New York: Touchstone Books.

8 Sarason, op. cit.

9 Kegan, R. (1994). *In over our heads: The mental demands of modern life*. Cambridge, MA: Harvard University Press.

10 Pacanowsky, M. (1995, Winter). Team tools for wicked problems. *Organizational Dynamics, 23* (3), 36–51.

11 Wheatley, M. J. (1992). *Leadership and the new science: Learning about organization from an orderly universe*. San Francisco: Berrett-Koehler.

12 Maturana, H. R., & Varela, F. J. (1992). *The tree of knowledge: The biological roots of human understanding*. Boston: Shambhala.

13 Kegan, R., & Lahey, L. (1984). Adult leadership and adult development: A constructivist view. In B. Kellerman (Ed.), *Handbook on socialization theory and research* (pp. 199–229). Chicago: Rand McNally.

14 Argyris, C. (1990). *Overcoming organizational defenses*. Boston: Allyn and Bacon.

15 Perkins, D. (1992). *Smart schools: Better thinking and learning for every child*. New York: Free Press.

16 Argyris, op. cit.

Chapter 11 Capacities for School Change

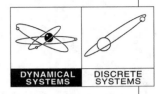

this chapter features:

Getting work done
Doing the right work
Working collaboratively
Managing systems
Developing groups
Adapting to change

ADAPTIVE schools develop when collaborative adults live their values and goals, pay attention to their decisions and behaviors in the moment, and increase their consciousness of multiple ways of seeing systems. Earlier chapters examined fundamental strategies for carrying out this work. In this chapter we expand on the 12 capacities for school change that were briefly introduced in chapter 2. The 12 capacities for school change (Table 11-1) interact with one another and cannot be addressed in isolation if schools and professionals are to become increasingly adaptive in response to the changing needs of the students they serve. These capacities are living examples of the dynamical principle that everything influences everything else.

The six organizational capacities and the six professional capacities form a synergistic whole that must be continually addressed. It is never a case of either/or but a case of both/and. We are persuaded that all the staff development in the world, and all the knowledge and skill building that we provide to individuals, will have only minimal impact if districts and schools do not also put energy and resources into altering the deep structure of the organization.

We introduced three focusing questions in chapter 1:

1. Who are we?
2. Why are we doing this?
3. Why are we doing this, this way?

These questions organize the short-form response to the "how" of adaptivity in schools. The twelve capacities structure the long-form answer.

Steven Covey reminds us of the need to balance production and production capacities.[1] His retelling of the fable of the farmer who killed the goose that laid the golden egg points to the ongoing need to develop the capabilities to do important work

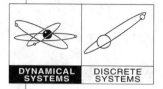

as much as the need to do the work itself. If we are not careful, the "goose" of school improvement dies from a lack of food and water.

This is a perennial problem in schools starved for time: to do the important work for students and to support continual adult and organizational learning. We will make the case here that time is just one element in the puzzle. Many factors organize time choices; the clock and the calendar are only two of the elements at work.

Table 11-1. 12 Capacities for School Change

Organizational Capacities	Professional Capacities
• Vision, values, and goal focus • Systems thinking • Initiating and managing adaptation • Interpreting and using data • Developing and maintaining collaborative cultures • Gathering and focusing resources	• Collegial interaction • Cognitive processes of instruction • Knowledge of the structure of the discipline(s) • Self-knowledge, values, beliefs, and standards • Repertoire of teaching skills • Knowing about students and how they learn

These twelve capacities are both diagnostic tools and curricula for school improvement.

Schools are living organisms, and like all healthy living organisms they are characterized by continual flow and changes in their metabolism involving thousands of biochemical reactions. Stable systems are dying systems.[2] In scientific terms, chemical and thermal equilibrium leads to death. Vital schools, like all living organisms, continually maintain themselves in a state far from equilibrium. This is the state of life. Stability emerges through the average, over time, of the ebb and flow of energy through the system. Attention to the six organizational capacities for adaptivity and the six professional capacities for adaptivity helps this energy flow.

As you read this chapter, please have in mind some of the persistent problems you see in the schools around you. As with the low-performing high school profiled in chapter 2, you may notice particular capacities that are underdeveloped. We hope that you also notice specific capacities that are well-developed in your settings. The essential question, then, is: "Where should leaders now focus the system's attention to make a difference in the situation?"

Organizational Capacities for Adaptivity

Schools do not develop organizational capacities as abstractions.
They do so by addressing meaningful problems. Skilled leaders use
problems as opportunities for learning. This approach meets both
production and production capacity needs. Working alongside
leaders who understand this informs our learning as well. Recently
we spent time with a school that addressed the six organizational
capacities (Fig. 11-1) in the following manner.

Figure 11-1. Six Organizational Capacities

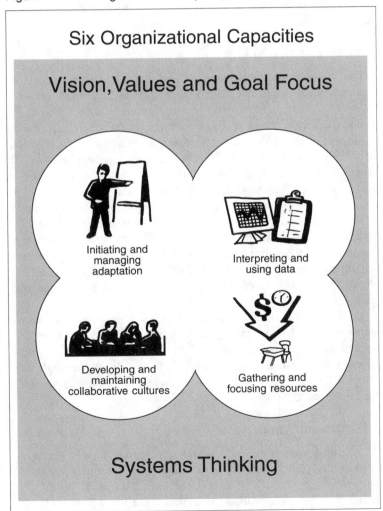

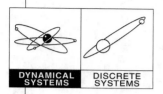

DYNAMICAL SYSTEMS DISCRETE SYSTEMS

Last year Sea View Elementary School[3] engaged the issue of low scores on a statewide fourth-grade writing assessment. The test was new to both this school and others in the state. It emphasized narrative and expository writing. While the fourth-grade teachers were not happy about the scores, they were not terribly surprised. When they first saw the test, they realized that the school's writing program had some gaps, given the expectations embedded in the examination. As a clearer picture of student writing performance began to emerge, the principal organized a series of meetings. We were fortunate enough to participate in some of them. Appendix H and Appendix I offer some practical approaches to structuring conversations about data and for engaging others in collecting and reporting data.

Vision, Values, and Goal Focus

When we learned about the writing problems at Sea View, our first question was, "In what way is this issue about raising test scores, and in what way is it about long-term improvements in student writing and in the writing program?" The principal assured us that the change effort was aimed at long-term systemic improvements in the teaching of writing. In fact, she was willing to take some political heat from parents and central office administrators, if necessary, to keep the focus long-term and not just fix what was showing.

Several other values contributed to the project's success, such as a belief in the power of cumulative effects for learners. As we describe in the systems thinking section, collective efforts matter. September of the fourth grade is much too late to start a concentrated writing program. The assessment of the system at that point was viewed by the school as an assessment of the whole, not that specific part.

The other operating value and vision was an image of continual improvement for all students. The emerging writing skills matrix was seen as a developmental road map, not as a curriculum to be covered by each grade level in turn. If a third grader had difficulties crafting simple sentences, that is where the teacher started. Paragraphs could wait until foundational skills were in place.

Systems Thinking

The writing problem at Sea View was soon seen by the teachers as a systems problem. A fledgling sense of collective responsibility for student learning motivated the work of vertical teams. K–3 staff members were openly supportive of their fourth- and fifth-grade colleagues and agreed to work collaboratively on an improvement plan and effort.

One of the vertical teams produced a draft skills matrix for the teaching of both narrative and expository writing. This systems view was developed through rotating 2-hour planning sessions, with each new team adding to and filling in gaps in the work of previous teams. Several teachers even looped back on their lunch breaks to participate with colleagues on other teams.

One by-product of this work was increased confidence on the part of lower grade teachers that their efforts in developing fundamental writing skills would be appreciated by their upper grade colleagues. When they could see the system of which they were a part displayed in matrix form on the wall of the meeting room, they could see where their efforts led and view with ease their part in the whole.

Upper grade teachers also benefited when they spotted gaps in writing instruction on the grid. One glaring example was the lack of emphasis on expository forms. The state assessment first pointed this out. The skills matrix reinforced it. This also inspired changes in another part of the system, because the district writing rubric did not provide guidance or standards in this area. Several Sea View teachers volunteered to be on the revision committee tackling the rubric. With their draft skills matrix in hand, they greatly influenced the process. In the course of this work, they shared their efforts informally with several other schools and engineered a resource swap with teachers in other buildings who were working on different parts of the writing and literacy development puzzle.

Systems thinking is a critical skill in a world of messy and wicked problems. In this emerging field, practitioners model systems using mathematics, complex diagrams, and rigorous analysis of variables. Ultimately, such work leads to leverage points in the system that can be modified or perturbed enough to positively influence systems change. One challenge here is that both "thing" and "energy" models apply to the same system. Finding and modifying systems requires both ways of seeing and acting.

Systems analysts concern themselves with the "state of the system." Numbers, stocks, delays, flows, feedback, and rules all organize the state of the system at any given point in time. Systems thinker Donella Meadows offers 10 ways to see systems and positively intervene to make productive changes.[4] We have adapted her work and present it in a modified form later in this chapter.

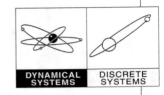

DYNAMICAL SYSTEMS   DISCRETE SYSTEMS

In a messy world, systems thinking is essential.

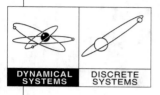

DYNAMICAL SYSTEMS | DISCRETE SYSTEMS

Initiating and Managing Adaptation

The principal at Sea View intuitively knew that shared dissatisfaction is the first step in initiating change. This, coupled with shared vision and knowledge of practical tools and strategies, must be strong enough to outweigh the costs of any change.

The following simple formula captures these factors.

$$\text{Change} = (A \times B \times C) > X.$$

X = the cost of change

A = shared dissatisfaction

B = shared vision

C = knowledge of practical tools and strategies

Without shared dissatisfaction, all the vision and strategies in the world do not promote a desire to change. Too much dissatisfaction without practical tools will shut down the system. Vision that is neither shared nor connected to the other two resources sputters out into inspirational vagueness. All change has costs for both individuals and organizations. The left side of the change formula must overcome the right side.

The work of William Bridges is a useful guide to this area of the map.[5] He points out that change in organizations is not the problem; it is transitions that are bewildering. Transitions are the psychological readjustments to change. They have three phases: (a) ending, (b) neutral zone, and (c) new beginning. Each phase has special characteristics and special requirements to be navigated successfully.

Endings must be marked concretely and symbolically. Many change processes stall because people in the organization have not let go of the old. Curriculum changes in schools often meet this difficulty. Teachers cling to the tried and true, in some cases hoping to leap to the new like a trapeze artist high above the crowd. They are often unwilling to let go and hang suspended in midair with one hand on each trapeze.

At Sea View, the writing meetings that were initiated marked the transition from old ways of working to new. They were symbols of a new order and at the same time marked the ending of isolation and scapegoating. The principal did not have to name this. Freeing teachers for these meetings with substitutes symbolically and practically conveyed this message.

During an ending, a group needs to ask, "Who is losing what in this change?" and "Who needs what support to work through the

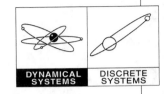

transition?" At Sea View this took the form of a change in curriculum materials for language arts. While it was widely recognized that the textbooks were outdated and falling apart, some teachers still needed an opportunity to express their concerns about the new materials and the need for greater planning and lesson preparation time. Early meetings provided opportunities for these conversations and the emotional support needed by these staff members.

The neutral zone is a time of anxiety and discomfort for many participants, but it is also a time of great creativity. At Sea View, dialogue, reflection, and sharing of practical materials and tools organized this phase. The principal was always supportive and nonjudgmental, allowing teachers to express their feelings and concerns about increased accountability and their work-in-progress.

Willliam Bridges reminds us that new beginnings require selling the problem and not the solution. At Sea View, the writing issue was owned by the staff. In fact, as they began this project, they knew much more about the shortfalls in student writing performance than they did about the solutions.

Bridges also admonishes readers to remember the marathon effect. Thousands of runners compete in the Boston Marathon each year. The world-class runners, with their faster qualifying times, line up at the start of the pack. By the time the runners in the rear cross the starting line, these leaders are several miles up the course.

In school change processes, early adapters must remember and pay attention to those who follow. To produce cumulative effect in schools, these "omnivores" must pace themselves and support the learning of their colleagues. The race is not fully underway until everyone crosses the starting line. Appendix J describes five stages of change and maps a process for productive action.

Interpreting and Using Data

The assessment results from the state had merely confirmed the fourth-grade teachers' expectations of low performance by their students. Thus, rather than discounting the results or questioning the validity of the test, these teachers began an informal dialogue with the principal and other teachers. Part of this dialogue explored comparisons between the state assessment and writing samples collected from fifth-grade students in the school. This in turn led to conversations with third-grade teachers and examinations of writing samples from their students.

As this example illustrates, data can be both quantitative and qualitative. The number of Sea View students in each performance

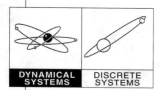

quartile carried some meaning for the teachers. Actual samples of student writing carried other meanings. In these ways, teachers with a variety of mind styles had opportunities to engage with the problem in a manner best suited to their preferences. Numbers spoke to some people, whereas artifacts of learning spoke to others.

Developing and Maintaining Collaborative Cultures

A sense of collaboration governed this project from the beginning. A leadership team composed of a cross-section of teachers and the principal organized the project and monitored progress. This team steeped itself in the collaborative tools described in chapter 3. They kept communications open between grade levels and provided a bird's-eye view of the school and the project.

Vertical teams attended the meetings. In this way, each group had information about K–5 writing approaches and access to knowledgeable practitioners from every grade level.

At one point it became obvious that all teachers in the school were not teaching and using the same proofreading marks. Group members said, "You know, we don't all need to talk about this." So we asked them to name three people in the school whom they all respected and who had the technical knowledge to handle this task. They quickly named three people, who agreed to develop a simple set of grade-level appropriate proofing marks for faculty approval at the next whole-group meeting.

Gathering and Focusing Resources

This project demonstrates the power of this capacity. Our contract with the district and school emphasized the development of collabo-rative skills and process tools. Schools need an engaging vehicle to carry this work. At Sea View, the principal and leadership team used the writing issue as their mode of transport.

Time and money were budgeted for meetings, for some staff members to attend in-depth training in expository writing, and for new curriculum materials. Other issues in the school that could be set aside were done so. A bulletin board in the hallway near the office proudly displayed an ever-changing sampling of student work in this area. The parent newsletter provided updates and progress reports.

One of the innovations that most contributed to project success was the use of floating substitutes and careful scheduling of the vertical-team meetings to best align with teacher preparation periods. In this way teachers were free, while school was still in session, to participate in 2-hour sessions for planning and problem-solving

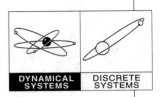

purposes. On most project days this required the services of six to eight substitutes.

The district staff development director understood the nature of this work and readily agreed to cover the cost of substitutes. District staff development practices are moving beyond the notion of course-based training as the only means of professional development. Time with peers in focused work sessions contributes to learning for all participating adults and simultaneously supports direct payoffs for student learning.

10 Places to Intervene in a System

The paradigm offered by Donella Meadows begins with the least effective intervention, labeled 10, and proceeds in increasing order to 1, the most effective.

Systems thinking and vision, values and goal focus forge the context for the other four organizational capacities.

10. Numbers.   Numbers form parameters in the world of systems thinking. Taxes, subsidies, and standards are examples of numbers that planners try to regulate to change systems. Interest rates, the minimum wage, and the number of hours required for teacher recertification are other examples of numbers regulation within systems. The poverty level is an official number that influences schools; it determines cutoff points for receiving free or reduced school lunches, which in turn relate to equity-funding formulas.

Academic standards and graduation requirements are another form of numbers that school planners are trying to regulate. With related measurement and record-keeping systems, this form of intervention attempts to define the parameters of the system. It is within this frame that school systems define how good is good enough. Meadows notes the following:

> All these are . . . adjustments to faucets. So, by the way, is firing people and getting new ones. Putting different hands on the faucets may change the rate at which they turn, but they are the same old faucets, plumbed into the same systems, turned according to the same information and rules and goals; the system isn't going to change much.[6]

9. Material stocks and flows.   In education systems, material stocks and flows consist largely of people. The baby boom and the current "baby boomlet" influence the system by sheer number. As these children flow through the system, they affect each level of schooling they encounter. Subsets of this population also make a difference, as districts with high immigration rates have discovered.

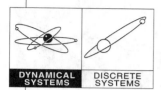

DYNAMICAL SYSTEMS   DISCRETE SYSTEMS

How many children, speaking how many languages, flow in the system?

This frame also applies to the adult professional population. Early retirement systems are directed here, as are teacher recruitment drives. The number of minority teachers available to hire is another example, as is the number of novice teachers who need support and training.

The only serious way to influence this part of the system is by establishing buffers. A bank account is a buffer against income fluctuations. A river floodplain is a buffer against flood damage only if humans do not build there. The available supply of teacher candidates is a buffer against unsupervised classrooms. This is one reason that policy makers are reluctant to raise entrance standards to the profession. Higher standards initially lower the available pool unless the greater teacher-training system also adjusts. Instead, most states have emergency certification provisions.

8. Negative feedback loops.   In this frame we make a transition from the physical or "thing" part of the system to the "energy" part. In this case, the energy is in the form of information. A thermostat loop runs by negative feedback; it regulates a system state called room temperature. All negative feedback loops require goals, such as "70° F." When the system parameters slip away from the goal, negative feedback loops kick in and return the system to the desired system state. In the thermostat example, valves open, burners fire, hot water and air pump into conduits, and rooms become warm.

The mental trick to understanding negative feedback is to not get lost in the word *negative*. Antibiotics provide negative feedback to infectious bacteria. The human immune system operates by this same principle. The federal Freedom of Information Act takes this parameter into public policy to control the excesses of government officials by kicking in when information does not flow to citizens.

Standardized test scores used to drive punishment and reward systems are an example of this idea at work in school systems. Published in the local newspaper, they attempt to shame schools into compliance. Parameters are set by political pressures. In some settings, operating within the 60th percentile nationally is good enough; in others, the principal might be fired.

Exercise and good nutrition are also negative feedback loops and strengthen the body's immune system. Organic gardeners constantly build up their soil. The 12 capacities described in this chapter keep school systems healthy when properly maintained.

7. Positive feedback loops.   Negative feedback loops in a system balance the positive feedback loops. Again, some mental

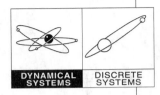

gymnastics are required to understand this frame. Flu viruses run by positive feedback; they infect one person after another until they run out of hosts. Unless you've had a flu shot or your body's immune system is hardy, the negative feedback system is not strong enough to overcome this positive feedback. Unregulated population growth, erosion, and unchecked epidemics eventually destroy the system that initially supported them.

The howl of an amplified speaker system is another prime example of this principle at work. Each time the signal runs from the microphone to the amplifier, it gets stronger and stronger, until everyone present is covering their ears or until someone pulls the plug.

The trick at this level is to encourage positive feedback.

The trick at this level is to encourage positive feedback that feeds the system and sets up "success to the successful" loops. The seven norms of collaboration are an example of productive positive loops. Healthy dialogue and discussion about student work are another.

6. Information flow.   Deciding what information should flow where is important for planners, policy makers, and practitioners. Getting information where it is most useful, in the most usable form, influences systems change.

Meadows relates a classic systems thinking tale.[7] In a subdivision of identical houses, the electric company installed its meters in the basement of some of the houses and in the front hall of others. In the latter case, the inhabitants could easily see the meter spinning in its glass case every time they walked in or out the door. In these houses, electricity consumption was 30% lower than in the other houses.

The real point of improved assessment systems in schools is not grading and class placements but to provide information to learners, parents, and teachers about gaps in knowledge and skills and about areas of strength and weakness. High-level accountability systems in the form of norm-referenced tests usually do a poor job of providing this information. They hide the essential details in quartiles and percentages instead of providing the more direct information required for learning.

5. Rules of the system.   This refers to incentives, punishments, and constraints. Suppose, just for a minute, that parents and students evaluated teachers and principals. How do you think the system would change? The power to regulate behavior is real power. That is why people run for school boards and lobbyists gather where governing bodies make laws.

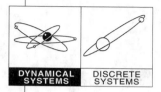

Teacher contracts, discipline policies, graduation requirements, and the like are all examples of rules at work in the education system. Rules set up both negative and positive feedback loops. Both productive and unproductive behaviors are kept in place by the rules of the system. One reason that collaboration in schools is so difficult is that rules establish the workday and the work year. These rules, as much as lack of knowledge and skills on the part of caring adults, get in the way of adaptivity and positive change.

4. Power of self-organization Natural systems change themselves. In biology this is called evolution, and sometimes coevolution—when plants and insects or plants and birds adapt to one another through changes in flowering structures and in beak length, for example.

The system elements discussed so far all power self-organization. To study self-organization is to study patterns. What are the arrangements of people and projects in this setting? In what ways do they interact? What is most valued here? How are conflicts resolved? Where does information flow, and where is it stalled? These and other patterns form the self-organizing backbone of the school and district.

The power of self-organization is the reason that biologists value biodiversity and hate the forces of extinction. Diversity, with its accompanying flexibility during changing circumstances, is a sign of the ultimate health of a system. Monocultures are highly susceptible to disease, pests, and other fluctuations in the system. As Meadows says, "Any system, biological, economic, or social, that scorns experimentation and wipes out the raw material of innovation is doomed over the long term on this highly variable planet."[8]

To intervene at this level, change agents work on pattern creation (the five dynamical principles introduced in chapter 1 apply here), goal clarification, and challenging paradigms.

3. Goals of the system. We loop back here to one of our other capacities for adaptivity. Goals change systems. Earlier we explained how negative and positive feedback loops work. Each of these has goals. The goal of negative loops is to constrain the system, whereas the goal of positive loops is to feed themselves.

In this case, we are talking about the big goals of the system that define success or failure. An experienced high school principal explained this to us one day when he remarked that "all this standards stuff is good, I guess, but until someone demonstrates to me that high ACT scores and college admissions success have gone away, we're not going to change the way we operate."

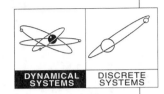

Goal clarity sets up the rest of the system. Putting on the hat of an anthropologist is a helpful way to seek out the goals of a system. Many important goals are buried beneath rhetoric and mission statements. Searching for who wins and who loses in the current design brings you closer to the true goals of the system.

2. Mindset of the paradigm out of which the system arises. To see the mindset of a system, you must step outside of it for perspective. Graphic displays are one way to do this. This super balcony view exposes the mental models that govern the organization. Change agents then gently tug at mismatches in the system between espoused values and goals and actual results. They intentionally perturb the system to motivate self-organization around some new operating principles.

Pyramids were built by cultures that believed in an afterlife. The symbols and structures of the system display the thinking behind it. In schools, beliefs about learning and teaching do not often change through staff development alone. Explorations of the mental models that educators hold about learners, learning, and teaching can create major shifts.[9]

1. Power to transcend paradigms. No paradigm is absolutely true. We have mental models to hold mental models. The path of mastery in this area is to release oneself from one's mindset. Earlier we referred to this as post institutional thinking, getting outside the institution of our own minds. This book offers a host of ways for individuals and groups to do this. Meadows deserves the closing words here.

> I don't think there are any cheap tickets to system change. You have to work at it, whether that means rigorously analyzing a system or rigorously casting off paradigms. In the end, it seems that leverage has less to do with pushing levers than it does with disciplined thinking combined with strategically, profoundly, madly letting go.[10]

Professional Capacities for Adaptivity

Professional capacities for adaptivity (Fig. 11-2) work in tandem with the six organizational capacities described earlier in this chapter. In the example from Sea View Elementary School, improvements in the writing program arose from attention to both areas. Within this arena, individual teachers and teams of teachers set out to get smart about both writing and the teaching of writing.

No paradigm is absolutely true.

Figure 11-2. Six Professional Capacities

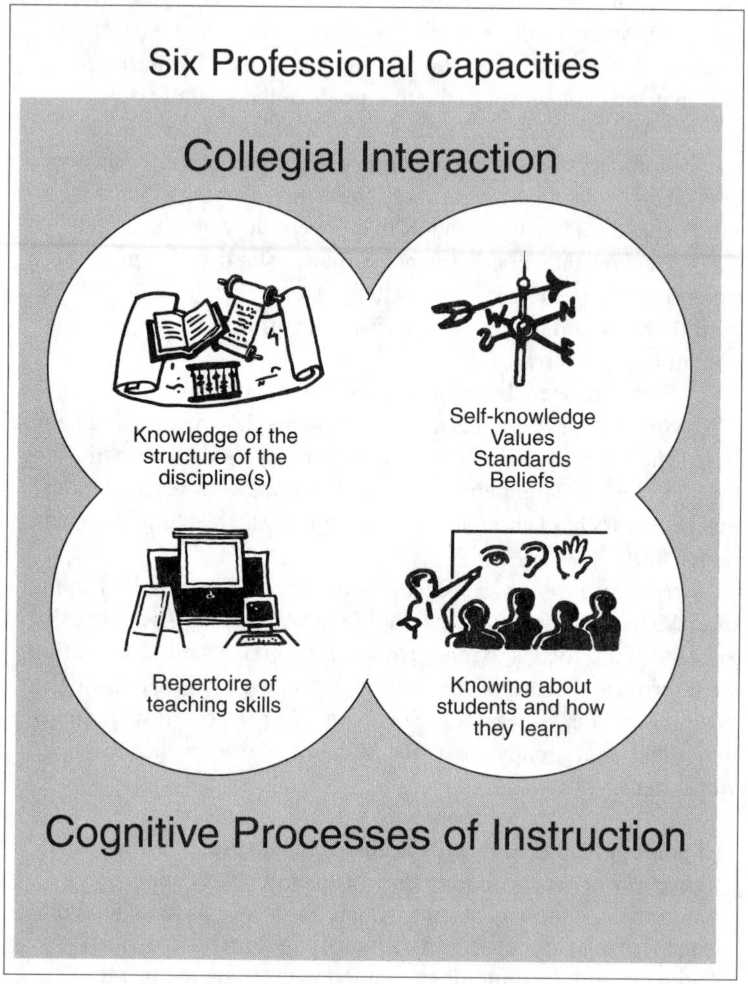

Six Professional Capacities

Collegial Interaction

Knowledge of the structure of the discipline(s)

Self-knowledge
Values
Standards
Beliefs

Repertoire of teaching skills

Knowing about students and how they learn

Cognitive Processes of Instruction

Collegial Interaction

Who teachers are to one another matters. In a sometimes lonely profession, isolation within the individual cells of an egg-crate school does not promote personal or professional growth. Parallel play may socialize youngsters in sandboxes, but it limits learning for adults.

To be a colleague requires sharing one's knowing and not-knowing. It means sharing and creating materials together. It means teaching each other about the craft of teaching. We are still somewhat surprised when we find out how many teachers in a given school have

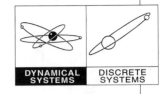

never seen each other teach. Their experiences of one another consist mostly of passing in the hallways with or without students in tow.

In study after study, we run across findings stressing the importance of collegial interactions for growth in teaching and growth in student achievement.[11] Adult learning, like all learning, is both an individual and a collective act. Where collegiality is strong, communities of practice bloom.[12] These communities support distributed cognition, which means that people get smart together.

At Sea View Elementary School it was OK not to know everything there was to know about teaching writing. Several teachers immersed themselves in learning to teach expository writing. As they tried out these ideas in their classrooms, they shared their successes and shortfalls with other teachers and encouraged them to adopt the techniques that seemed to be working.

A new kindergarten teacher brought a wealth of experience in language development for early childhood programs. The first- and second-grade teachers opened up a dialogue with her as they eagerly awaited the next school year and the arrival of these youngsters in their classrooms.

The hallway bulletin board, with its rotating display of student work, became a focal point for conversations about student writing and teaching students to write. These conversations led to lesson swapping and more conversations.

Collegiality is different than conviviality. The teachers at Sea View were both, but they didn't confuse lunch-table chatting with professional dialogue. Mindfully talking about one aspect of the instructional program allowed the school as a community to focus its energy and use talk as a vehicle for learning and productive change.

The Cognitive Processes of Instruction

Teaching is a cognitively demanding profession. Decisions made in quiet moments and decisions made on the fly influence success and failure in the classroom. Many variables add to the complexity of the thinking tasks that confront teachers every day. Planning and reflecting skills energize and organize good teaching.

In planning, teachers consider the following:

1. Information about students—who they are, what they know and can do

2. The nature of the instructional task—subject matter, activities, materials

3. The context of the school—class size, scheduling, grouping

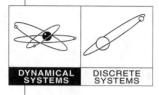

DYNAMICAL SYSTEMS | DISCRETE SYSTEMS

4.   Their own beliefs—their conception of learning, of teaching, and of the particular subject or topic[13]

In reflecting, skilled teachers consider three areas—the technical, the practical, and the critical.[14] Technical reflection focuses on whether objectives were met, based on specified criteria for success. Practical reflection focuses on the effectiveness of actions and the ends to which those actions led. Critical reflection focuses on the purposes of education and the assumptions that underlie practice.

The "bookends" of planning and reflecting frame lesson execution. It is here that additional cognitive resolving power pays off for students and teachers as learning comes into focus. A teacher's "with-it-ness" supplies the necessary cognitive and emotional flexibility to maintain concentration on the big picture while modifying and adjusting along the way. One of the early and ongoing challenges for the Sea View writing project was to not get hung up on lesson plans during the actual lesson. Learning to write is a messy business. Following the students and their needs was much more important than following the plan.

Sea View teachers are still hard at work learning to plan for, teach, reflect upon, and apply new understandings from their writing skills matrix. Becoming better teachers of writing calls upon all of their cognitive processes of instruction.

A teacher's "with-it-ness" supplies the necessary cognitive and emotional flexibility to maintain concentration on the big picture.

Knowledge of the Structure of the Discipline

What teachers know and can do greatly influences student learning. A teacher's knowledge of the structure of a given discipline translates directly into daily instructional decisions, curriculum choices, and lesson designs. Individual teachers teach different subjects differently.[15] An elementary teacher's math lesson will be structured and conducted in a manner different from the same teacher's literature circle.

Expert teaching calls for an understanding of subject matter that is thorough enough to organize topics so that students can create meaningful cognitive maps.[16] Teachers with this level of knowledge can then use it flexibly to address ideas as they come up in the course of learning and teaching. Real learning is messy. Students do not always stay within or even fit within the boundaries of lesson plans. Teachers' knowledge of content topics and of fields of learning must therefore always be wider and deeper than that of their students. This enables fluid movement within subject matter and enables responsiveness to student questions and perceived student needs.

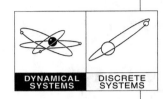

Lee Shulman breaks down knowledge of the structure of disciplines into several important subsets. One is content knowledge itself. If teachers do not know a subject, students will not come to know the subject. Another area is knowing not just the contents of a domain but also the structure of subject matter—the organizing principles and concepts.

A second grader sorted out an important idea in mathematics one day when he observed with excitement, "Numbers are made up of other numbers—you can take them apart!" Many second graders never reach this conclusion on their own. It is more likely to happen if their teachers understand this big idea themselves.

It is also important to know the habits of mind in a given field. The principles of inquiry are different in literature than they are in physical science. How are ideas developed in social studies? Who is a valid source in literary criticism? How do mathematicians solve problems? These are all examples of this idea applied to different content areas. This supports students in understanding how new ideas are added to a field and how deficient ones are dropped by those who produce knowledge and knowing in a domain.

Students too have habits of mind. Each content area is a minefield of misconceptions and error patterns. Knowing these allows the expert teacher to anticipate, carefully structure lessons and units, and respond appropriately to the fragile half constructions of their novice learners. Shulman calls these adaptations pedagogical content knowledge. This blending of content knowledge, learner knowledge, and teaching knowledge binds subject matter to specific learning devices. Expert teachers draw from a rich menu of analogies, models, and explanatory devices that support them and their students in representing ideas and understandings in a variety of ways.

The writing project at Sea View struggled with all of these issues. Teachers' knowledge of writing and writing processes grew alongside that of their students. A practical developmental continuum for stages of student writing began to emerge, and teachers forged important connections between student writing and other areas of literacy, such as student reading difficulties. This triggered inquiry into the structure of the reading program as teachers wondered aloud about the most appropriate balance of fiction and nonfiction books to use with students at all grade levels. They are still exploring the connections between exposing students to quality nonfiction through guided reading experiences and translating that into writing lessons.

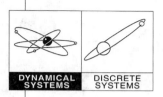

Self-Knowledge, Values, Standards, and Beliefs

Little children playing school vividly demonstrate beliefs about teaching that shape the rules of this play and the power relationships between the players. When some of these children grow up and become real teachers, beliefs, values, and personal standards implicitly and explicitly guide decisions about what and how to teach.

Values and beliefs influence the perceptions and judgments that carry teachers through their days. They are not always consciously understood or named by individuals, but their presence shimmers beneath the surface of a teacher's practice. Values shape the standards that teachers hold for their own work and that of their students. They are filters for what elements of the vast subject matter are emphasized and reinforced. Ultimately, they are each teacher's true curriculum and true lasting lessons.

One of the central issues at Sea View was—and is—What is good writing? This standards issue is an interactive construction forged by individual teachers and collaborative colleagues. The ebb and flow of changes in their students' writing focuses this clarification process and at the same time challenges their beliefs about teaching and learning. This clarification process is the deepest level of inquiry at Sea View. Teaching writing is a vehicle for exploring the ways and means of learning about learning, both for students and for adults.

Repertoire of Teaching Skills

Teaching is a craft skill built on action-knowledge honed by trial and error. It begins with the teacher's own understanding of what is to be learned by students and how this learning is most appropriately orchestrated for the population being served. Understanding teaching is a lifetime journey. There is always something new to learn about oneself, one's students, content, process, and the dynamical interactions of these elements.

Master teachers, like concert artists, consciously expand their performance repertoires. They develop and assemble micro routines that can be combined and reconstituted to fit a wide variety of settings. These experts automatize many routines to free cognitive space for more complex perceiving and more sophisticated instructional problem solving. This unconscious competence is the hallmark of the expert in the classroom.

One of the tensions and energy drains for the novice writing teachers at Sea View was this very lack of automaticity. Daily writing tasks demanded that conscious attention be placed on seemingly mundane lesson details. When everything is important, sensory overload sets in. Peripheral vision, both literal and metaphoric, was not a sufficient resource for managing the physical, emotional, and cognitive demands of high-quality writing instruction at this stage of teacher learning.

Knowing About Students and How They Learn

Learners and teachers need one another. Each is incomplete without the other. Who they are in this relationship forms a delicate balance of minds, hearts, and souls. The desire for smaller class sizes and smaller schools is a response to this need to know one another. In an increasingly diverse world, direct and personal knowledge is even more necessary as old assumptions and operating rules lose their guiding power.

All the teaching repertoire in the world is wasted if it is not well matched to the needs of learners.[17] The exploding knowledge base about learning styles, multiple intelligences, developmental differences, and cultural variation supports Lee Shulman's notion of the need for pedagogical learner knowledge on the part of all teachers.

Developmental differences do not end in the third grade. Grade by grade, the span, in Piagetian terms, widens. Many learners in middle schools and high schools operate at a solidly concrete operational level. They often stumble when they bump head-on into a curriculum organized by abstraction and taught through symbol systems. When flexible teachers start with the concrete and scaffold learning to the abstract, these same students grasp complex ideas and perform at high levels.

Developing culturally respectful teaching approaches is an increasing need in many schools. Methods and materials that work with one population may confuse or offend another. Language differences play an important role here. One often unnoticed variable is the difference between students' social discourse and their knowledge of the structure and norms of academic discourse. Researchers Okhee Lee and Sandra Fradd refer to this sophisticated matching as instructional congruence.[18] This means that teachers mediate the nature of academic content with students' language and cultural experiences. This makes content accessible, meaningful, and relevant.

Learning about student writers at Sea View energized and at times terrorized the teachers. The more they looked, the more differences they spotted. This led to dialogue and discussions about

All teaching repertoire is wasted if not matched to learners.

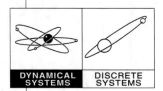

DYNAMICAL SYSTEMS | DISCRETE SYSTEMS

the best ways to intervene with individuals—when and how do you coach young writers, and when and how do you consult with them in a more directive manner? Other conversations explored alternative ways to group students for instruction. One direction this took was to experiment with cross-grade groupings for targeted minilessons.

A World of Both/And

Neither the organizational nor the professional capacities for adaptivity would have sufficed on their own to make a difference at Sea View. In this world of both/and, the twin goals reinforced one another. Developing each capacity within a spirit of collegiality and inquiry led to a natural flow within and among the areas.

These 12 capacities frame windows for looking at schools and districts. Current project successes can usually be located here. Current log jams in the system also have roots in these territories. This, then, is a diagnostic tool and a curriculum for organizational and professional development.

End Notes

[1] Covey, S. R. (1989). *The seven habits of highly effective people.* New York: Fireside Books.

[2] Capra, F. (1996). *The web of life: A new scientific understanding of living systems.* New York: Anchor Books.

[3] This is not the school's real name. For reasons of confidentiality we created this pseudonym.

[4] Meadows, D. (1997, Winter). Places to intervene in a system (in increasing order of effectiveness). *Whole Earth*, pp. 79–83.

[5] Bridges, W. (1991). *Managing transitions: Making the most of changes.* Reading, MA: Addison-Wesley.

[6] Meadows, p. 79.

[7] Meadows, p. 82.

[8] Meadows, p. 83.

[9] Caine R. N., & Caine, G. (1997). *Education on the edge of possibility.* Alexandria, VA: Association for Supervision and Curriculum Development.

[10] Meadows, p. 84.

[11] Little, J. L., & McLaughlin, M. (1993). *Teachers' work: Individuals, colleagues, and contexts.* New York: Teachers College Press.

[12] Brown, A. (1994). The advancement of learning. *Educational Researcher, 23* (8), 4–12.

[13] Borko, H., Livingston, C., & Shavelson, R. (1990). Teachers' thinking about instruction. *Remedial and Special Education, 11* (6), 40–49.

[14] Calderhead, J. (1996). Teacher beliefs and knowledge. In D. C. Berliner & R. C. Calfee (Eds.), *Handbook of educational psychology*. New York: Simon & Schuster Macmillan.

[15] Shulman, L. (1987). Knowledge and teaching: Foundations of the new reform. *Harvard Educational Review, 57* (1), 1–22.

[16] Darling-Hammond, L. (1997). *The right to learn: A blueprint for creating schools that work*. San Franciso: Jossey-Bass.

[17] Saphier, J., & Gower, R. (1997). *The skillful teacher*, Carlisle, MA: Research for Better Teaching.

[18] Lee, O., & Fradd, S. H. (1998). Science for all, including students from non-English-language backgrounds. *Educational Researcher, 27* (4), 12–21.

Chapter 12 Community Doesn't Just Happen

*A*nd thou shalt have the grace of great things.

—Rainer Maria Rilke

Community doesn't just happen in schools. It is simultaneously a fragile resource and a state of being. "Community is an outward and visible sign of an inward and invisible grace, the flowing of personal identity and integrity into the world of relationships."[1] These networks of relationships bind people to each other and to important ideas and work.

The modern sense of schools as communities is relatively new. Not long ago, the individual teacher was the center of most attempts to improve the quality of teaching and learning in schools. Today, new promise is held in the growing recognition of the power of school-based professional communities to support teacher development and improve student learning.[2] As mentioned in chapter 2, Karen Seashore Louis and colleagues found that professional communities in schools are characterized by a shared sense of purpose, a collective focus on student learning, collaborative activity, de-privatized practice, and reflective dialogue. Such communities develop collective responsibility for student learning, producing schoolwide gains in student achievement.

Other studies[3] have found that a major difference between stuck schools and moving schools was teacher talk and teacher efficacy. Studies of secondary schools find that teacher membership in a learning community is strongly related to students in specific subject areas and entire schools, significantly exceeding the learning of control groups.[4] However, Richard Elmore[5] cautions that efforts at school restructuring may or may not result in student learning. In fact, he finds only a weak relationship between the two. Reorganizing the school by modifying schedules, grouping patterns, and teaching arrangements does not automatically ensure a collaborative climate.

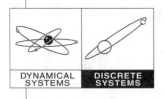

True collaboration arises from beliefs and skills. In this dynamic, teachers are reinventing instruction and cocreating responses to educational dilemmas. In chapters 2 and 3 we stressed that for professional community to exist, it is important that teachers talk. Equally important, however, is what they talk about. Chapter 11 identifies sources for professional conversations that lead to improved student learning. It seems that when teachers talk about real students, real student work, and ways to reinvent instruction to support greater student learning, achievement soars.

Developing school communities is even more complex because all group members belong to other groups as well. The site-based decision-making team has members who think of themselves as primary teachers, special education teachers, parents, administrators, taxpayers, and many other roles. To be a member of a given group, each individual must sort out and resolve conflicting loyalty and identity issues. This is a central "Who am I?" question that each group member must clarify.

Principles of Community

Creating such communities requires vision, values, perseverance, hard work, and time. Community doesn't just happen. Sergiovanni notes that schools are more like a functional family than a fast-food chain.[6] Like any healthy family, community building requires work to develop it and keep it together. We offer the following seven principles in this important journey:

1.   Community doesn't just happen.
2.   Community is the other face of conflict.
3.   Diversity enriches community.
4.   Both things and energy matter.
5.   We cannot not be connected.
6.   Community lives within.
7.   Community doesn't last forever.

Community Doesn't Just Happen

If values are the heart of community, communications are the pulse, bones, and physiology. Most teaching groups, isolated from peers for so many years, need to learn ways of talking together. The task is complicated because it requires at least four languages. First is the language of emotion and passion, providing speech for that which

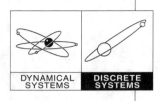

moves us. After nearly 2,000 years in Western civilization, the role of emotion in professional life and its necessity for sound decision making is finally being legitimized by Goleman,[7] Damasio,[8] and others. Second is the language of logic and analysis, to apply a variety of perspectives in reasoned reflection and planning. Third is the language of dialogue, to develop shared understanding, and fourth is the language of discussion, to make decisions that stay made. We described these last two languages in chapter 4. They are ways of talking that are fundamental to the success of any community.

Developing community also requires attention to the environmental level of the nested levels of learning schema described in chapter 8. Teachers need space and time to collaborate. Linda Darling-Hammond[9] describes how "push-in" efforts in a number of restructuring elementary and high schools provide more time for collaboration, staying with the same students for two or more years, and teaching teams with distributed expertise. These schools are eliminating "pull-out" services to students, and special staff are reassigned to reduce teacher-pupil classroom ratios. She describes an elementary school in Chicago in which teachers teach four full days of academic classes each week and spend the fifth day planning in multigrade teams as students rotate to resource classes in music, fine arts, computer lab, physical education, library science, and science lab.

At an elementary school in South Carolina, teachers have 80 minutes per day for planning. In Cincinnati, an elementary staff reorganized the schedule to free up 5½ hours per week for planning time and reduced pupil-teacher ratios to 15:1 using "push-in" strategies. We've even heard of a school in the central valley of California where an impenetrable fog sometimes delays the start of school. Buses are delayed until visibility is safe. School leaders realized that if fog could keep kids home, so could teachers' need for collaborative work time. Once a week, now, schools in the district have a "teachers' fog day."

Only 32% of instructional-staff time is spent teaching in regular high schools, compared to 60% to 85% of staff time in elementary schools, intermediate schools, and alternative high schools, according to Cooper, Sarrel, and Tetenbaum.[10] Yet high schools, too, are creating more time for the school's major purpose—teaching. The same study finds that nonteaching time in traditional high schools is not spent on collaborative planning and curriculum work, as is the case in other countries. Changing this is not easy, yet restructuring high schools are modifying these realities, most often at

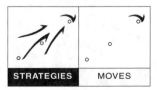

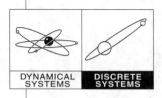

a great cost in terms of the psychological factors of change.

Darling-Hammond describes International High School, in which the principal, assistant principals, and all other staff work with students in advisories. Guidance counselors are attached to teaching teams. The librarian is a teacher with classes. Full-time teachers constitute 67% of the staff. At Central Park East Secondary School, virtually everyone works with students, and full-time teachers constitute 73% of the staff. Darling-Hammond observes:

> Shared time for planning, professional development, and governance is much more extensive in the restructured schools. In International High School, cluster teachers share 70 minutes of planning time daily and a half day each week for staff development and collective work while students are in clubs.[11]

To accomplish the structural changes described above requires more than communications skills. Communities must keep their values clear and continue developing the resources to see themselves and their students through rough times. Not the least of these resources are the five energy sources for high performance that we have discussed—efficacy, flexibility, craftsmanship, consciousness, and interdependence.

Community Is the Other Face of Conflict

Conflict is a manifestation of interdependence.

Conflict is a manifestation of interdependence. Without a need for one another, there would be no conflict. Conflict is necessary in order to have community. Conflict forges new life forms. Canyons, beaches, and mountains are created from conflicting energies. Because human conflict is uncomfortable, groups often seek to avoid it. When they do so, they live in a state of community building that Scott Peck[12] calls *pseudocommunity.* This is a stage of extensive politeness. Being comfortable is the goal. Members of pseudocommunities ignore or make light of problems, withholding their true feelings. They ignore individual differences and avoid people or issues that make them uncomfortable.

Groups move from this stage by asking transition questions: "Who are we?" "Why are we doing this?" "What is our purpose?" Challenging nominalizations and generalizations will also move the group to the next stage of development—chaos.

Peck's use of the term *chaos* is different from, but not totally unlike, the meaning of the term in quantum physics: a dynamical system in which many variables are constantly interacting—each affecting another, which affects another, and so on. In Peck's model,

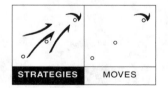

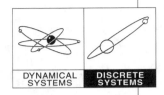

chaos is a time of fighting and struggling. Differences move into the open. Most often the fighting at this stage is neither respectful nor skillful. Members try to convert others to their views. They demonstrate fix-it behaviors and try to heal. Others resist the attempts to change. They look for someone to blame and develop cliques and alliances.

Groups have two choices at this point, either toward community or away from it. Many groups and leaders attempt to achieve peace by overregulating potential problems. Organizations attempt to resolve differences by developing policies, structuring committees, and establishing chains of command, but these only treat the surface manifestations of conflicts.

The way toward community at this point is through engaging conflict and embracing it with special tools. Peck calls this stage *emptiness.* Members empty themselves of the need to convert or fix others. They empty themselves of the need to control, of the sense that there is one right way, of ideologies and prejudices about other people. Members empty themselves of barriers to communication and work to make a transition from rigid individualism to an acceptance of interdependence. Individualism is valued, but so is collegiality. Ways are sought to achieve the best of both worlds. Silence is an asset. Also prominent in the tool kit are the metacognitive strategies of suspension and the balcony view described in chapter 4. Concepts and tools from chapter 9 on conflict are also helpful.

At Peck's fourth stage, groups realize *true community.* Here, people are open, lucid, vulnerable, and creative. They bond together across their differences for common purposes.

Diversity Enriches Community

Healthy biological cultures are diverse. Monocultures are at greatest risk for disease and trauma. If only one type of pine tree grows in the forest, one species of insect, fungus, or other parasite can destroy all the trees. Botanists cross-pollinate, splice genes, and graft stems to different root stocks to increase resistance to pestilence and disease. On the edges of ecosystems, at points of transition between habitats, life-forms are the most profuse and evolving.

As long as the group and its subgroups know that they are a system, diversity of cognitive style, educational beliefs, ethnicity, culture, gender, role, and age range increase the quality of group decisions and offerings to students. In fact, there are some indications that a staff too heavily weighted with males will have greater difficulty working collaboratively than a group that has more gender balance.[13]

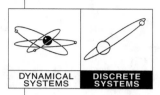

DYNAMICAL SYSTEMS   DISCRETE SYSTEMS

Diverse ideas help groups to form rich responses to educational perplexities. Disagreements that focus on substantive, issue-related differences of opinion actually improve team cohesiveness, commitment, and effectiveness. Disagreements that become expressed as personal attacks or judgments about others, however, insert a destructive energy flow into group work. What groups need to know and be able to do in order to engage in cognitive conflict without affective conflict are the topics of chapter 3 (collaborative norms), chapter 4 (dialogue and discussion), and chapter 9 (using conflict as a resource).

Both Things and Energy Matter

Throughout this book we have advocated for building the energy resources of schools, yet energy is not enough. Prairie Ridge High School in the Crystal Lake District in Illinois was designed as an adaptive facility, capable of supporting independent and interdependent activities within the building.[14] Constructed to allow the building to operate as an 1,800-student high school, it can also be transformed to work as two 900-student schools or four 450-student schools. The thoughtful placement of special spaces, such as science labs, and the flexibility of interior walls that are not weight bearing make this so. Prairie Ridge was designed to serve the interrelationships between the mind (classroom and academic areas), body (physical education and athletic areas), and spirit (the theater and art area). Each of these areas is zoned to be able to act independently from one another, yet in the course of a normal school day the three areas interdependently form a total learning community. Additionally, each of these areas contains design elements intended to support staff and students in developing the five energy sources of high performance: efficacy, flexibility, craftsmanship, consciousness, and interdependence. A prime example of this is the lack of separate offices for each academic department. Teachers share a well provisioned common preparation area.

Although this example is exceptional in its scope and execution, things do matter in achieving educational aims. The "surround," as David Perkins terms it, is tantamount to being a thinking member of the human community, interacting in countless ways to influence human learning.[15] One of the authors is reminded of his first year as a fully credentialed teacher. The principal met him outside the building on the first day of school and asked, "Are your desks in rows?" Trembling with anger and anxiety, the young teacher asked if the conversation could be continued in the principal's office. Once there,

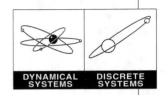

he asserted that he understood his role to be the responsibility for learning in that class, and if that was the case, he would decide the furniture arrangement that would best suit that purpose.

Values matter. Values have life as energy. Statements of mission and beliefs are things that are printed, framed, and hung on the wall. Things without energy may not be enough. The things must support the energy. We've visited staff rooms with posters on the walls: seven norms of collaboration, five meeting standards, or four group-member capabilities. In each case these "things" represent ideas important to the group and are used as checkpoints and reminders in the heat of group work.

Thoughtful groups create forums and places for dialogue. Such physical and psychological space is essential to supporting and transforming the total community.

We Cannot Not Be Connected

If there is no other, there will be no self. If there is no self, there will be none to make distinctions.

—Chuang Tzu

Wherever we look, we find only ourselves. This appears to be true at every level of organization that we can conceive.

Physicist Fritjof Capra, writing about quantum theory, explains that subatomic particles are not isolated grains of matter. Rather, they "are probability patterns, interconnections in an inseparable cosmic web that includes the human observer and her consciousness."[16]

Albert Einstein disclosed that even space and time are products of our five senses. We see and touch things and experience events in sequential order.

Depak Chopra advises that the atoms of hydrogen, oxygen, carbon, and nitrogen you exhale were just a moment ago locked up in solid matter. "Your stomach, liver, heart, lungs and brain are vanishing into thin air, being replaced as quickly and endlessly as they are being broken down."[17]

Scientists and sages seek to understand a universal connectedness in which individual entities exist but have no separation. About the process of self-creation, Margaret Wheatley and Myron Kellner-Rogers say:

Differentness comes into the world, a desire to be something separate. From a unified field, individual notions of self arise. This process, like all those that describe self, is enticingly paradoxical. First, something appears for which there is no

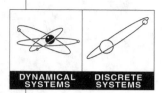

DYNAMICAL SYSTEMS   DISCRETE SYSTEMS

known antecedent. Where does the self that is organizing originate? Or why does it attempt to separate itself from the unified fields? Why does this movement toward differentiation even start?[18]

Akido master Thomas Crum recommends that personal boundaries not determine our identity.[19] Boundaries are misperceived if we interpret them as separations from others. If the self does not remember its connectedness, it will expire. Each act of yours creates the conditions for other lives.

Fritjof Capra also reminds us that to understand our essential interdependence is to understand our relationships to other people and other things. "It requires the shifts in perception that are characteristic of systems thinking—from parts to the whole, from objects to relationships, from contents to patterns."[20]

Community Lives Within

As a friend of ours used to say, "This one is an inside job." Being in community involves a tension, nearly always present, between self-assertion and integration. It requires acceptance of self as both whole and part, a dichotomy described by Arthur Koestler as *holonomy*.[21] The word comes from the Greek *holos,* meaning "whole," and *on,* meaning "part." This conveys a combination of opposites, functioning autonomously while working interdependently. While all five energy sources contribute to consciously holonomous living, interdependence makes the most direct contribution.

Ultimately, the success of individuals depends on the success of the community as a whole, and the success of the community depends on the growth and development of each member.

Since there seems to be no objective reality out there, perception combined with intention creates reality. As you see a thing, that is what you will have. As you describe a thing, that is what you will see.

Community Doesn't Last Forever

Of one thing we are certain: things change. Experiences accumulate; learning occurs at different rates in different areas for different people. Life stages bring new developmental challenges to the young adult, the middle-age professional, the person near retirement. Although community is robust and can prevail for long periods, it is also fragile and subject to changing conditions. Groups that lose their capacity to work effectively with conflict plunge back into chaos.

They may recover or may move back toward organizing conflict away or into pseudocommunity. We must ask:

> As we act together in the world, our organization's identity grows and evolves. It helps periodically to question what we have become. Do we still love this organization? Do we each organize our work from the same shared sense of what is significant? We return to the place where our community took form, where we first became inspired by what we could be in the world. From remembering that place, together we can decide what we want to be now.[22]

Widening Our View

We've been talking about collaboration and being in true community as the cutting edge of our work, the leading edge of professional learning. Yet it may be the oldest story of all the human stories. Our ancestors on the plains of Africa lived in collaborative communities: the hunters and the gatherers, the fishers and the cooks, the weavers and the spinners, working together and sharing a life.

But what are the organizers for community? For West African cultures, it is the drum. It is from these cultures that drumming music has become an essential element in the music of much of the world: In South America, Central America, and North America, the beat is present. The Afro-Cuban rhythms sound through salsa, blues, jazz, rock, and country music. The essential difference in the music of the villages of West Africa is that the beat is polyrhythmic—twos, threes, fours, interacting, intertwining, setting the rhythms for the dance. As West African women pound corn, the little ones don't mimic the beat, they clap and pat counter rhythms, seeking their voice within the village.

To be a drummer in this culture is to be a person of distinction. For the drummer not only keeps the rhythm but also knows the history of the people. The drummer calls people to the dance by naming their ancestors: Bring all of who you are to the center and dance. The tradespeople are called to the dance with their own signature rhythm—the carpenter, the potter, the weaver, the shepherd. The dancers, too, play off the beat, adding their own rhythm to the mix. The African dancer may pick up and respond to the rhythms of one or more drums, depending on his or her skill.[23] But in the best dancing, the dancer, like the drummer, adds another rhythm, one that is not there. The dancer's ear is tuned to hidden beats, responding to gaps in the music.

You don't have to dance on the beat to be part of the village, but you are expected to honor the beat and blend your movement with the movements of others. In fact, to dance with disregard for the beat is considered to be mentally disturbed, because this represents a breakdown of communication, awareness, and community. The goal is to find the beat, honor the beat, add your voice, and dance.

Welcome to the dance!

End Notes

[1] Palmer, L. J. (1998). *The courage to teach: Exploring the inner landscapes of a teacher's life.* San Francisco: Jossey-Bass, p. 90.

[2] Louis, K. S., Marks, H. M. & Kruse, S. (1996). Teachers' professional community in restructuring schools. *American Educational Research Journal, 33* (4), 757–798.

[3] Rosenholtz, S. (1988). *Teachers' workplace.* New York: Longman.

[4] Little, J., & McLaughlin, M. (Eds.). (1993). *Teachers' work: Individuals, colleagues, and contexts.* New York: Teachers College Press.

[5] Elmore, R. (1995). Structural reform and educational practice. *Educational Researcher, 24* (9), 23–26.

[6] Sergiovanni, T. (1994). *Building community in schools.* San Francisco: Jossey-Bass.

[7] Goleman, D. (1995). *Emotional intelligence: Why it can matter more than IQ.* New York: Bantam Books.

[8] Damasio, A. (1994). *Descartes' error.: Emotion, reason, and the human brain.* New York: Avon Books.

[9] Darling-Hammond, L. (1997). *The right to learn.* San Francisco: Jossey-Bass.

[10] Cooper, B., Sarrel, R., & Tetenbaum, T. (1990, April). *Choice, funding, and pupil achievement: How urban school finance affects students.* Paper presented at the meeting of the American Educational Research Association, Boston. Cited in Darling-Hammond, p. 181.

[11] Darling-Hammond, p. 185.

[12] Peck, S. (1987). *The different drum: Community making and peace.* New York: Touchstone.

[13] Louis, K., Kruse, S., & Associates. (1995). *Professionalism and community: Perspectives on reforming urban schools.* Thousand Oaks, CA: Corwin Press.

[14] Saban, J., Wensch, T., Costa, A., Garmston, R., Battaglia, A., & Brubaker, W. (1998, Spring). Designing the holonomous school building. *Journal of School Business Management, 10* (1), 35–39.

[15] Perkins, D. (1992). *Smart schools.* New York: Free Press.

[16] Capra, F. (1982). *The turning point: Science, society, and the rising culture.* New York: Bantam, pp. 91–92.

[17] Chopra, D. (1993). *Ageless body, timeless mind: The quantum alternative to growing old.* New York: Crown, p. 9.

[18] Wheatley, M., & Kellner-Rogers, M. (1996). *A simpler way.* San Francisco: Berrett-Koehler. p. 51.

[19] Crum, T. (1987). *The magic of conflict.* New York: Touchstone Books.

[20] Capra, F. (1996). *The web of life; A new scientific understanding of living systems.* New York: Anchor Books, p. 298.

[21] Koestler, A. (1972). *The roots of coincidence.* New York: Vintage Books.

[22] Wheatley & Kellner-Rogers, p. 62.

[23] Chernoff, J. M. (1981). *African rhythm and African sensibility: Aesthetics and social acton in African musical idioms.* Chicago: University of Chicago Press.

Appendix A   Naive Questions

1.   How much detail do we need to move this item?

2.   Who is making this decision?

3.   What is the process for making this decision?

4.   What parts of this issue live in our sandbox?

5.   Who will do what by when?

6.   I'm trying to understand: Is this a matter of principle or a matter of preference?

7.   What conditions might cause us not to follow through on these agreements?

8.   How will we know when we are successful?

9.   Is there something we're not talking about that is keeping us stuck?

10.   What questions would be useful to ask ourselves?

11.   What are our assumptions about this?

Appendix B Norms of Collaboration Inventory

Norm	Rarely	Occasionally	Frequently
Pausing			
• Listens attentively to others' ideas with mind and body			
• Allows time for thought after asking a question or making a response			
• Rewords in own mind what others are saying to further understand their communications			
• Waits until others have finished before entering the conversation			
Paraphrasing			
• Uses paraphrases that acknowledge and clarify content and emotions			
• Uses paraphrases that summarize and organize			
• Uses paraphrases that shift a conversation to different levels of abstraction			
• Uses nonverbal communication in paraphrasing			
Probing			
• Seeks agreement on what words mean			
• Asks questions to clarify facts, ideas, stories			
• Asks questions to clarify explanations, implications, consequences			
• Asks questions to surface assumptions, points of view, beliefs, values			
Putting Ideas on the Table and Pulling Them Off			
• States intention of communication			
• Reveals all relevant information			
• Considers intended communication for relevance and appropriateness before speaking			
• Provides facts, inferences, ideas, opinions, suggestions			
• Explains reasons behind statements, questions, and actions			
• Removes, or announces the modification of, own ideas, opinions, points of view			

Paying Attention to Self and Others			
• Maintains awareness of own thoughts and feelings while having them			
• Maintains awareness of others' voice patterns, nonverbal communications, and use of physical space			
• Maintains awareness of group's task, mood, and relevance of own and others' contributions			
Presuming Positive Intentions			
• Acts as if others mean well			
• Restrains impulsivity triggered by own emotional responses			
• Uses positive presuppositions when responding to and inquiring of others			
Pursuing a Balance Between Advocacy and Inquiry			
• Advocates for own ideas and inquires into the ideas of others			
• Acts to provide equitable opportunities for participation			
• Presents rationale for positions, including assumption, facts, and feelings			
• Disagrees respectfully and openly with ideas and offers rationale for disagreement			
• Inquires of others about their reasons for reaching and occupying a position			

Appendix C Assessing the Seven Norms of Collaborative Work in a Key Work Setting

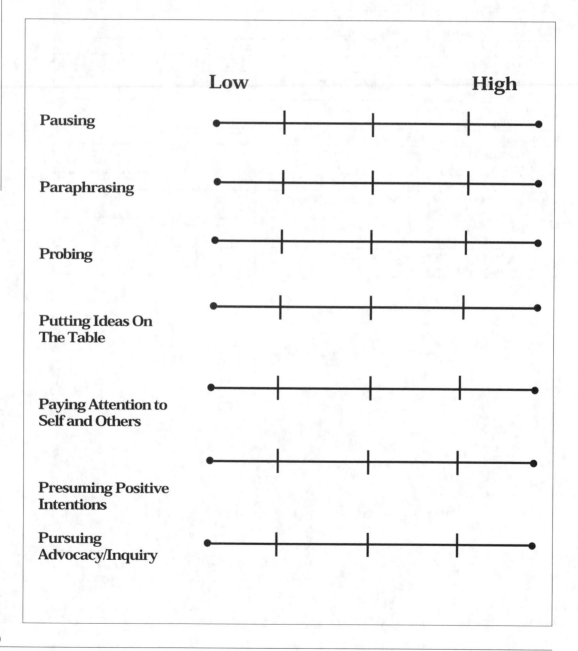

	Low			High
Pausing				
Paraphrasing				
Probing				
Putting Ideas On The Table				
Paying Attention to Self and Others				
Presuming Positive Intentions				
Pursuing Advocacy/Inquiry				

Appendix D

The Responsibilities Dilemma of the Teacher–Facilitator Person

Teachers in school-based leadership positions whose responsibilities include facilitating school improvement efforts, and whose roles have been determined in part by special funding sources or district policy, often face the dilemma of needing to sort out their working relationship with the school principal or other administrator to whom they normally report.

This is complex for two reasons. First, any employee-supervisor relationship is governed by multiple factors: district policy, negotiated agreements with employee organizations, the management and leadership style of the principal, the work culture in the school, style characteristics of the employee, and the interpersonal relationships existing between the principal and teacher-leader.

Because informal personalized factors have a greater influence on the actual working procedures than the hypothetical relationships described in program descriptions, the realized relationship is somehow negotiated between the two people.

However, getting clear about the working relationship is further complicated because knowing who is to be served in a support role is complex for even the most practiced consultant or facilitator.

Because one cannot serve two masters, an early task for a consultant or facilitator is to learn who the primary and ultimate clients are. It is these parties whom the resource person is committed to serve. So, questions of teacher-principal working relationship aside, the teacher-leader and the principal need to address several questions.

1. Because of the potential for having role requirements given to the teacher-leader from sources beyond the principal, who exactly is the teacher leader's primary and ultimate client, and what is the teacher-leader's responsibilities to those clients?

2. Under what conditions can the principal be a primary client?

3. Under what conditions can a working committee of the entire faculty be a primary client?

4. What are the core values that will guide this work?

Who is the client?

A *contact* client is a person who makes the initial contact with the teacher-leader. This establishes an expectation for serving a principal or school according to the goals and descriptions of the funding program. Sometimes the contact comes from the following:

- A personnel office
- A staff development office
- An administrator in charge of special programs

An *intermediate* client is involved in the early contracting arrangements between the teacher-leader and the school. Often this person is responsible for administrating the districtwide program under which each teacher-leader has been assigned. The intermediate client will communicate program goals, procedures to follow, and job descriptions for the teacher-leader. These guidelines set the parameters within which the principal and teacher-leader are to work.

The *primary* client is the group with which the facilitator will work. Because specific goals and working procedures can only be developed with the primary client, the teacher-leader must be clear about who this is. Three prerequisites for being successful as a primary client are as follows:

- The primary client has made a free and informed choice to ask the facilitator for services.
- The primary client has accepted responsibility for the problem being worked on.
- The primary client has or can access the information necessary to develop solutions.

Communicating client status

The *ultimate* clients are the stakeholders whose interests should be protected even if they are not in direct contact with meeting processes. These would include the organization as a whole, students, parents, and community members.

The larger the school system, the greater chance that communications between the support-role person and the contact, intermediate, and primary clients will be incomplete, contradictory, or confusing. Large school systems, even with the best of intentions, have communication problems. This is a systems problem, not a people problem. The most effective level for aligning incongruent understandings about role and function is with the two persons closest to the action, the teacher-leader and the principal. If necessary, the district resource teacher or administrator leading the program can help.

In some situations, a primary client may also be the contact and intermediate client. For example, a department chairperson asks you to facilitate a meeting to develop faculty consensus on a set of educational values. The chairperson now works with you to develop agreements on mutual responsibilities as well as the goals and agenda for this meeting. During the meeting that you facilitate, the chairperson is also a member of the group receiving your services.

Under what conditions can a principal be the primary client?

The principal can be the primary client when he or she will receive, or be a member of the group that receives, direct services from the facilitator; the principal will be an *effective* primary client when he or she has done the following:

- Made a free and informed choice to ask for services
- Accepted responsibility for the problem being worked on
- Has or can access information necessary to develop solutions

Under what conditions can a working committee of the entire faculty be a primary client?

- A subgroup of the whole can be a primary client when it represents the full range of opinions of the faculty.
- It can be an *effective* primary client when the same three conditions for principal effectiveness as primary client have been met.

What are the core values that will guide the work?

The ideas that follow are recommended as generic values for all facilitation work.

What is the presenting problem, diagnosis, and plan?

Facilitators should not assume that the client has accurately *or* inaccurately defined and diagnosed the problem.

The *confident* client has already defined the problem, its causes, and a method for solving it, and asks, "Can you help me accomplish this?"

The *searching* client has identified the problem but is not clear about its causes or methods to solve it, and asks, "How can you help us with this problem?"

The *puzzled* client has not yet identified the problem, and so asks, "Can you help us figure out what is going on and what to do about it?"

The *reluctant* client talks with a facilitator because job expectations require it; this person asks, "What does the project want you to do?"

What are the resources and motivation for change?

An often overlooked resource for change is the group's strengths. Another often overlooked resource is the critical voices of selected group members.

Just because a group seeks help does not mean that it is interested in changing its behavior.

Groups need resources to change. These include time, information, skills, knowledge, and motivation.

Motivation to change can result from several forms of discomfort:

- An internal dissatisfaction with the status quo
- Organizational pressure to improve
- An unachieved vision
- A drive toward craftsmanship and continual improvement

What type of facilitation services are being requested?

In *basic facilitation,* the group seeks only to solve a substantive problem. The group engages a facilitator to temporarily improve its processes in order to work on the problem. When the problem is resolved, the group's process knowledge and skills are relatively unchanged. The basic facilitator is like a mechanic who fixes the group's car well enough to get it to a destination. Facilitation and agenda development tend to be done by one or two persons, and the group expects the facilitator to use whatever processes he or she considers effective.

In *developmental facilitation*, the group seeks to permanently improve its processes while solving a substantive problem. When the problem is resolved, the group will also be more knowledgeable and skilled at solving future problems. The developmental facilitator is like a staff developer who leads the group in learning how to monitor, repair, and redesign their own car so they can use it to reach any destination they seek. Facilitation and agenda development are shared, and the group periodically reflects to learn from its experience.

Appendix E   Contracting for Facilitation Services

1. ENTER and develop the RELATIONSHIP

    Goals

    - Establish trust
    - Develop relationship
    - Establish mutual learning and empowerment as goals
    - Determine mutual expectations

    Questions

    - Are the people here who need to be here?
    - Whose voices are we not hearing?
    - Who are the contact and intermediate clients?
    - Who is the primary client?
    - Who is the ultimate client?
    - How does the person I'm talking to fit within the system?
    - What are the client's expectations?
    - What should be the nature of the consulting services?

    See Appendix D.

2. ELICIT and process INFORMATION

    Goals

    - Distinguish between presenting problem and underlying problem
    - Collaboratively determine desired state
    - Determine specific facilitator goals, plan, working procedures, and assessment design
    - Understand the systems in which facilitation is to occur

    Questions

    - Who will be involved in defining the problem?
    - Who will be involved in determining the desired state?
    - How will you know if you and the client are successful?
    - What lenses are represented by the primary client and the systems in which the client works?
    - What data is relevant?
    - What data-gathering and reporting mechanisms will be used?

- What values and principles will guide decision making?
- What feedback loops should be established?
- Who will assume which responsibilities for this endeavor?

3. EXECUTE and monitor A PLAN

Goals

- Facilitator provides appropriate interventions into the system
- Consultant and primary client "doing"
- Learning from "doing"
- Desired state achievement
- Client empowerment

Questions

- What will you do to keep the relationship a priority?
- How will you keep your communications descriptive and nonjudgmental?
- What will you do to maintain personal authenticity?
- How will you keep your eye on the ball in a confetti storm?
- How will you know the interventions are working and the client is learning?
- How will you know if revising goals or strategies is called for?
- How will you know that you are done?

4. EXIT and complete a RELATIONSHIP

Goals

- A decision to extend the facilitation relationship, recycle on a new problem, or end it
- Client clarity and commitment to personal next steps
- Client empowerment to act independently
- Client feedback to facilitator regarding the facilitator's services

Questions

- How will we know if the relationship should be extended, recycled, or ended?
- How do I know if the client has the resources to success-fully pursue next steps?

- How can I clarify and transfer my own learnings from this relationship?

In the contracting phase, the primary client and the facilitator are jointly responsible for identifying a presenting problem, a way to get started, and mutual responsibilities.

There is never a guarantee that consulting or facilitation services will successfully lead to school improvement. However, the odds for success are enhanced when the principal and teacher-leader form a trusting, candid, and shared responsibility partnership. In effective projects persons in these two roles develop clarity about the following:

Relationship

- Determine mutual expectations
- Develop and maintain trust
- Establish mutual learning goals
- Identify the primary and ultimate clients

Goals

- Distinguish presenting from underlying problem
- Determine desired state
- Determine specific facilitation goals, plan, working procedures, and assessment design
- Incorporate tests for environmental impact
- Understand the system in which the facilitation is to occur
- Who will be involved in defining the problem and desired state?
- How will you know when the project is successful?

Data

- What data is relevant?
- What data gathering and reporting mechanisms will be used?
- What perceptual filters do stakeholders have?
- What values and principles will guide decision making?
- What feedback loops will be established?
- Who will take responsibility for specific portions of this endeavor?

Plan

- What projects will have to be set aside to accomplish this?
- Identify interventions
- Develop a timeline
- How will you know if revising goals or strategies is called for?
- How will you know if the improvement efforts should be extended, recycled, or ended?
- How will relationships and positive energy be monitored and maintained?
- Who will take responsibility for specific portions of this endeavor?

Appendix F

The Facilitator's Contracting Conversation

Purpose	Possible Process
1. Make person-to-person connection to increase the comfort level of the client	• Rapport skills • Personal disclosure
2. Communicate understanding of the problem, issue, or task	• Gather information about the client's perception of the problem • State your understanding of the client's perception, acknowledge any "uniqueness" the client may feel about the problem, and express positive presuppositions regarding the client's resources and intentions • Inquire about aspects of the problem not yet stated • Summarize an expanded description of the problem and watch for confirming nonverbal responses

3. Clarify the desired state for:
  • the intermediate client
  • the primary client
  • ultimate clients
	• Inquire about the client's ultimate goals
	• Ask how the client will know that the goals have been achieved.
	• Present data you as a facilitator have gathered from other sources that might influence the client's framing of outcomes
	• Assist in suggesting additional behavioral descriptors of the desired state

4. Test opportunity costs	• What's the worst possible outcome of expending energies on this issue? • What's the worst possible outcome of not dealing with this issue? • By addressing this issue, what else might have to be set aside or delayed?
5. Clarify what the client wants from you	• Test a well-formed goal statement by observing affirming nonverbal responses • Ask directly, "What do you want of me?"

6.	State what you want in the relationship	• Inquire as to constraints the client wants in the working arrangement with you
		• Be clear with yourself about which wants are essential agreements you must have in order to make this facilitation relationship work and which wants are merely desirable
		• Describe what you want
7.	Describe what you can and cannot offer	• Describe services you feel qualified to provide that are appropriate to your understanding of the client's wants and to achieving the desired state
		• Describe the support services required for project success
		• Clarify any constraints you believe you will have in this relationship
		• Forecast the results you believe the two of you will be able to produce
8.	Define the principles and values that will guide the facilitation work	• Who will decide what?
		• Who will recommend what?
		• What is within and beyond the scope of the group's authority?
9.	Get and test the strength of the agreement	• Many facilitation contracts are faulty for one of three reasons:
		1. The client felt some kind of coercion, however subtle or indirect
		2. The client agreed to the arrangements but increasingly felt inadequate control over what was happening
		3. The client talks a more participative game about decision making than he or she is really comfortable with
		• Ask, "Is this project something you really want to see happening? Are you fully satisfied with the way we have set things up? Do you feel you have enough control over how this project is going to proceed?"
10.	Provide support	• Make genuine supportive statements about the client's willingness to proceed
11.	Summarize next steps	• Clarify who will do what by when

Adapted from Peter Block. (1981). *Flawless Consulting: A Guide to Getting Your Expertise Used.* San Francisco, CA: Jossey-Bass Pfeiffer.

Appendix G

Team Development Survey/ Group Inventory

Teams can be distinguished from working groups by their conscious attention to the processes they use to develop as a team. This survey is one instrument that teams can use to increase their awareness of their development through the use of perceptual data. The survey is intended to be diagnostic, not evaluative; it is a springboard for reflection and planning.

The authors of the survey are in the process of conducting factor analysis for reliability of the items. Even without statistical analysis, teams that have used the instrument have found it to be a valuable tool for dialogue. Further analysis will result in revisions to the instrument, which will be available for purchase.

Used with permission of Kaleidoscope Associates, L.L.C.

Carolee Hayes, Co-Director
8770 Forrest Drive
Highlands Ranch, CO 80126
Phone: (303) 683-1740
Fax: (303) 683-1810
Carolee_Hayes@ceo.cudenver.edu

Jane Ellison, Co-Director
6094 S. Kingston Circle
Englewood, CO 80111
Phone: (303) 773-8661
Fax: (303) 773-8661
Jane_Ellison@ceo.cudenver.edu

Kaleidoscope Associates

Team Self-Assessment

- This survey is intended to be a diagnostic instrument to assist teams in examining their development. It is designed to provide data for team analysis, reflection, and goal setting.

- In considering the statements, it is important to remember that you are responding in a way that best describes your thinking about your team development as a whole, *not your own* development as a team member.

Directions: As you read each statement, circle the appropriate response to indicate whether you strongly agree, agree, disagree, or strongly disagree, with the statement. (SA = Strongly Agree, A = Agree, D = Disagree, SD = Strongly Disagree)

1.	We pay little attention to team development.	SA	A	D	SD
2.	We are good at predicting and managing time.	SA	A	D	SD
3.	We find it difficult to work when we don't have complete information.	SA	A	D	SD
4.	We get our work done as quickly as we can.	SA	A	D	SD
5.	Some members of our team are clearly more important than others.	SA	A	D	SD
6.	We are quick to find answers and solutions.	SA	A	D	SD
7.	We have diverse goals and values.	SA	A	D	SD
8.	We strive to improve ways to do things.	SA	A	D	SD
9.	We feel separated from the larger systems in which we work.	SA	A	D	SD
10.	Our meetings are efficient and effective.	SA	A	D	SD
11.	We consider the impact of our work and our decisions before we act.	SA	A	D	SD
12.	We are aware of organizational goals with which we must coordinate our team's goals.	SA	A	D	SD
13.	We seek support from and give support to each other.	SA	A	D	SD
14.	We adjust our norms and change our procedures in order to be more effective.	SA	A	D	SD
15.	We are aware of where we are in our development as a team and where we want to be as a team.	SA	A	D	SD

16.	We draw on our experience and use the knowledge and skills we have to be an effective team.	SA	A	D	SD
17.	Others control most of what happens to us.	SA	A	D	SD
18.	Our goals have little importance to us.	SA	A	D	SD
19.	Our work has less effect than we would like it to have.	SA	A	D	SD
20.	We often feel uncertain and fearful in our interactions.	SA	A	D	SD
21.	We are often confused about who is supposed to do what.	SA	A	D	SD
22.	We are aware of where we are in our work and where we want to be with our work.	SA	A	D	SD
23.	As we think about specific issues, we expand our thinking to encompass a larger view.	SA	A	D	SD
24.	Members of our team are uncomfortable speaking their minds.	SA	A	D	SD
25.	We view situations through our own eyes and the eyes of others.	SA	A	D	SD
26.	We are in the process of becoming an even more effective group.	SA	A	D	SD
27.	We pay little attention to group process.	SA	A	D	SD
28.	Our team has control over what happens to us.	SA	A	D	SD
29.	Our communication with each other often needs clarification.	SA	A	D	SD
30.	We aren't clear about why we're using a particular process to get something done.	SA	A	D	SD
31.	We accomplish less than we hope to in most of our meetings and are often frustrated by lack of closure.	SA	A	D	SD
32.	We share similar perspectives on most issues.	SA	A	D	SD
33.	We stop our work during meetings to monitor and adjust our processes to become more effective.	SA	A	D	SD
34.	We are often unsure about the progress we are making.	SA	A	D	SD
35.	We examine the positive intentions of others' behaviors.	SA	A	D	SD
36.	We are satisfied with our processes and procedures.	SA	A	D	SD
37.	The way we work on things stays pretty much the same.	SA	A	D	SD
38.	Members are supportive of the team's efforts and decisions.	SA	A	D	SD
39.	We usually don't get through our agendas.	SA	A	D	SD
40.	We know why we are a team.	SA	A	D	SD
41.	We calibrate our progress against established criteria for excellence.	SA	A	D	SD
42.	We communicate with specificity.	SA	A	D	SD
43.	We adjust our work during meetings in order to become more effective.	SA	A	D	SD

44.	We consider several ways of doing something before deciding what might work best.	SA	A	D	SD
45.	The whole is greater than the sum of its parts.	SA	A	D	SD
46.	We can articulate the processes we use (e.g., decision making, problem solving).	SA	A	D	SD
47.	We hone in on issues and look at the specific facts relevant to the issue.	SA	A	D	SD
48.	Our common values and goals provide us with a sense of community.	SA	A	D	SD
49.	We tend to divide things up and work as individuals.	SA	A	D	SD
50.	We all know who is accountable for what.	SA	A	D	SD
51.	We feel safe as members of this team.	SA	A	D	SD
52.	Our team's work impacts important issues.	SA	A	D	SD
53.	We tend to forget what we have learned and don't use it to help us become more effective.	SA	A	D	SD
54.	We don't usually think about what will happen to others as a result of our work.	SA	A	D	SD
55.	We each feel valued as a member of the team.	SA	A	D	SD
56.	We are about as good as we can get.	SA	A	D	SD
57.	The goals of our team have real meaning for us.	SA	A	D	SD
58.	We are critical of each other.	SA	A	D	SD
59.	We frequently have to revisit decisions we have made.	SA	A	D	SD
60.	We are not sure why we exist as a team.	SA	A	D	SD

SCORING: Record the corresponding score for each number and total. State-of-mind scores range from 12–48. Total score ranges from 60–240.

CONSCIOUSNESS		
1	SA=1 A=2 D=3 SD=4	__
4.	SA=1 A=2 D=3 SD=4	__
11.	SA=4 A=3 D=2 SD=1	__
15.	SA=4 A=3 D=2 SD=1	__
22.	SA=4 A=3 D=2 SD=1	__
27.	SA=1 A=2 D=3 SD=4	__
30.	SA=1 A=2 D=3 SD=4	__
33.	SA=4 A=3 D=2 SD=1	__
40.	SA=4 A=3 D=2 SD=1	__
46	SA=4 A=3 D=2 SD=1	__
54.	SA=1 A=2 D=3 SD=4	__
60.	SA=1 A=2 D=3 SD=4	__
TOTAL SCORE		____

EFFICACY		
16.	SA=4 A=3 D=2 SD=1	____
17.	SA=1 A=2 D=3 SD=4	____
18.	SA=1 A=2 D=3 SD=4	____
19.	SA=1 A=2 D=3 SD=4	____
20.	SA=1 A=2 D=3 SD=4	____
24.	SA=1 A=2 D=3 SD=4	____
28.	SA=4 A=3 D=2 SD=1	____
51.	SA=4 A=3 D=2 SD=1	____
52.	SA=4 A=3 D=2 SD=1	____
53.	SA=1 A=2 D=3 SD=4	____
55.	SA=4 A=3 D=2 SD=1	____
57.	SA=4 A=3 D=2 SD=1	____
TOTAL SCORE		____ _

FLEXIBILITY		
3.	SA=1 A=2 D=3 SD=4	____
6.	SA=1 A=2 D=3 SD=4	____
14.	SA=4 A=3 D=2 SD=1	____
23.	SA=4 A=3 D=2 SD=1	____
25.	SA=4 A=3 D=2 SD=1	____
32.	SA=1 A=2 D=3 SD=4	____
35.	SA=4 A=3 D=2 SD=1	____
37.	SA=1 A=2 D=3 SD=4	____
43.	SA=4 A=3 D=2 SD=1	____
44.	SA=4 A=3 D=2 SD=1	____
47.	SA=1 A=2 D=3 SD=4	____
58.	SA=1 A=2 D=3 SD=4	____
TOTAL SCORE		____

CRAFTSMANSHIP		
2.	SA=4 A=3 D=2 SD=1	____
8.	SA=4 A=3 D=2 SD=1	____
10.	SA=4 A=3 D=2 SD=1	____
21.	SA=1 A=2 D=3 SD=4	____
29.	SA=1 A=2 D=3 SD=4	____
31.	SA=1 A=2 D=3 SD=4	____
34.	SA=1 A=2 D=3 SD=4	____
36.	SA=1 A=2 D=3 SD=4	____
39.	SA=1 A=2 D=3 SD=4	____
41.	SA=4 A=3 D=2 SD=1	____
42.	SA=4 A=3 D=2 SD=1	____
50.	SA=4 A=3 D=2 SD=1	____
TOTAL SCORE		____

INTERDEPENDENCE		
5.	SA=1 A=2 D=3 SD=4	____
7.	SA=1 A=2 D=3 SD=4	____
9.	SA=1 A=2 D=3 SD=4	____
12.	SA=4 A=3 D=2 SD=1	____
13.	SA=4 A=3 D=2 SD=1	____
26.	SA=4 A=3 D=2 SD=1	____
38.	SA=4 A=3 D=2 SD=1	____
45.	SA=4 A=3 D=2 SD=1	____
48.	SA=4 A=3 D=2 SD=1	____
49.	SA=1 A=2 D=3 SD=4	____
56.	SA=1 A=2 D=3 SD=4	____
59.	SA=1 A=2 D=3 SD=4	____
TOTAL SCORE		____

TEAM TOTAL
Consciousness (12-48)
Efficacy (12-48)
Flexibility (12-48)
Craftsmanship (12-48)
Interdependence (12-48)
Total (60-240)

Appendix H Structuring Conversations About Data

1. What types of data will best inform improvement efforts?

Outcome Data	Demographic Data	Process Data
Norm-referenced test results	Ethnicity, primary languages, language proficiency levels, redesignation, gender and age mix	Curriculum, Instruction, Assessment: alignment; variety of curricular materials, instructional strategies; instructional delivery system; consistency across programs, grade levels, subjects, courses; quantity, quality, appropriateness of books and instructional materials; etc.
Performance assessments (portfolios, exhibitions, performance tasks)	Attendance patterns— including all students and special populations, dropout, mobility and stability, suspension and expulsion data	Resources: distribution of resources across programs, grade levels, disciplines, courses, special populations; decision making processes relative to allocation of resources; etc.
Report card grades	Socioeconomic status, participation in free or reduced lunch program, family situations, health issues, child abuse	Staff: composition, training, credentials, certification for assignment, experience, expertise, etc.
Course enrollments, graduation and dropout rates, promotion and retention rates	Categorical programs, special needs populations, support services	Professional Development: needs assessment; nature, quality, frequency of training opportunities; participation; level of implementation; follow-up; etc.
Aggregated and disaggregated data, matched and unmatched data, longitudinal data, etc.	Parent involvement, community and business supports, volunteers	School Organization: staff/pupil ratios by grade level, program, discipline; structure of school day and year; use of facilities, support services; governance structures and decision-making processes, communication processes (among staff, with parents), etc.
	Schoolwide trends of student intentions after graduation, by sub-population (high school only)	School and District Growth Needs: external factors, including state and federal program mandates, community and foundation programs, school and business relationships, parent and community organizations, national and international community projections and trends (high schools)
	Staff mobility, attendance, ethnicity, gender, etc.	

2. What organization of data will best inform improvement efforts?

Quantitative—Using Numbers	Qualitative—Using Description
Count events, products, instances Display in tables, charts, graphs Organize by frequency, central tendencies, dispersion	Review holistically Examine documents, anecdotals, artifacts Create categories Search for patterns

3. What types of analysis will best inform improvement efforts?

Asking Inquiry Questions	Generating Theory
What *is* the data? What important ideas seem to "pop out"? What patterns or trends appear? What are similarities with data from other sources? What are differences with data from other sources? What are we seeing at the levels of the class, department, grade level, and school? What seems to go together? What seems unexpected? In what other ways can this data be viewed?	What inferences might we make from this data? How might we explain this data? What might this data be telling us about the following: <ul><li>Learning environment</li><li>Student attitude</li><li>Student performance</li><li>Student knowledge or skill</li><li>Teachers' work culture</li><li>Teacher attitude</li><li>Curriculum</li><li>Instruction</li><li>Assessment</li></ul>How does this data compare with what we would hope to see in these areas? How does this data compare with the literature?

Appendix I   Engaging Others in Collecting and Reporting Data

Some or all of these items may need to be addressed in a school improvement plan. Decide who should be involved and at what levels of authority.

Which Person or Group Should Address?	Items:	What Should Be the Level of Authority?	Levels of Authority
_____	Question(s) data should answer	_____	1. React to ideas
_____	How data will be used	_____	2. Adapt from a model
_____	Types of data to collect	_____	3. Provide ideas
_____	Data-gathering plan		4. Select from options
_____	Data-dissemination plan	_____	
_____	Instrument development	_____	5. Develop criteria
_____	Protocol development		6. Develop recommendations
_____	Data-analysis plan	_____	7. Design
_____	Feedback-to-faculty plan	_____	8. Decide
_____	Action-planning design	_____	9. Act
		_____	10. Evaluate

Appendix J   Five Stages of Change

1. Accepting the Existing Condition
   - Seeking information on perceptions, processes, and results of schooling
   - Examining, understanding, and owning the information
   - Recognizing strengths and weaknesses in system performance
   - Determining how perceptions, processes, and results might be related

2. Owning the Problem
   - Focusing dissatisfaction within the existing condition
   - Defining the dissatisfaction as a problem inherent in the system, not in individuals
   - Understanding that individuals are part of the system that has a problem
   - Understanding that individuals working systematically together can resolve the problem
   - Committing to active solution seeking

3. Owning the Solution
   - Developing a shared understanding of probable causes for the existing condition; a vision of a desired condition; the skills, knowledge, and attitudes necessary to achieve it; related assumptions; and available knowledge and resources
   - Generating a range of possible solutions appropriate to the problem and the situation
   - Analyzing the feasibility of suggested solutions, given the nature of the particular situation
   - Adapting a solution to fit the situation
   - Committing to actively participate in implementation

4. Implementing the Plan
   - Being involved in the activities designed to change the system's processes and results

5. Monitoring/Evaluating the Processes and Progress
   - Monitoring for implementation mutations
   - Adopting healthy mutations, excising others
   - Identifying and solving implementation problems as they arise
   - Celebrating progress
   - Accepting and owning the new reality

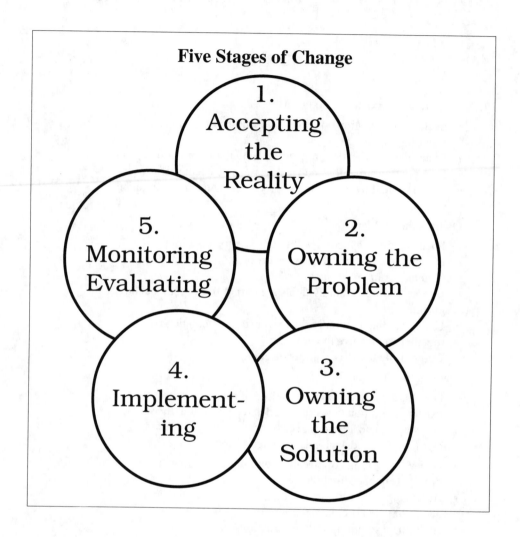

Five Stages of Change

1. Accepting the Reality

2. Owning the Problem

3. Owning the Solution

4. Implement-ing

5. Monitoring Evaluating

Author Index

A

Albert, S. 162
Amason, A. C., 185
Argyris, Chris, 230, 231

B

Bailey, Suzanne, 189
Baker, Bill, 37
Bateson, Gregory, 163
Berliner, David, 156
Beyer, Barry, 57
Bohm, David, 55
Bridges, William, 205, 248, 249
Briggs, John, 2

C

Capra, Fritjof, 271, 272
Chopra, Depak, 271
Costa, Art, 29, 177, 214
Covey, Steven, 243
Crum, Thomas, 196, 198, 199, 272
Csikszentmihayli, M., 174
Cuban, Larry, 3

D

Damasio, Antonio, 209, 212, 267
Darling-Hammond, Linda, 267, 268
Dawes, R., 18
Dilts, Robert, 163
Doyle, Michael, 64, 77, 89, 92
Drucker, Peter, 1
Dunton, Kathy, 9, 11

E

Einstein, Albert, 271
Ekman, Paul, 212
Ellison, Jane, 172

Elmore, Richard, 5, 165, 265

F

Fradd, Sandra, 261
Fullen, Michael, 3, 173

G

Garfield, C., 173
Garmston, Robert, 29, 174, 177, 214
Glickman, Carl, 28, 59
Goleman, Daniel, 211, 212, 267
Grinder, Michael, 207, 213

H

Hargreaves, A., 18
Hayes, Carolee, 172
Horvath, J., 156
Hyerle, D., 174

J

Joyce, Bruce, 18

K

Kanter, Rosabeth Moss, 220-221
Kegan, Robert, 167, 225, 229
Kellner-Rogers, Myron, 162, 271
Koestler, Arthur, 272
Kreutzer, D., 169
Kruse, Sharon, 16, 17
Kuhn, Thomas, 223

L

Laborde, Genie, 206
Lahey, Lisa, 167, 229
LeDoux, Joseph, 210, 211
Lee, Okhee, 261
Lewin, Kurt, 221

Subject Index

About the Authors

ROBERT J. GARMSTON makes presentations and conducts workshops for educators, managers, and professionals throughout the United States, and in Canada, Africa, Asia, Europe, and the Middle East. Professor Emeritus of Educational Administration at California State University, Sacramento, he is Executive Director of Facilitation Associates, an education consulting firm specializing in leadership, learning, and personal and organizational development. Formerly a classroom teacher, principal, director of instruction, and superintendent, Dr. Garmston is co-developer of the Cognitive Coaching model and co-director of the Institute for Intelligent Behavior with Dr. Arthur Costa. He lives near Sacramento, California with his wife Sue and close to his five adult children, and grandchildren, who are, of course, cute and bright.

BRUCE M. WELLMAN consults with schools, professional groups and organizations throughout the United States and Canada. He is co-director with Dr. Laura Lipton of Pathways to Understanding, a training and consulting firm specializing in enhancing student learning, developing collaborative practices and improving schools. Mr. Wellman is a Senior Associate with the Institute for Intelligent Behavior and has spent more than eight years co-developing the principles and practices of Adaptive Schools with Robert Garmston. To this work he brings a rich background as a classroom teacher, curriculum consultant, staff developer and author of numerous educational publications. He lives in Guilford, Vermont with his wife Leslie Cowperthwaite, where they garden, walk in the woods and enjoy watching birds and wildlife.

About the Designer

MICHAEL BUCKLEY works as an illustrator, graphic designer, and fine artist. His graphic work appears in books, magazines, newspapers, and on labels, logos, posters, and tee shirts. His paintings and drawings are exhibited and collected locally, nationally, and internationally. These days he teaches, paints, draws, and leads workshops in presentation graphics. Occasionally he collaborates on special projects such as this one.